# JAMES BOND
# UNMASKED
### by Bill Desowitz

*Best Wishes*
*Bill Desowitz*

To my late parents, Doreen and Stan, who introduced me to
the movies (including an indelible evening with *Goldfinger*), and
to my wife, Robin, who encouraged me to continue this journey with Bond.

# James Bond Unmasked

Copyright © 2012 by Bill Desowitz

Cover by Stanley Chow
Designed and published by Charles Helfenstein

ISBN-13: 978-0-9844126-1-7
ISBN-10: 0-9844126-1-1

Jamesbondunmasked.com

## Acknowledgements

I wish to thank the Bond actors for enlightening me about 007, and obviously without whom this book would not have been possible: Sean Connery, George Lazenby, Roger Moore, Timothy Dalton, Pierce Brosnan, and Daniel Craig. I'd additionally like to thank Michael Wilson, Barbara Broccoli, Michael Apted, Lee Tamahori, Martin Campbell, and Marc Forster for providing their insights in support of my journalistic coverage throughout the last decade. I'd especially like to thank my publisher, Charles Helfenstein, for having faith in my vision and for his continued support. And I'd like to thank Stanley Chow for his elegant illustration. Thanks to Steve Chagollan at *Variety* for giving me the initial assignment to round up the Bonds; Sean Dudas and Larry Garrison for facilitating my Connery interview — the Holy Grail; Jerry Pam for getting Moore; Marvin Paige for persuading Lazenby and Dalton to talk about Bond with me; and Ron Barbagallo, who's been my Jiminy Cricket throughout this project.

# CONTENTS

# INTRODUCTION: BONDING WITH 007

**"You want to talk about the Bonds."**

It was Sean Connery, calling from Prague in 2002, where he was shooting *The League of Extraordinary Gentlemen* (the Bond-influenced film, which, as of this writing, is his final screen appearance). He rarely talks Bond anymore, but I was on an unprecedented mission to interview all the actors for an anniversary tribute in *Variety*. So, with a great deal of persistence and luck, I got Connery to reminisce about the super-cool and free-spirited world savior he made famous with *Dr. No* in 1962.

"They were exciting and funny, and had good stories and pretty girls and intriguing locations and a certain kind of style," Connery remembered. "And [they] didn't take anything for granted."

Connery also cited four factors for the initial popularity of the longest-running film franchise, which incredibly turns 50 this year (and has amassed $5 billion at the box office worldwide and counting): 1) JFK listing Ian Fleming's *From Russia with Love* among his top 10 favorite books in *Life Magazine* in 1961 — the best possible publicity for *Dr. No* and for Bond in general; 2) an exhilarating escape from the sullen "kitchen sink" dramas about angry young men rebelling against their working class roots, revitalizing a dispirited post-war generation of Brits; 3) the importance of director Terence Young, who imbued Bond with his suave sensibilities and molded Connery in his own image; 4) and the surprising success of *Dr. No*, which cost $1 million, grossed twice as much domestically and $4 million overseas — and changed pop culture.

Of course, the biggest factor was Connery himself, who personified the greatest wish-fulfillment fantasy in film history as Bond. And what was the secret of his success? "The movement, the fights, and whatever else are absurd situations," he suggested. "But you have to work very hard to make something look easy."

In other words, the essence of Bond for Connery was always being effortless in his actions. "When

you take somebody on physically, to be able to do the dance, the dance is the movement," he told *The South Bank Show* in 2006. "So that when there was any movement, it was important. It was a message that something was coming." Then Bond would dispatch the baddies in a pantomime of elegant force that justified his license to kill.

With that, nothing deterred me from getting George Lazenby, Timothy Dalton, and Roger Moore in quick succession. Since I had already interviewed Pierce Brosnan earlier about *The World Is Not Enough* (1999), it wasn't hard arranging more time to discuss *Die Another Day* (2002). Then, when Daniel Craig replaced Brosnan for *Casino Royale* in 2006, *USA Today* assigned me to cover all six members of this League of Extraordinary Gentlemen, and I've continued reporting Craig's progress ever since.

After Connery defined Bond, the other actors have redefined him through the force of their own personalities: Lazenby succeeded Connery with cockiness while introducing vulnerability to Bond; Moore embraced the lighter side of Bond to disarm the baddies; Dalton countered with a brooding Bond driven over the edge; Brosnan offered a neo-classical Bond confronted with a changing world; and Craig began again as Fleming's "blunt instrument" for a post-modern Bond.

Yet for each actor, there's a common denominator: "You do a Bond and it's bigger than anything," Dalton proclaimed. "The role overtakes the individual, you incorporate it as part of your history; it rises out of proportion."

But as a novice, Lazenby had "to stay within the frame of Connery. I couldn't be me — the swaggering Australian," he recounted. "So here I was a non-actor: I changed my accent, I changed my walk, everything. But I had the self-assuredness."

Moore had the easiest transition to Bond, thanks to the great success of *The Saint* TV series (1962-69). "Fortunately or unfortunately, whichever you want to look at it, I was born with the looks of a leading man and I sort of fit the heroic roles," he conceded. "I know my strengths and limitations as an actor and have been able to capitalize on this very successfully. All I had to do was *be* James Bond."

It was a lot more complicated in Brosnan's case: he landed Bond, then lost him, and finally got him in his grasp. "Bond remains a constant — he never changes," he emphasized. "He's the one stabilizer within the whole genre. And he's the one who remains somewhat timeless, somewhat trapped within a period of time as well. And my task was trying to find my own reality within it: How do you make it human but still keep the fantasy and mystique of the character?"

Craig has certainly grounded Bond in his own reality: "As a hero figure, he's a guy that just knows what's what," he offered. "And that's kind of exciting, because it's an unpredictability that it gives him. But also that things are gonna be OK — he's gonna work it out. I try to point to this a little bit more that maybe it isn't going to be OK, because I think that's more dramatically interesting."

Although I accomplished my mission to learn about the significance of Bond from each of the actors, I still wasn't satisfied. I wanted to use the roadmap they provided to see Bond through their eyes, actor by actor and film by film; I wanted to contextualize the experience and chronicle the evolution — hence *James Bond Unmasked*.

Cinematically, the Bond franchise was clearly influenced by Alfred Hitchcock's breathless *North by Northwest* from 1959 (Cary Grant, the first choice for 007, was best man at Bond producer Albert "Cubby" Broccoli's wedding with Dana Wilson). But Bond is no Roger Thornhill, who is befuddled by espionage. Bond controls his glam spy world with a license to kill as both a loyal member of MI6 and a defiant individualist. He's the ultimate insider/outsider, hero/anti-hero, possessing what everyone wants: complete power and freedom. And as a result of his ageless, doppelganger nature, Bond exists in a "floating timeline" from the Cold War through the current post-9/11 era, adjusting to changing geopolitical, technological, and cultural events.

Nonetheless, Bond is a creature of the Cold War and the rules of the franchise were established in the first three films: *Dr. No, From Russia with Love* (1963), and *Goldfinger* (1964). Yet there is more

to the fantastical formula than a steady stream of guns, gadgets, and girls. The films are typified by a highly stylized, ritualistic game of cat-and-mouse between the super baddies and Bond, initially conveyed by screenwriter Richard Maibaum's classy framework, production designer Ken Adam's techno/Expressionistic vibe, cinematographer Ted Moore's hyper real look, editor Peter Hunt's kinetic energy, and composer John Barry's sexy scores.

But as a cultural icon, Bond poses a challenge for the ambitious actor. "The character of Bond is often taken for granted because of the historical background," Dalton noted. "He's less well written, so his purpose is to get us through the action sequences that together build the narrative of the story. And that's difficult. You're there as the center of the story, but each script isn't developed to support that. The history supports that because we know *he's* James Bond. But in any other movie, you've got real scenes and real dramas going on, but not here. They're all different but the same."

Ironically, that's why Bond has lasted so long: his mystique has remained intact no matter what. That is, until Craig's origin reboot started delving into Bond's troubled psyche for the first time, giving us a rare glimpse behind what Fleming called the "taciturn mask." Now we are finally witnessing more fully the consequences of having a license to kill and the constant struggle with his inner demons.

"It's not that he's just been given a license to kill; he's been given a responsibility," Craig added. "His weakness lies in the fact that he's headstrong and he makes mistakes — and he makes mistakes that are severe. I want an audience to question that.... Because I want the audience to not only be on the edge of their seat with the excitement of the action, but also on the edge of their seat emotionally a bit and run ragged...."

Myths are mirrors. And Bond is the ongoing myth of our time. It's a great opportunity to explore how we've come from Connery to Craig in half a century — and why Bond means so much to us.

Bill Desowitz,
Los Angeles, April 2012

5

# SEAN CONNERY: THE BIRTH OF BOND

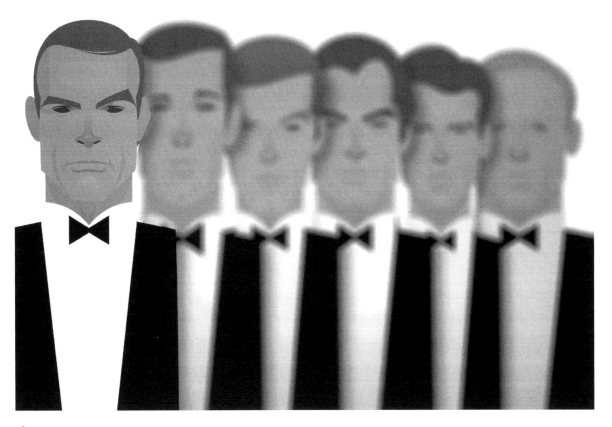

Looking back, it's hard to imagine Cary Grant, David Niven (who eventually starred in the 1967 *Casino Royale* spoof ), James Mason, or any other movie star portraying Ian Fleming's famous superspy on the big screen. It wouldn't have been unique and it wouldn't have lasted. And that's precisely what Cubby Broccoli and Harry Saltzman wanted when they teamed up in 1961 to produce the franchise for their Eon Productions. They were an intriguing pair between Broccoli's passion for glam showmanship and Saltzman's penchant for gritty realism (including the seminal "kitchen sink" drama, *Look Back in Anger* in 1959).

But since United Artists couldn't afford a star anyway, the shortlist apparently consisted of Patrick McGoohan, then starring in *Danger Man*, who turned it down reportedly because he didn't approve of Bond's promiscuity, eventual Bond Roger Moore, and an up and coming Scotsman, who definitely was on the prowl for Bond.

In retrospect, it's a good thing they went way outside the box with the charismatic newcomer from Edinburgh. A laborer, an artist's model, a bodybuilder (a Mr. Universe competition landed him a small part in a production of *South Pacific*), and footballer, Connery (born Aug. 25, 1930) caught Hollywood's attention after starring in, of all films, Walt Disney's *Darby O' Gill and the Little People* (1959).

But Connery was too unrefined for Fleming's image of Bond as an Eton-bred version of singer Hoagy Carmichael (he didn't win the audition and he refused a screen test). However, working class appeal was still fashionable and Connery was hardwired for superstardom — and the producers knew it: they were impressed by his supreme confidence and sexual allure. He strode with "the threatening grace

of a panther on the prowl," Saltzman observed.

As a matter of fact, Connery studied movement with famed Swedish ballet dancer and acting instructor Yat Malmgren (who espoused a technique that flows from the mind to the body). "I used strong and commanding movements, not with weight, but to show how Bond is always in control of a scene," Connery told *GQ* in July 1989.

Of course, it helped that Broccoli and Saltzman were already familiar with Connery's work, including *Operation Snafu* (1961), edited by Hunt, and that *Dr. No* director Terence Young had previously worked with him on *Action of the Tiger* (1957).

> ## The only real difficulty I found in playing Bond was that I had to start from scratch.
>
> ### *Sean Connery*

"Sean, of all the Bonds, has to be categorized the best," asserted Young in the *Dr. No* Criterion Collection laserdisc audio commentary. "But Sean does fit physically, better than any of them, the description of Bond by Fleming: lean, dark, sardonically looking."

Still, despite being groomed as a gentleman by Young, Connery had to discover Bond on his own since Fleming's first novel, *Casino Royale* (1953), was unavailable as part of the franchise package. "The only real difficulty I found in playing Bond was that I had to start from scratch," Connery divulged during the making of *Thunderball* (1965) and reprinted in the very revealing *Adrian Turner on Goldfinger*. "Not even Ian Fleming knew much about Bond.... He was born, kerplump, 33 years old. Bond is very much for breaking the rules. He enjoys freedom that the normal person doesn't get. He likes to eat. Likes to drink. Likes his girls. He is rather cruel, sadistic. He takes in a big percentage of the fantasies of lots of people."

Connery later told *Playboy* in November 1965 that Fleming described Bond to him as "a very simple, straightforward, blunt instrument of the police force, a functionary who could carry out his job rather doggedly. But he also had a lot of idiosyncrasies that were considered snobbish — such as a taste for special wines, et cetera. But if you take Bond in the situations that he is constantly involved with, you see that it is a very hard, high, unusual league that he plays in. Therefore, he is quite right in having all his senses satisfied — be it sex, wine, food, or clothes — because the job, and he with it, may terminate any minute."

Connery made six of the first seven Bond films from 1962-71 (returning in 1983 for the unofficial *Thunderball* remake, *Never Say Never Again*). He told me the first three were fun, but grew weary of salary battles, demanding production schedules, and an increasing reliance on gadgets and sci-fi. "And each one had become more and more successful; it's very difficult not to be influenced by that," Connery added.

But it's difficult to think of Bond without Connery and vice versa. He set an incredible standard (eventually winning over the skeptical Fleming, who reportedly thought of him as a truck driver). And the fact that Bond has endured beyond Connery is a testament to both his indelible stamp on the character and enormous cultural impact. We wanted Bond to continue. And his successors have been chasing his shadow, to varying degrees, ever since.

"I was hooked on Connery," Lazenby enthused. "I think that in part gave me the drive to become James Bond. I was a James Bond fan. Every time a movie came out, I was there. And not only that, for the life of me, I didn't believe I could be as good as Connery — he created the character."

For Brosnan, whose first memorable movie experience as a child was *Goldfinger*, "There's only one man who's played it and is Bond to this day — and that's Connery," he declared.

"It's that darkness that he brought into it," Craig added. "This is a complicated character — it's not two-dimensional. This guy has a past and there's a reason he's been made this way. That, for me, was one of the reasons I wanted to do this."

But leave it to the Shakespearean-trained Dalton to best sum up Connery's legacy: "For good or bad, Sean is the one that started it all," he said. "Those first three movies he did were the best James Bond movies there are. They captured the essence of the series. And they were responsible for establishing what has become the most powerful and probably the most enduring film image. There's nothing to compare with the notion of Bond in people's consciousness. He was great. He was one of the founders of some kind of dynasty."

# DR. NO

**Bond:** I admire your courage, Miss…?

**Sylvia Trench:** Trench. Sylvia Trench. I admire your luck, Mr…?

**Bond:** Bond. James Bond.

It's the most famous introduction in movies, of course, establishing Connery as Bond and his special mixture of danger and sex. Yet our first real intro to 007 is the more iconic gun barrel teaser by title designer Maurice Binder, which has become an indispensable part of the cinematic ritual.

White dots move across the screen and expand into the swirling rifling of a gun barrel, and then a silhouetted Bond walks, turns, and fires directly at us, causing blood to crawl down the screen and the barrel to wobble and fall. It's pure Pop Art and symbolic of Bond always in motion and always in danger, according to Binder (better known for creating the erotically silhouetted girls in the main titles as further stylization). Bond is actually portrayed by stunt double Bob Simmons instead of Connery in the first three films (shot in black and white). But the trope has obviously been tailored for each actor while also becoming a reassuring sign of Bond's return. That's why fans were thrilled at the gun barrel's deconstruction in *Casino Royale* but horrified when it was missing from the opening of *Quantum of Solace* (2008). Better late than never, though: the gun barrel appeared at the end to signal the completion of Bond's rite of passage.

But, as Connery suggested, he had to create Bond on the spot. So when we discover him playing *chemin de fer*, his face is obscured, dealing cards, winning, and flirting with the tantalizing Sylvia Trench (Eunice Gayson) to raise the stakes. Interestingly, our full glimpse of Bond in a tux, smoking a cigarette and looking self-satisfied, is both refined and rough (you can never take the Scot out of Connery). This makes Bond uniquely appealing and unpredictable.

Yet Connery couldn't do it alone and generously gives Young most of the credit: "Terence's contributions were enormous because he was always a great bon vivant," Connery recalled. "He was very much up on the latest shirts and blazers and was very elegant himself — whether he had money or not — and all the clubs and that kind of establishment. And also he understood what looked good — the right cut of suits [the landmark, pared down Conduit Cut from his tailor, Anthony Sinclair,] and all that stuff [custom shirts with turned back cuffs from Turnbull & Asser and a Rolex watch], which I must say was not that particularly interesting for me. But he got me a rack of clothes and, as they say, could get me to look convincingly dangerous in the act of playing it."

Finding the right tone with Young was also essential: they decided to mix it up with drollness and irony. This kept Bond playful and provided a defense mechanism for dealing with his precarious existence: "I took it seriously on one level," Connery recollected, "which was one had to be menacing, one had to be strong enough to do all this stuff. Or seem old enough to do it. And the humor was one element that was missing from the books of Fleming himself. And we did share a great deal of the same humor. So it was a combination."

The wit is immediately on display between Bond and Trench with the double-entendres and his famous intro (ushered in by Monty Norman's immortal "James Bond Theme"), and then later with gallows humor when leaving a dead body in the car ("Sergeant, make sure he doesn't get away"). But Trench is as game as Bond — if not more so — as they leave the club and make a tentative golf date for later in the afternoon.

Here we are introduced to Connery's graceful stride and instinctive ability to convey a sense of control. "You should be able to follow something of the drama by the walk and the body language without having to understand what the people are saying," Connery divulged in *GQ*.

The actor's sense of control is evident throughout, whether he's setting up a hotel room for surveillance; tossing, flipping, and punching a driver with ease after arriving in Jamaica; overtaking fisherman Quarrel (John Kitzmiller) and his restaurateur friend with no more difficulty; or simply following Quarrel across the street.

But facing M (Bernard Lee), his gruff boss and head of MI6, is the most daunting task of all. However, Bond brings his cheery mood with him when summoned to British Intelligence headquarters in the middle of the night. He opens the door, tosses his hat onto the stand (a ritual that oddly anticipates the deadly Oddjob in *Goldfinger*), and flirts with Miss Moneypenny (Lois Maxwell), the endearing secretary to M. At first glance, she's a clever go-between, using their witty repartee to defuse office tension between M and Bond ("Flattery will get you nowhere, but don't stop trying"). Yet she's also clearly smitten with Bond and fantasizes about domesticating him.

What's interesting is that the Canadian-born Maxwell lobbied for the role of Moneypenny, but was also offered the part of Sylvia Trench, which Maxwell declined because she was uncomfortable looking too risqué in the following scene in Bond's apartment. She had her chance to bed Bond. But it's just as well —Maxwell was much better suited as "the in and out girl": protecting Bond and keeping his misogyny in check (a role later expanded by Judi Dench's more maternal M during the Brosnan and Craig eras).

Yet duty calls and Bond apprehensively enters M's office for a briefing on the situation in Jamaica, where the station chief and his assistant have been murdered, and MI6 is helping the CIA investigate the disruption of Cape Canaveral missile launches by radio jamming.

The relationship between Bond and M is unquestionably the most fascinating and complex of the franchise. Its evolution from Lee (who appeared in 11 films) to Robert Brown (who appeared in four) to Dench (who makes her seventh appearance in the upcoming *Skyfall*, 2012) is important in understanding the psychology of 007. But it's clear from the introduction in *Dr. No* there's an adversarial tone. It's a holdover from the kitchen sink dramas: the disapproving authority figure that berates the defiant and undisciplined subordinate, who eventually fights back with his intellectual prowess in an escalating game of one-upmanship.

"And some of those meetings are my favorite moments in the early Bond films in that office," Craig admitted, "with that big padded door and coming in and throwing the hat and hooking it. And it was always a sort of dick-swinging exercise when he sat there and, 'Hello, he's from the ministry,' and all that bollocks going on. And I liked all that."

It's certainly fun watching Bond subvert M's authority later on, but here he slyly smokes his pipe and humiliates 007 by taking away his gun. Since Bond's Beretta jammed on his last mission and sent him to hospital for six months (derived from the *From Russia with Love* novel), M insists he switch to the now-famous Walther PPK. "When you carry a 00 number, you have a license to kill, not get killed," M lectures. Major Boothroyd (Peter Burton), the armorer, presents Bond with his new handgun, and he unsuccessfully tries to slip away with his Beretta. M, as always, must have the last word, and even stops Bond from picking up where he left off with Moneypenny.

Still on edge, Bond returns to his apartment with the new Walther drawn and finds Trench, as if out of a dream, putting golf balls into a glass with his 9 iron, wearing only one of his shirts and high heels. It's the first of only two glimpses thus far of Bond's home (the other being in *Live and Let Die*, 1973), which is located in the novels near The King's Road in Chelsea. "I felt that he was a sportsman and at the same time very British," suggested Ken Adam in the Criterion laserdisc commentary. "And [it's] a conventional apartment with a certain amount of antique furniture, but also showing a bit of his golf clubs to give him a personality, that this was a well-educated person."

Despite being caught off guard and having a plane to catch to Jamaica, Bond naturally finds Trench irresistible. She's the ideal girlfriend for him: sexy, available, competitive, diverting. Yet, even for the swinging sixties, she's ultimately frustrated by Bond being constantly on the go. But then a

committed relationship is out of the question for this free spirit — at least for now.

Fleming's second novel, *Live and Let Die* (1954), begins: "There are moments of great luxury in the life of a secret agent." One of the hallmarks of the Bond franchise has been taking us vicariously to the most exotic places in the world. Jamaica was the first with its tropical eye candy, easy fishing, calypso music, plentiful beer and rum, and Caribbean cuisine. No wonder Fleming adored it (Goldeneye, his retreat, inspired the title of Brosnan's first film in 1995). Bond does too: it's the ideal place for "having all his senses satisfied" and cinematographer Moore obliges with supersaturated colors.

As a result of his insider/outsider status, Bond fits in comfortably with both the British elite and local Jamaicans during his investigation of Dr. No's nefarious plot. However, there are moments when Connery appears impatient while sitting during expositional scenes or edgy during tense moments, not yet comfortable in Bond's skin. He's always much better on the move. Young faulted himself for allowing Connery to go "over the top."

And Bond needs help, so he's introduced to CIA agent Felix Leiter (Jack Lord), who briefs him about the mysterious Dr. No; he would become a semi-regular and trusted ally. They establish a friendly rapport and Lord, who dons sunglasses and also carries a Walther PPK, gives off his own cool vibe through body language. Too bad this was his lone appearance as Leiter (he has been succeeded by six other actors, the most recent being Jeffrey Wright's even cooler turn in the Craig films). Apparently Lord couldn't come to financial and creative terms with the Bond producers, later starring in the popular *Hawaii Five-0* TV series (1968-80).

Professor Dent (Anthony Dawson) turns out to be the franchise's first henchman, a nervous geologist that tips his hand too easily about the radioactive evidence, which inevitably leads Bond to Dr. No. But not before Dent pays an uninvited visit to No's reclusive island, Crab Key, to warn him. The weird, Expressionistic-looking waiting room he enters is the first of many imaginative set designs by Adam (who later created the War Room in Stanley Kubrick's *Dr. Strangelove*, 1964). It's simple yet sinister with a circular inclined ceiling that casts a web-like shadow across the back wall, ensnaring Dent in its grasp. Adam was forced to improvise at the last minute with no money left for anything elaborate. But less is definitely more in this case. Meanwhile, the disembodied voice of Dr. No (Joseph Wiseman) displays a quiet menace, instructing Dent to pick up the tarantula in the wooden cage on a nearby table. The tarantula is the embodiment of No's cunning evil and the perfect complement to the room.

Bond returns to his hotel room that night and realizes he's had a visitor. He sniffs a bottle of Smirnoff (the first of the Bond series with many product placements) and opens a new one just to be safe. He sits down, props his legs up on the table, and he tries to relax with his drink. It's a rare moment of contemplation for Bond — and the only one during Connery's tenure. In fact, Pierce Brosnan, who was frustrated by a resistance to navel gaze, wonders: "What is his relationship with M? What is his relationship with the women that he will encounter? How far can you push those relationships in a Bond film to the point where he just closes the door and sits and reflects?"

The respite is all too brief: Bond wakes up in the middle of the night with the tarantula creeping up his body. After sweating it out, he coaxes the spider off his arm and onto the headboard, flicks it onto the floor, and violently beats it to death with his shoe. Then Bond rushes into the bathroom to throw up off-screen. It's a singular instance of terror straight out of the novel (with a spider instead of a centipede), which Young insisted on retaining, and Connery's most frightened moment as Bond.

Bond then pursues, seduces, and double-crosses an enemy agent, Miss Taro (Zena Marshall) — the second sexual conquest— who tries to lure Bond to his death on the way to her house in the mountains. But he cleverly runs the Three Blind Mice assassins off a cliff in a scene that very likely influenced the *Quantum of Solace* pre-credit car chase, with Craig's Bond throwing off his pursuers with a submachine gun during the tense drive with Mr. White to Siena, Italy.

It's not surprising that Bond displays such anger with Taro at her house, squeezing a towel as though he wants to strangle her before they kiss. He treats her cruelly, particularly after sex, and takes pleasure in seeing her escorted by the police. It's a harbinger of greater, more notorious misogyny yet to come.

But that's just a prelude to the trap Bond sets for Dent in her house. Bond sits in a chair and appropriately plays Solitaire; Dent finally enters and empties his gun into the bed. But before Bond can learn anything significant, Dent slowly reaches for his weapon on the floor: "That's a Smith & Wesson, and you've had your six," Bond reminds Dent before calmly shooting him twice and blowing on the silencer with snobbish satisfaction.

It's Bond's defining moment and nothing else compares to the shocking way he sadistically murders Dent (not even when it's replayed with Stromberg in *The Spy Who Loved Me*, 1977), and Connery plays it very convincingly, particularly as a counterpoint to the tarantula scene. "Bond is dealing with rather sadistic adversaries, who dream up pretty wild schemes to destroy, maim, or mutilate him; he must retaliate in kind," Connery told *Playboy*.

That was Young's defense in fighting to keep the brutality when censors and execs at UA pressured him to cut it, though the number of shots Bond fires was trimmed by a third, somewhat dulling the impact of the extra bullet in Dent's back after he's dead.

"You know, people wouldn't let their kids go see James Bond when they first came out... they were restricted if you were under 16," noted Dalton. "He was a bit of a sensation. He *killed* people. Good guys didn't do that. And he didn't kill them fair and square."

In fact, the "sex, snobbery, and sadism," which Paul Johnson blasted in his 1958 *New Statesman* review of Fleming's *Dr. No*, has endured throughout the franchise as a kind of holy trinity, re-emerging in full force with Craig's origin story, and in keeping with the Fleming template of a ruthless assassin.

Now ready to confront Dr. No, Bond travels to Crab Key later that night with the cagey Quarrel in his boat. But in the morning, his plans are complicated by the appearance of nature lover and shell collector Honey Ryder (Ursula Andress, who was a sex symbol in her own right, and later

appeared in the *Casino Royale* spoof). Indeed, her iconic, bikini-clad entrance out of the water not only inspires Bond to join her in singing "Underneath the Mango Tree," but also caused quite a sensation that has been unmatched. It even resulted in two homages: Jinx (Halle Berry) in *Die Another Day* and Craig in *Casino Royale*.

Honey completes the pattern of basically three Bond girls per film, ranging from friendly to antagonistic to resistant-turned romantic. Throughout the second-half, though, Honey crucially brings out a gentler, more caring side to Bond, in keeping with the novels. Typically, Bond alternates between predator and protector when it comes to women (which will culminate with *On Her Majesty's Secret Service* in 1969). Yet he's sincerely impressed with Honey's toughness (she placed a black widow spider under a rapist's mosquito netting) and fearless attempt to defy Dr. No, who apparently killed her marine zoologist father.

Dr. No's guards eventually take Bond and Honey captive with the help of a mechanical "dragon," a disguised flame-throwing tank that incinerates Quarrel during a fight. Bond is so used to being in control, however, that when they are being decontaminated from radiation, he orders a guard to clean Honey first. Bond soon meets No and the power struggle begins. He knows Bond so well, in fact, that he not only serves him his favorite vodka martini, but also ushers in the unforgettable line, "Shaken, not stirred."

As for No's flamboyant lair, it's a combination resort and nuclear-powered facility, containing both European and Asian influences, in keeping with his German and Chinese heritage, and highlighted by a large, distorted-looking aquarium. From the outset, Adam conveys a sense of megalomania through a combination of the avant-garde and electronics, mixing up styles, materials (where else would you find copper?), and technology, which was radically new to movies.

Dr. Julius No magnificently set the standard for Bond super villains, thanks to Wiseman's brief but simmering performance. The prominent New York stage actor was already a standout as the volatile druggie in *Detective Story* (1951), his first major film appearance. No transcends Fu Manchu: he wears stylish Nehru suits, surrounds himself with beauty, and has a touch of larceny (possessing the recently stolen portrait of Wellington by Goya). Not surprisingly, No even has a fondness for Nietzsche: "The successful criminal brain is always superior," No proclaims. "It has to be!" But like many subsequent Bond adversaries, No contains a physical flaw that enhances his sociopathic tendencies: metal hands as a result of a radiation accident.

Shunned by East and West, No works for SPECTRE (Special Executive for Counter-Intelligence, Terrorism, Revenge, and Extortion), a global terrorist organization that is dedicated to destroying the Old World Order and establishing a fiendish new one. SPECTRE was actually introduced in the *Thunderball* novel (1961), which has a complicated history. It began as an unfulfilled film project with Fleming teaming up with producer Kevin McClory and screenwriter Jack Whittingham. Then Fleming repurposed the material as 007's ninth literary adventure, and Broccoli and Saltzman seized on *Thunderball* as their first Bond film. However, they quickly switched to *Dr. No* when McClory and Whittingham sued Fleming for his unauthorized novelization. After the suit was finally settled in 1963, Eon partnered with McClory to make *Thunderball* the fourth Bond film.

Still, it was a wise decision on the part of the producers to immediately switch Bond's organized nemesis in *Dr. No* from the Soviets in the novels to the more ideologically neutral SPECTRE, especially given the tense geopolitical climate and their global distribution plans. For his part, screenwriter Maibaum was fairly adept at using SPECTRE as a Cold War linchpin.

Thus, No proudly declares over dinner that his immediate plan to wreck the U.S. missile program is merely the first step in a more elaborate scheme by SPECTRE. Bond is not impressed: "World domination. Same old dream," he scoffs. He then rejects No's attempt to recruit him for SPECTRE (Bond even quips that he would have to be put in charge of the Revenge division).

Perhaps No thinks Bond is merely corruptible or sees a like-minded social misfit. In any event, the tense dinner exchange represents a more extreme example of Bond's issue with authority. Bond will put up with MI6 and M because it affords him a luxurious lifestyle as a civil servant, but he'll be damned if he's going to switch sides and work for SPECTRE and No (let alone future arch-nemesis Ernst Stavro Blofeld).

But when No orders them locked up and insinuates that his guards can have their way with Honey, Bond threatens to break a bottle of champagne. "That's a Dom Perignon '55," he protests. "It would be a pity to break it." "I prefer the '53 myself," Bond condescendingly replies in setting up a joke that will later be paid off in *Goldfinger*.

Yet No knows precisely how to erase Bond's smugness. He orders his guards to "soften him up," and provides a grueling obstacle course through a steamy shaft as Bond's only escape, which leaves him battered and bloodied (he won't bleed again like this until 1989's *Licence to Kill*). After strangling a technician and stealing his radiation suit, Bond makes his way to the control room containing the nuclear reactor and toggling beam aimed at a U.S. missile. It is pure Adam, with vertical metallic beams and multi-level wood floors. Bond overheats the reactor and fights No above the cooling vat reminiscent of a *Flash Gordon* serial, and the doctor's metal hands prevent him from crawling out of the vat and he boils to death — a fitting retribution for his sadism.

Amid the chaos, Bond rescues Honey from drowning: she's tied to the bottom of a spill basin rapidly filling with water. It's a dry run, if you will, for the pivotal rescue of Tracy (Diana Rigg) by Lazenby's Bond during the pre-credit sequence of *On Her Majesty's Secret Service*.

Water, of course, figures prominently as a sexual motif in the Connery films, as Bond and Honey escape by boat when the reactor blows. Leiter comes to the rescue with the Coast Guard, but Bond releases the tow and sends them adrift so he can continue his tryst with Honey. It's the first of many similar climaxes for 007, alone with the lady he's just rescued, usually at sea (in *Goldfinger* it's nearby a body of water), with the reassuring tag, "James Bond Will Return…"

# FROM RUSSIA WITH LOVE

If *Dr. No* was a landmark as the first Bond film, then *From Russia with Love* was a milestone as a dramatic leap forward in overall quality and performance by Connery. Based on the fifth Fleming novel, *FRWL* offers the best espionage story and is arguably the best Bond film as a result.

"I think the one that worked for my money the best was *From Russia with Love*," Connery declared, because of its intriguing story and locations in Istanbul, Turkey, and Venice, Italy. Connery also thought it was refreshing coming directly after *Dr. No* as a more down-to-earth spy thriller.

Likewise, director Terence Young hailed it as the greatest Bond film along with Connery's best performance as 007: "He was more assured in every way," Young explained in the Criterion laserdisc of *FRWL*. "He was a little too eager in *Dr. No*. Now he's cool. When you analyze it, he was the first really cool star in the business. I would say, already, there were signs of it in *Dr. No* and that was Ian Fleming and then what we added to the script. That sort of flip humor gave the impression that he didn't care, that he was above such worldly problems. He was at his most comfortable in this picture. He looked good; he put on weight. He was very proficient already; he got into the skin of the part. By the time he came to this, he had much more confidence in what he was doing."

Exactly: Connery has also taken some of the edge off Bond, who appears more effortless in his actions and unflappable in his manner, even when surveying a hotel suite in Istanbul for spy bugs with feline authority. But you wouldn't know it by the franchise's first pre-credit sequence (which has become a veritable movie within a movie). Imagine opening with "the death of Bond": an innovative idea devised by producer Saltzman to startle the audience and introduce unpredictability to the opening of every film, according to the indispensible *James Bond: The Legacy* by John Cork and Bruce Scivally.

A pasty-looking and fearful Bond is stalked by a blond-haired assassin (Robert Shaw) in a sculptured garden directly lifted from Alain Resnais' lavish *Last Year at Marienbad* (1961). But Bond is helpless, as the assassin quickly strangles him with a garrote wire from his watch in less than two minutes. Of course, it's not Bond, but a victim with a mask as part of a training exercise on SPECTRE Island.

As part of a quasi-sequel to *Dr. No*, SPECTRE has devised a trap to heat up the Cold War and lure Bond to his death: a simple plot with a complex narrative. More important, we are mysteriously introduced to the head of SPECTRE (Number One) aboard his yacht in Venice. His face is unseen but he's viewed wearing an octopus signet ring (the symbol of the organization) and stroking a white Persian cat, which is a nice humanizing touch later adopted by Marlon Brando's Don Corleone at the opening of *The Godfather* (1972). Anthony Dawson provided the hands and Viennese actor Eric Pohlmann the voice (both uncredited), so part of the fun was trying to figure out who played Number One while enjoying early glimpses of his Machiavellian mischief. It wasn't until *You Only Live Twice* (1967), of course, that we were formally introduced to Number One as Ernst Stavro Blofeld.

Blofeld takes delight in metaphorically explaining SPECTRE's strategy to his latest recruit from SMERSH, Col. Rosa Klebb (Lotte Lenya): "Siamese fighting fish, fascinating creatures. Brave, but on the whole, stupid. Yes they're stupid. Except for the occasional one such as we have here, who lets the other two fight while he waits: Waits until the survivor is so exhausted that he cannot defend himself, and then, like SPECTRE, he strikes!"

Enter Kronsteen (Vladek Sheybal), arrogant Czech chess grand-master and chief planning officer for SPECTRE, who we've just witnessed winning a match in Venice with ease (visually underscored by art director Syd Cain's pawn motif). Kronsteen explains how Bond will be lured to Istanbul to steal a Lektor decoding machine from the Soviet consulate with the help of a beautiful clerk, handpicked by Klebb.

The Soviets will blame the British; SPECTRE will kill Bond; and sell the Lektor back to the Soviets.

Interestingly, Umberto Eco in *The Bond Affair*, co-authored by Oreste Del Buono, characterizes the Fleming novels as a series of chess matches. The analogy is never more apparent than here. Yet despite Kronsteen's assurances that he has anticipated every possible move and countermove, Blofeld remains somewhat skeptical. This is clearly an organization plagued by fear, distrust, and envy, but they view Bond's wild reputation as a weakness they can exploit to exact revenge.

Although it takes 17 minutes for Bond's entrance, he remains the focal point, with "real scenes and real dramas going on," as the plot now shifts to Klebb. She flies to SPECTRE Island, where she meets the head of training, Morzeny (Walter Gotell), and assigns the psychopathic Donald Red Grant (Shaw) to stalk and kill Bond. She also tours the latest weaponry at the training facility, influenced by *Spartacus* (1960). In fact, the pre-credit sequence was supposed to show off the elaborate set, but the filmmakers didn't want to give it all away, so they came up with the more modest cat-and-mouse exercise. But in later devising the pre-credit sequence of *The Man with the Golden Gun* (1974), they figured out how to introduce a similar situation with Scaramanga's funhouse without spoiling all the fun.

In briefing and intimidating the stunning Soviet clerk, Tatiana Romanova (Daniela Bianchi) in Istanbul, Klebb wears glasses with thick lenses that distort her eyes; she displays a notorious hint of lesbianism by caressing the girl's knee, as well as a fondness for sadism by cracking her whip (she previously greeted Grant with brass knuckles). Lenya, the famous Austrian singer married to German composer Kurt Weill ("Mack the Knife"), was Oscar-nominated for her supporting role in *The Roman Spring of Mrs. Stone* (1961), but her maniacal Klebb has left an indelible mark on Bond villainy.

We finally catch up with Bond beside a river (wouldn't you know it?). He tries to pick up where he left off with Trench on a picnic, only to have Moneypenny page him. Trench was intended to be a regular girlfriend, but when Young was replaced by Guy Hamilton on *Goldfinger*, she was never seen

again. At least they get to finish their "lunch" before Bond is whisked away in his Bentley (making its lone appearance) back to London.

Bond's briefing with M is more cordial than the last. After learning that the clerk has supposedly developed a crush on him and wants to defect (a cute inside joke about the growing Bond mania), Bond even displays rare self-effacement related to "coming up to expectations" in the flesh. "Just see that you do," M instructs.

We are also introduced to the latest head of Q Branch (Desmond Llewelyn), who presents Bond with a special attaché case with ammunition, flat throwing knife, an Armalite AR-7 folding rife, 50 gold sovereigns (25 on either side), and tear-gas cartridge, to which Bond replies, "That's a nasty little Christmas present, but I shouldn't think I need it on this assignment."

Yet Bond will require every "gadget" to survive the grueling mission, thanks to Q's tireless ingenuity. Beginning with *Goldfinger*, Q figures very prominently in the MI6 ensemble as the proud purveyor of gadgets, and Llewelyn plays the part with verve in a record 17 films, serving as yet another gruff guardian to 007.

Once in Istanbul, Bond contacts Ali Kerim Bey (Pedro Armendariz, part of the famous John Ford acting company), the local British Intelligence station chief. Bey is an agreeable ally, who efficiently runs his organization with the help of his sons, relaxes with his secretary/mistress (Nadja Regin), and even enjoys amicable relations with SMERSH. He tells Bond he's wasting his time and that he should just have fun in Istanbul for a couple of days. In contrast to Jamaica, Instanbul offers a darker, richer, more Byzantine setting for espionage, with its mixture of Persian, Greek, and Roman influences.

A warm kinship develops between Bond and Bey distinguishing it from the other Connery films: "Pedro Armendariz was terminally ill and wanted to finish the film, so we changed everything around and it was a very strong, wonderful character," Connery recounted.

But Bey is soon shaken from his complacency after SMERSH bombs his office the next day in an attempt to assassinate him. He leads Bond by gondola in an underground tunnel to eavesdrop on the Soviet consulate using a periscope. The Bulgarian spots a rival assassin, Krilencu (Fred Haggerty), who works for the Soviets, and whisks Bond to a local gypsy camp that night to keep out of site and figure out their next move. However, they've picked a bad time as the camp prepares for a ritualistic fight to the death between two women (Martine Beswick and Aliza Gur) competing for the chief's son. After dinner and entertainment from a belly dancer, the girls start brutally fighting: biting, clawing, kicking, and punching, to Bond's amusement.

But then Krilencu and his men launch a surprise attack, and all hell breaks loose, with Bond and Bey helping the gypsies. It's the franchise's initial major action sequence and the first opportunity for Bond to display his great marksmanship, as noted Bond historian Steven Jay Rubin pointed out in the Criterion commentary: firing a pistol without blinking, thanks to the way it's staged and cut. Bond moves from one kill to the next with panache, amid the chaos. Still, Grant has to step in at one point as guardian angel to shoot an assailant that blindsides Bond. It's the first hint of Grant's slyness. Afterward, in an attempt to rescue the girls, Bond persuades the gypsy leader to stop the fight, so he suggests 007 selects the winner, which makes for a long night.

The following night, Bey (who was wounded in the arm) and Bond stake out Krilencu's hideout and wait for him to escape through a hatch opening from Anita Ekberg's mouth in a large movie poster from *Call Me Bwana* (also produced by Broccoli and Saltzman). Bond assembles his AR-7 and prepares to shoot Krilencu, but Bey insists on doing the honors despite his injury, so Bond obliges both out of professional courtesy and fondness for Bey. "She should have kept her mouth shut," Bond retorts in one of the few instances of gallows humor in *FRWL*.

> **Essentially the bulk of the movie was simply this one proposition: How and when Connery finds out that he's going to be murdered.**
>
> *Timothy Dalton*

Upon returning to his hotel suite, exhausted, Bond discovers Tatiana in his bed, wearing only a black choker, surpassing Trench's surprise visit in *Dr. No*. He is astonished at her beauty and takes the opportunity to satisfy her (though both are unaware they are being filmed by Klebb's men).

One clandestine turn deserves another, as Bond records Tatiana the following day aboard a ferry boat so he can authenticate the Lektor. She's already begun falling in love with Bond and asks how she compares with girls in London and if they'll make love all the time.

Bond asks Tatiana for a copy of the consulate floor plan and they rendezvous at Hagia Sophia, a former cathedral and mosque, and now a museum: iconic for its intricate architecture. Bond then steals the Lektor in spectacular fashion (on the 13th, no less) as Bey arranges an explosion from under the building that sets off tear gas. Bond finds Tatiana and flees with the Lektor during the chaos. The three then escape on the Orient Express.

The centerpiece of *FRWL* is the long train sequence, which, to this day, remains a highlight of the franchise and as suspenseful as anything the genre has delivered. Dalton offered the best analysis of its significance: "The interesting thing….is that it's memorable for the train sequence, with the audience knowing that Robert Shaw was a double-agent, who was going to kill him, and knowing that Sean Connery didn't know that. Essentially the bulk of the movie was simply this one proposition: How and when Connery finds out that he's going to be murdered….All on a train! Now we couldn't do a sequence like that [for 30 minutes] in a modern movie. Nowadays, a sequence is five minutes! BAM! BAM! BAM! And this was all about the look in the people's eyes, what was going on — it was a real piece of drama!"

Yes, there's a lot more than murder on the Orient

Express: it's an opportunity for Bond and Tatiana to grow closer, pretending to be a proper English couple, David and Caroline Somerset. She falls madly in love with Bond, fantasizing about life in London, and he transitions to being her protector while arranging for agent Nash from "Station Y" to meet him at Zagreb with the escape route to London. Meanwhile, Bey spots a Soviet security officer on the train named Benz, who recognizes Tatiana, and keeps him occupied.

However, Grant kills them both off-screen and makes it seem like a double-murder. Bond's response is to explode at Tatiana when they are alone together in their compartment. We have never seen such anger from him and he is ready to kill her for the death of Bey, but she pleads ignorance and divulges Klebb's name as a last resort.

The train stops at Zagreb and Grant kills Nash and impersonates him in time to rendezvous with Bond. Grant plays Nash as a stereotypical Brit, someone who's only done his homework and can't hide his true nature, repeating the expression "old man" and inappropriately ordering Chianti with his grilled sole, which naturally strikes the bon vivant Bond as odd. Then Bond notices him putting something in Tatiana's wine glass (chloral hydrate), and he confronts Grant, who explains that the escape route is only for two. Bond plays along, but when he bends over to look at the map, Grant hits him over the head and momentarily knocks him out.

Bond regains consciousness and suffers through Grant's arrogance and British hatred to learn about the plan: it's a turning point when Bond fully realizes the power and ambition of SPECTRE. "That must have been a pretty sick collection of minds to dream up a plan like that," Bond responds. It's also a humbling moment for Bond — the greatest of Connery's tenure. And yet it's an opportunity for Bond to outwit Grant and, ultimately, Kronsteen, with his own counter chess moves because Grant takes his sweet time for revenge: "The first one won't kill; not the second, not even the third… not till you crawl over here and you kiss my foot!"

After Bond unsuccessfully tries to bribe Grant, he offers the gold sovereigns to buy a cigarette. Grant takes the bait: falling for the 25 sovereigns in the suitcase but then insisting on opening the attaché case himself, which explodes in his face, resulting in the best hand-to-hand fight in franchise history — or "the dance," as Connery calls it. And since it's dark and occurs in such close quarters (shot with multiple cameras, including a hand-held one), there's an extra frisson. Viewed today, in contrast to the extremely gritty and disorienting *Bourne* fight sequences, not to mention the *Quantum of Solace* action, you appreciate the clarity of the cutting as well as the brutality of the struggle. You feel the force of the blows. Bond even appears over matched until the last-second use of the hidden knife, allowing him to stab Grant and strangle him with his own garrote wire.

The entire two-minute fight showcases Bond's extraordinary physical and mental adroitness, which Hunt brilliantly emphasizes with his pioneering "crash cut" editing style: removing unnecessary transitions and utilizing jump cuts to heighten the experience. "Hunt cut on internal rhythms, constructing a scene as if he were a jazz musician," Cork and Scivally suggest. "The result changed the way we watch movies….Quite simply, he brought the Bond films into the avant-garde."

With Grant finally disposed of, Bond reaches into his coat pocket to take his money ("You won't be needing this, old man"). Bond then awakens Tatiana and they leave the train with Grant's escape plan, leaving Blofeld to play Klebb and Kronsteen

off each other. Morzeny enters as an observer, as Blofeld appears to side with Kronsteen, making Klebb sweat, before Morzeny kills the surprised chess master with a poisoned toe-spike in his shoe. Klebb promises to make the most of her reprieve. But Bond outmaneuvers SPECTRE twice along the way with his fine marksmanship: first in a *North by Northwest*-influenced shootout with an enemy helicopter (the AR-7 comes in handy again) and then in a speedboat chase with Morzeny and his squadron of boats, culminating with Bond firing a signal flare into the discarded fuel tanks and engulfing Morzeny and his cronies in flames.

*FRWL* concludes as it began, in Venice. Bond and Tatiana hurriedly try to leave their hotel with the Lektor and are stopped by Klebb dressed as a maid, who holds Bond at gunpoint. For the first time, Bond appears truly helpless. That is, until Tatiana comes to his rescue by knocking the gun loose. Klebb then activates the poison toe-spike in her shoe and tries to kick Bond, who pins her with a chair like a matador holding off a bull. But just before Klebb stabs Bond, Tatiana, who's matured considerably, saves his life by grabbing the gun and shooting Klebb. As Bond sits down, he's visibly shaken, humbled, and realizes that he's lucky to be alive. But his only recourse is gallows humor: "She's had her kicks." We leave Bond with Tatiana in a gondola, as he looks at the incriminating film from their bridal suite in Istanbul, before discarding it in the water and waving goodbye. We not only hear the first franchise pop theme song (sung by Matt Monro) during the end credits, but are also informed that the next film will be *Goldfinger*.

In the end, Bond has been tested and alerted to the global threat of SPECTRE and ready for more fantastic missions ahead. And, as a franchise, Bond was poised to become a phenomenon. But this didn't necessarily suit Connery: "Well, once you had done the first two, you just moved forward because the rules were established," he emphasized. "One wound up doing less and less, as it were, because you did what you were expected to do and whatever else only up to a point."

That's because once you've created an icon, it takes on a life of its own.

# GOLDFINGER

*Goldfinger* was the game-changer for Bond and the first modern blockbuster (it was listed in *The Guinness Book of World Records* as the fastest grossing film of all time, earning its $3 million back in two weeks, and grabbing around $125 million worldwide). All the elements converged into a sleek and powerful machine like the tricked out Aston Martin DB5 that 007 drives. That's because Broccoli and Saltzman raised Bond to a whole new level of style and excitement. The production values were more lavish, the plot more outrageous, the pace swifter, and the score more pulsating. The action, sex, gadgets, and humor were appropriately elevated as well in an experience that glistened in gold. We were totally immersed in Bond's world and followed his exploits almost exclusively, allowing us to identify with him more vicariously.

Then again, the timing was right for Bond mania to strike in 1964. The world was a dangerous place with the U.S. still in a funk over the assassination of JFK, the Cold War getting hotter, and Vietnam escalating. However, there was also an unbeatable attitude, thanks to passage of the civil rights legislation, the rise of the Labor party in the UK, and the Beatles becoming a sensation on both sides of the Atlantic. Not only that, but, as Cork and Scivally recall, the greater emphasis on technology and physicality in *Goldfinger* nicely coincided with the accomplishments on display at the New York World's Fair and Summer Olympics in Japan.

A lot of credit goes to new director Guy Hamilton (Carol Reed's assistant on *The Fallen Idol*, 1948, and *The Third Man*, 1949). Hamilton previously said no to *Dr. No* but yes to *Goldfinger* after Young departed (like Connery, he was unable to become a franchise partner).

"Bond was only as good as his villains and there was a great danger in him becoming Superman," Hamilton cautioned in *Turner on Goldfinger*. "Consequently, tension goes if you know he's going to win every time. The villain has to be a convincing threat."

Connery also recognized the need to shake things up:"[The] interesting thing was to surprise people who thought they knew how he was going to react to a situation," he told *The New York Times* in 1987. "You'd play the reality, play the humor, have a bit of playful repartee with the audience, and do something unexpected."

As a result, the narrative was refined into a series of set pieces choreographed like an obstacle course with Bond at its center (which Dalton referred to earlier). This meant Connery had to step up everything he learned about "strong and commanding movements." The *Goldfinger* template not only determined the direction of the franchise, but also the future of the action/adventure genre. One might even argue that it further served as the forerunner of the video game.

We notice the difference immediately in the dazzling pre-credit sequence. Bond swims to a dock, throws off his snorkel mask camouflaged as a seagull, and emerges in a dry suit; he then scales a wall with a grappling hook gun, knocks out a guard, trips a switch, and calmly enters the interior of a South American heroin lab "decorated like the Plaza," courtesy of another outlandish set by Ken Adam that's oval and metallic. Then, with utter confidence and grace, Bond applies plastic explosives to the red Nitro tanks and sets a detonated timer synchronized to his famed Rolex Submariner watch. He exits and casually removes his dry suit to reveal a white dinner jacket underneath, and tops it off with a red carnation; then walks into a noisy cantina to admire a sexy dancer (Nadja Regin). Bond lights a cigarette, looks at his watch, and the bomb explodes outside, which causes everyone to clear out.

Bond has just destroyed the local drug trade ("At least they won't be using heroin flavored bananas to finance revolutions"). Yet rather than taking the first flight to Miami, Bond has some "unfinished business" with the dancer in her room. In other words, dangerous sex, just the way he likes it. But as they kiss, he spies a thug (Alf Joint) creeping from behind in a reflection in her eye. He spins her around to block the assailant and the dancer's knocked out. They fight and Bond throws the thug into the bathtub. While he struggles to grab Bond's gun from the nearby holster, Bond electrocutes him with an electric heater: it's a harbinger of more climactic fireworks and a resourcefulness that will serve 007 well throughout the franchise: "Shocking. Positively shocking," Bond quips before exiting so Shirley Bassey can belt out the brassy main title song (the franchise's first pop hit), and we can luxuriate in a golden glimpse of things to come, courtesy of Robert Brownjohn's graphic title sequence.

What we've just witnessed in only four minutes — and will continue to experience for the remainder of the film — is the emergence of the iconic Bond that defined masculinity for the baby boom generation. You never have to worry about telling Bond to Man Up.

However, when we next meet up with Bond at the Fontainebleau in Miami, it represents his first appearance in the U.S. He's getting a massage by Dink (Margaret Nolan, the buxom golden girl in the main titles). But Bond is immediately interrupted by Felix Leiter (now played by the more mundane-looking Cec Linder), and dismisses Dink ("man talk") and slaps her on the ass, demonstrating that his sexism has been escalated too. Felix relays a message from M that he's to keep an eye on Auric Goldfinger (German actor Gert Frobe), who's taken a mark named Simmons (Austin Willis) for $10,000 at gin rummy by the pool.

It only takes Bond a moment to deduce that Goldfinger has been cheating, and sneaks into his suite with the unwitting help of a chambermaid, where he finds the golden-haired and black bikini-clad Jill Masterson (Shirley Eaton) assisting in the scam. Bond busts it up with his usual charm and rubs it in by blackmailing Goldfinger into losing $15,000.

Back in Bond's bed in post coital bliss (she's wearing his pajama top and he's wearing the bottom), 007 realizes that the champagne has lost its chill. In fact, Bond can't resist showing off his snobbishness as he heads for the fridge: "My dear girl, there are some things that just aren't done, such as drinking Dom Perignon '53 above the temperature of 38 degrees Fahrenheit. That's just as bad as listening to the Beatles without earmuffs!" This refers back to his Dr. No put down while at the same time poking fun at the Fab Four, who were his only serious cultural rivals. But then the Beatles would strike back the following year when they riffed on the "Bond Theme" in the title song for *Help!* (released as the U.S. version of the single).

Suddenly one of the surprises Connery alluded to occurs when Bond is knocked unconscious by Goldfinger's henchman, Oddjob (former wrestler Harold Sakata). In keeping with Hamilton's mandate, the mute Korean is much more formidable than Red Grant: strong enough to crush a golf ball and a master at tossing his steel-rimmed bowler with deadly aim. But when Bond regains consciousness, he discovers Jill's naked corpse covered in gold paint (a result of skin suffocation). Talk about shocking. Judging by his reaction, Bond has never encountered anything as nasty as this before.

This sequence not only displays the holy trinity of sex, sadism, and snobbery at its best, but also represents the first time a woman has been murdered because of Bond's reckless pursuit of pleasure. It's a blatant reminder of the dark side that he'd rather not confront and why he must avoid attachments. Still, he struggles to keep that famous ironic detachment.

And yet Bond has a hard time concealing vengeance in his subsequent meeting with M. "This isn't a personal vendetta, 007," scolds M. "It's an assignment, like any other. And if you can't treat it as such, coldly and objectively, 008 can replace you…"

"Sir, I am aware of my shortcomings," Bond replies in a rare admission of weakness. "And I am prepared to continue this assignment in the spirit you suggest — if I knew what it was about!" Why, gold bullion, of course. From now on, Connery's Bond becomes emotionally untouchable.

On his way out, Bond asks Moneypenny what she knows about gold. In another twist, she swings into action and goes straight for the marital answer; then asks him over for dinner and grabs his hat and tosses it onto the stand. When Bond admits he has a business appointment, she refuses to believe him until M confirms it. The scene ends with the warmest exchange between Bond and Moneypenny, giving her a minor victory and calming him down.

By contrast, we get a strange sense of déjà vu from the *Goldfinger*-inspired drowning of Strawberry Fields (Gemma Arterton) in crude oil in *Quantum of Solace*. One of the benefits of the origin story is that it allows us to compare Bond in similar circumstances at different stages of his career. While Connery's Bond is mature enough to perform his job "coldly and objectively," Craig's newbie Bond is emotionally scarred and still "solidifying his place in the world."

Still, Connery's Bond gets even with M by showing off his superior knowledge of brandy during a black tie meeting at the home of Col. Smithers (Richard Vernon) when discussing Goldfinger's international smuggling operation. "I'd say it was a 30-year-old fine, indifferently blended, sir... with an overdose of bon-bois," Bond offers about the disappointing brandy. "Col. Smithers is giving the lecture, 007," M fires back, but then sniffs the brandy in puzzlement.

They concoct a plan for Bond to meet Goldfinger socially for golf in London using a recovered Nazi gold bar as bait. Then, by following Goldfinger, Bond can figure out how he smuggles his gold out of the country. *Casino Royale* would follow in the same vein: they're depending on Bond to win and then crush the more insidious threat.

Our first visit to the Q Branch lab is similar to SPECTRE Island with its explosive and often ridiculous experiments, only much better, thanks to the introduction of the tricked out Silver Birch Aston Martin DB5 (designed in collaboration with Adam). The high-tech sports car is a remarkable step up from Q's "nasty little Christmas present." With its front firing machine guns, tire spikes, rear oil spray, smoke screen, and bullet proof shield (not to mention homing radar), the DB5 instantly became the official Bond car: an outward manifestation of his personality and profession — the constant adrenalin rush that comes with living on the edge.

At first, Bond would just as soon keep his green Bentley or at least test drive the DB5 on his own rather than suffering through Q's demonstration. But Q takes artistic pride in his work and hates the way Bond recklessly destroys his equipment,

which is the way Hamilton instructed Llewelyn to behave. Thus, Q comes off as a strict school master in a further nod to the kitchen sink ethos. This is most evident when Bond thinks he's joking about the ejector seat, and Q replies, "I never joke about my work, 007!"

One of the key debates among the filmmakers was whether to go for surprise or suspense in revealing the DB5's special features, and, as with the attaché case, they chose the latter. It always worked for Hitchcock and they obviously made the right choice considering how thrilling the DB5 works in action and the sustained cultural impact it has enjoyed (selling for $4.1 million at a London auction in 2010).

Significantly, the rest of *Goldfinger* revolves around the cat-and-mouse game already initiated by Bond, continuing with the golf match. In fact, when I asked what he enjoyed most about the film, Connery replied that it was his introduction to golf, which began a lifelong love affair with the sport. Golf fits in perfectly with the Malmgren method and Connery's physical imperative. He even met his current wife, Micheline Roquebrune, at a Moroccan golf tournament in 1970. Although she is French and couldn't speak English and he couldn't speak French, they immediately hit it off non-verbally.

"It wasn't until I was taught enough golf to look as though I could outwit the accomplished golfer Gert Frobe in *Goldfinger* that I got the bug," Connery explained in his autobiography, *Being a Scot.* "I began to take lessons on a course near Pinewood film studios and was immediately hooked on the game. Soon it would nearly take over my life. I began to see golf as a metaphor for living, for in golf you are basically on your own, competing against yourself and always trying to do better. If you cheat, you will be the loser, because you are cheating yourself. When Ian Fleming portrayed Auric Goldfinger as a smooth cheater, James Bond had no regrets when he switched his golf balls, since to be cheated is the just reward of the cheater."

Indeed, Bond could easily beat Goldfinger on skill alone, but it's much more fun topping him at his own game, tit for tat. And yet Goldfinger's inferiority complex makes him much more

vulnerable and interesting than most of the other super baddies. His immersion in gold is the ultimate attention grabber. His compulsion to cheat even extends to his reliance on Oddjob, whose deadly bowler is a shortcut, too. And his Operation Grand Slam is a cheat as well, with Goldfinger planning to destroy the gold in Fort Knox rather than stealing it (an improvement over Fleming's 1959 novel). Curiously, the billionaire has no connection with SPECTRE (the only respite during the Connery era) and instead works with agents for the Chinese government, which supplies the atomic bomb.

After the golf match, Bond follows Goldfinger to Switzerland to learn about his operation. High in the mountains, dressed more casually in a tan sports jacket and slacks (complementing the gold motif), Connery demonstrates a freer side to Bond, which the Aston Martin helps bring out. But he runs into another obstacle when Tilly Masterson (Tania Mallet) attempts to assassinate Goldfinger to avenge the death of her sister, Jill. Bond first avoids pursuing Tilly after she overtakes him in Ford's newly released Mustang ("Discipline, 007, discipline"), but his curiosity is piqued by her lousy aim. He chases her white convertible and slices the tires with the spikes like Ben-Hur's chariot to get her inside his DB5.

Later that night, Bond and Tilly are thrown together again after separately trying to infiltrate Goldfinger's factory, and escape together in the DB5, allowing Bond to show off the oil spray and bullet shield when cut off and forced to stop. That's when tragedy strikes twice for the Mastersons. In trying to protect Tilly by telling her to make a run for it, Bond inadvertently allows Oddjob to kill her with his hat. This forces Bond to use all the tricks in the DB5 to elude Goldfinger's thugs: a thrill ride with its own mixture of excitement, danger, and absurdity, commencing with the hilarious ejector seat gag. Bond is like a kid with a new toy and we enjoy seeing the gadgets in action along with him. But, alas, Bond is fooled by another Goldfinger cheat: a trick mirror in an alley, forcing him to crash into a wall.

Bond has truly run out of tricks in Goldfinger's factory, strapped to a table with an industrial laser (the first in movie history) slicing its way to his famous crotch. "Do you expect me to talk?" "No, Mr. Bond, I expect you to die!" After observing that Goldfinger melts the gold and smuggles the pieces in his solid gold Rolls Royce, Bond's only hope is to bluff his way out by pretending to know about Operation Grand Slam.

When Bond awakens from the tranquilizer dart aboard Goldfinger's private jet, he is greeted by

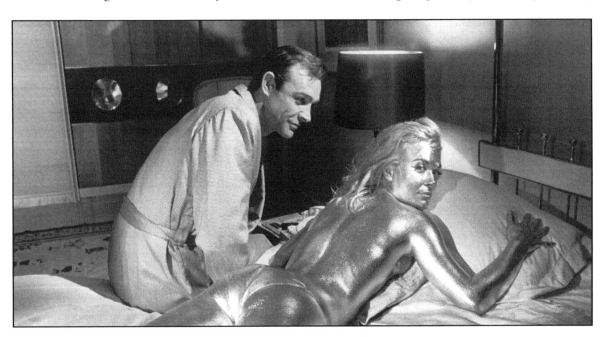

the infamous Pussy Galore (Honor Blackman): "I must be dreaming." Blackman, fresh from playing the leather-clad, judo expert, Cathy Gale, in *The Avengers* (1962-64), eases right into Pussy: the blond lesbian "immune" to Bond's charm, which is just another obstacle for him to overcome.

For the rest of the film, Bond remains Goldfinger's prisoner: first at his stud farm in Kentucky; then inside Fort Knox, handcuffed to the atomic bomb; and finally when held at gunpoint by Goldfinger in a presidential jet. This not only freezes Felix and the military until the climax but also demands even greater agility from Bond to outwit his opponents.

In fact, Bond's imprisonment necessitates leaving his point of view, most notably during Goldfinger's meeting with several rival American mob bosses in his extravagant wood and stone rumpus room. They have been part of his smuggling syndicate, and Goldfinger swindles and later gasses them in one of the franchise's most hideous displays (an uncooperative gangster is escorted off the stud farm and killed by Oddjob and then crushed in a compactor). If it seems Hitlerian, it's no accident: Adam, a German-Jewish refugee, designed the Frank Lloyd Wright-influenced hideaway with painful images of Hitler's Bavarian Berghof retreat in mind.

Fortunately, Bond escapes from his cell in time to hear enough about Operation Grand Slam before being recaptured and escorted by Pussy. At first, he derides Goldfinger's plan; then marvels at its brilliance: Pussy's Flying Circus of lesbian pilots will neutralize the area with the same Delta-9 nerve gas; Goldfinger will break in with the laser and irradiate the gold with the bomb, increasing the value of his gold while creating "economic chaos in the West."

The exchange of judo flips between Bond and Pussy in the barn, of course, represents a more sexually charged version of the dance. She likes to play rough (an S&M throwback to Gale), and so does Bond, who enjoys seducing her over to his side. This later becomes vital in destroying Goldfinger's operation by switching the nerve gas ("I must have appealed to her maternal instincts").

The absurd dance with Oddjob, though, is unlike any of the other choreographed fights during the Connery era. Bond is completely trapped and overmatched in this magnificent cathedral-like vault made of steel and granite with gold bars stacked to the ceiling (Adam at his most inventive). No punch, kick, flip, or karate chop will answer the henchman's considerable strength; no gadgets from Q to bail him out; not even a metal pole or gold bar will harm him. Bond is stripped of his hubris as Oddjob tosses him around like a rag doll and then grins and beckons for him to get up and continue the fight. In a way, it anticipates Richard Kiel's insurmountable Jaws in *The Spy Who Loved Me* and *Moonraker* (1979). The difference is that Connery takes the threat more seriously than Moore so the fight seems more dangerous.

There's only one thing that scares Oddjob: his hat, which Bond gets a hold of. However, our hope of sweet revenge is immediately denied with Bond's errant toss into the metal bars (so much for all that practice in the MI6 office). But then, as though remembering the heater from the pre-credit sequence, Bond alertly grabs a stray live electric cable and electrocutes Oddjob when he turns to retrieve his hat from the bars ("He blew a fuse"). Still, Bond must frantically defuse the bomb before it explodes, and a technician comes to the rescue to turn it off just as the counter reaches… 007.

But there's Goldfinger left to deal with on the way to a hero's welcome with the President. He has hijacked the plane and forced Pussy to pilot it. But, in spite of Bond's earlier warning to her about shooting guns inside aircraft, he forces Goldfinger to fire his gold revolver, which shatters a window and depressurizes the cabin. Bond uses all of his strength to hold on while Goldfinger gets sucked out and winds up "playing his golden harp."

With the plane now out of control, Bond redeems himself by rescuing Pussy and they safely escape before crashing into the ocean. He's earned his sex with Pussy. But first he must avert another rescue attempt by Felix before finishing their frolic underneath the parachute.

So, after enduring the rigors of Operation Grand Slam, Bond will finally go underwater for Operation Thunderball to resume his struggle with SPECTRE.

Timing is everything with Bond. Imagine, for instance, if *Thunderball* had been made first, as originally planned, instead of fourth when the lawsuit was finally settled (bumping *On Her Majesty's Secret Service*). Our introduction to Bond and his world would've changed considerably along with our perception of Connery as Bond.

But not for the better, according to director Terence Young, who was lured back one last time to film his favorite Bond novel and was grateful for the postponement. "*Thunderball* was an immensely expensive picture, and if we had started the series with *Thunderball*, I think it would've been poorly made," he admitted in the audio commentary for the *Thunderball* MGM Ultimate Edition. "It would've been skimped, it would've looked cheap, and we never would've been able to make it properly."

But, of course, *Thunderball* became the most phenomenally successful film of the Connery era, grossing $141.2 million worldwide, which still ranks number one in ticket sales. It capitalized on *Goldfinger's* momentum and the insatiable craving for everything Bond, and solidified 007's cultural dominance as "Mr. Kiss Kiss Bang Bang." *Thunderball* also fittingly introduced Connery's first gun barrel appearance — the epitome of grace under fire, as it were.

By 1965, though, Bond mania had spawned spy mania, led by the two anti-Bonds: *The Spy Who Came in from the Cold*, the John le Carré adaptation starring Richard Burton, and *The Ipcress File*, the first of the Harry Palmer trio of espionage thrillers starring Michael Caine and produced by Saltzman.

Yet it wasn't merely a matter of spending more lavishly on *Thunderball* to stay ahead of the competition (although the Oscar-winning underwater action, Bahamas eye candy, abundance of high-tech gadgets, and widescreen Panavision splendor certainly helped). The real success had more to do with playing up Bond's appetite for sex and violence, using water as the central metaphor.

Young also made Bond less of a pawn in the fight with SPECTRE, and returned to the more realistic action of his first two films.

But, as screenwriter Richard Maibaum suggested, it was just as important to stay ahead of the audience by acknowledging Bond's cultural status and making his humor more self-reflexive. Thus, when postponing a sexual tryst with his physical therapist, Bond utters, "Another time, another place," referring to the title of the 1958 melodrama Connery appeared in with Lana Turner. Or, when Bond refuses to toss his hat onto the stand at MI6 headquarters, it's surely a reminder of the bad aftertaste left by Oddjob.

The pre-credit sequence, meanwhile, literally pokes fun at the Bond mystique with some playful deceptions. We zero in on the initials JB on a coffin in a French chapel; but Bond safely stands on the balcony, explaining to a female operative that JB stands for Col. Jacques Bouvar, a SPECTRE agent who murdered two of his colleagues. He's clearly upset that he couldn't do the honors himself, but brightens when noticing Bouvar's widow opening her own car door.

Bond surprises her in a chateau to pay his condolences, and then slugs the widow, who turns out to be Bouvar in drag (ironically played by stunt double Simmons). A nasty and noisy street fight ensues in this incongruous setting in which they hurl every object within reach at one another (including a china cabinet, a clock, and a curtain). Editor Peter Hunt shrewdly speeds up the tempo and utilizes the jump cut to create the illusion of violent impact, anticipating even greater experimentation in *On Her Majesty's Secret Service*. Finally, they go at it with a poker until Bond strangles Bouvar with the object and throws flowers at his corpse, but not before suffering some painful blows to his back. (Remarkably, Daniel Craig appeared as Bond in drag in a 2011 PSA about gender inequality in the UK, with an off-screen Judi Dench as M challenging his misogyny.)

Bond then makes a wild retreat with the famous Bell Textron jet pack ("No well-dressed man should be without one"), landing beside his Aston Martin DB5. Fittingly, Bond drives off with the female operative and fends off his assailants with a high-pressure water sprayer.

As for SPECTRE, we peek inside the distinctive Paris headquarters (a glossier version of Adam's *Dr. Strangelove* War Room, with low ceiling, slanted walls, a gangway in the center, and chairs with consoles). Number One (Blofeld) sits high above on a platform, hidden by Venetian blinds, petting his cat, and discussing the financial reports of the latest terrorist activities in a capitalistic metaphor that predates *The Godfather*. SPECTRE has prospered considerably since *FRWL*, but, like the Bond franchise, requires greater funding for its major operations. And yet despite fees from an assassination, political blackmail, and a British train robbery, the projections have come up short. It seems there's an embezzlement problem with the flow of drugs from China into the U.S. So, reprising his fatal bait and switch routine, Blofeld makes Number 11 sweat and electrocutes Number Nine in his chair, which humorously disappears.

Number Two, Emilio Largo, then provides an update on their most ambitious project: ransoming £100 million from NATO. Looking like a silver-haired fox with an eye patch, (portrayed with panache by Adolfo Celi), Largo informs them that agent Count Lippe is making necessary preparations at a health clinic in the South of England, conveniently located near the NATO air base.

As luck would have it, Bond stays at the same gothic-inspired Shrublands clinic to treat his back. But he's bored and getting nowhere seducing his pretty physical therapist (Molly Peters), so bumping into the suspicious-looking Lippe (Guy Doleman, who also played Harry Palmer's stern boss) is just the inspiration he needs to have some mischievous fun and wreak havoc with SPECTRE and the clinic. He snoops around Lippe's room and notices a mysterious patient next door with his face covered

in bandages. Lippe then nearly kills Bond on a spinal traction machine, but the therapist returns in time to turn it off, prompting Bond to coerce her into having sex in the sauna to keep her job. Now Bond's energized. He gets even with Lippe by boiling him in a sweat box and then massages the therapist with a mink glove. Thus, sex and violence are more directly linked for Bond in *Thunderball*.

But this is just a sideshow. It turns out that the bandaged man at the clinic has undergone plastic surgery; he's an assassin hired by Lippe to murder and replace a NATO pilot on a training mission. However, the assassin greedily tries to extort more money. Lippe balks, but his accomplice, a voluptuous redhead, Fiona Volpe (Luciana Paluzzi), agrees to the new terms. The assassin hijacks a NATO Vulcan Bomber with two atomic bombs, gasses the crew, and deposits the plane undersea in the Bahamas, where Largo and his men camouflage the Vulcan and transport the bombs to a temporary hiding place before putting them aboard his craft, the Disco Volante, a hydrofoil with a catamaran around it. For good measure, Largo executes the extortionist.

The persistent Bond then uncovers the corpse of the real pilot at the clinic, and spoils a second attempt on his life when smashing the assassin through the window. Unfortunately, Fiona deprives Bond the pleasure of executing Lippe on his way back to London when she fires a missile into his car from her motorcycle (the penalty for hiring such a disloyal contractor).

Moneypenny catches Bond's customary hat toss; he's late for his meeting. For the first time, we view MI6's classically ornate conference room, a stunning contrast to SPECTRE's headquarters, where the other eight Double-0 agents sit impatiently and wait for Bond along with his superiors. But Bond redeems himself when identifying the deceased NATO pilot in a photograph during the briefing. Blofeld has given them a week to pay up or he will destroy an unnamed city (which turns out to be Miami). So Bond flies to Nassau to interrogate the beautiful sister of the deceased pilot, Domino

(Claudine Auger), and has four days to locate the bombs.

Bond in the Bahamas — it's an even a better fit than Jamaica in bringing out his easygoing side, courtesy of Connery. No wonder the actor became a lifelong resident. In fact, after Bond quickly learns that Domino is Largo's mistress, he plays a very easygoing game with Number Two: pretending to be non-threatening yet undermining Largo to impress her. For his part, Largo finds Bond mildly amusing and wants to detain him long enough to complete the mission. Besides, he thinks he's unstoppable and proudly wears his SPECTRE octopus ring.

However, handling Domino is tricky: she's young and sensitive, if headstrong, and Bond avoids telling her about the death of her brother for as long as possible, especially after learning how close they were. Even so, Bond uses his skill and charm to win Domino over and pit her against Largo when necessary. First, Bond baits Largo by casually beating him at baccarat ("It's your spectre against mine"); then he offers to buy Domino a drink and just acts cool when Largo finds them dancing together. And when Bond later catches one of Largo's goons in his hotel room and scalds him in the shower, he sends him back to Largo, who ruthlessly feeds him to his pet sharks.

But Bond can't find the bombs alone: he's nominally assisted by Felix (Rik Van Nutter, in a return to the cool-looking CIA agent) and an obliging Nassau contact, Paula (Martine Beswick from the gypsy fight in *FRWL*). Bond also requires Q's assistance, who meets him in a safe house dressed like a tourist. While initially protesting the way Bond treats everything he gives him "with equal contempt," Q delivers, among other goodies, a Geiger counter disguised as a watch, an underwater infra red camera, a re-breather, a miniature Veri pistol, and a radioactive pill to keep track of 007. The technology overall in *Thunderball* is much more authentic, including the sophisticated vehicles and underwater propulsion unit that Bond later uses, containing spear guns, explosive bottles, and searchlight.

That night Bond steps into action, swimming underneath the Disco Volante to photograph its hull. He survives an attacker and several grenades, and feigns his own death to escape. But then he's picked up on the road by Fiona (who also flaunts the SPECTRE ring). She tests Bond with a high-speed car ride back to the hotel where they're both staying. You'd think Bond would enjoy the dangerous adrenalin rush, but he gets a bad vibe from Fiona and tells her he doesn't like "being taken for a ride." Of course, not: he'd prefer taking her for a ride. There couldn't be a sharper contrast between Domino and Fiona, and Bond's relationship with both of them is the film's most fascinating aspect.

Bond visits Largo's luxurious island estate, Palmyra, where they play out their charade. Largo boasts about his passion for fishing while making fun of his personal assistant, Vargas (Philip Locke), who doesn't drink, smoke, or have sex; Bond pretends to have no passions either while glancing at Domino. Largo then tries to best Bond in skeet shooting; Bond pretends to have no facility with guns and then rapidly hits four targets while shooting from the hip. Largo shows off his dangerous Golden Grotto sharks, insinuating that he's going to feed Bond to them; but to further tweak Largo, Bond hints that he'd like to check out the Disco Volante.

Largo's had enough of Bond, so he orders his men to abduct Paula from the hotel while Bond is preoccupied with Domino at the Junkanoo festival, the local Mardis Gras. However, when Felix informs Bond that Paula's missing, he immediately arranges for a power blackout so he can sneak back into Palmyra and search for her. Unfortunately, she kills herself before Bond can rescue her, but he evades capture by carefully swimming through the other side of the shark pool.

It's time for Bond to confront Fiona, the franchise's first true femme fatale. He surprises her while she's taking a bath. She asks if he's in the wrong room and he slyly remarks, "Not from where I'm standing." From then on, there's no pretense between them and sex is part of the game. But Bond signals that he's in control when she asks for something to put on and

he merely dangles her shoes.

In bed, Fiona acts like a savage cat, complaining about the bars as though she's locked in a cage, and wondering if Bond likes "wild things." Bond looks bored, but she describes him afterward as a "sadistic brute." Francois Truffaut famously wrote that Hitchcock filmed scenes of love as though they were scenes of murder and vice versa, and the first part certainly applies.

Afterward, Fiona is joined by Largo's men, but Bond undercuts her authority by admitting that he's been on to her all along: "My dear girl, don't flatter yourself: What I did was for King and Country. You don't think it gave me any pleasure do you?" Then Fiona attempts to smash Bond's vaunted ego in the most memorable self-reflexive exchange: "James Bond, who only has to make love to a woman and she starts hearing heavenly choirs singing. She repents and immediately returns to the side of right and virtue — but not this one!" To which Bond famously shrugs, "Well, can't win them all."

Stuck in traffic in the middle of the Junkanoo, Bond seizes his chance to escape from Fiona and her cohorts in the car by knocking a bottle of rum from a beggar into a lit cigarette; a flame erupts and he leaps out. But he's shot in the calf before getting lost in the crowd. It's the most thrilling moment: no gadgets, just Bond on the run, hiding and fighting for survival amid the festive, colorful parade. He deftly slips into a float, but the trail of blood quickly gives him away. He creeps into the Kiss Kiss Club (an inside joke about "Mr. Kiss Kiss Bang Bang," which was also the title of an alternate theme song); and heads for the bathroom to clean and bandage his wound, and picks up a girl at the bar to dance with. Fiona cuts in, and Bond maintains his sense of humor while dancing and looking for a way out ("Strange as it may seem, I've grown accustomed to your face"). But Bond spies an assassin waiting for the right crescendo of the conga drum to fire,

**Director Terence Young takes a tea break on the set of *Thunderball* with Molly Peters and Sean Connery. Connery credits Young's style as a pillar of the series' success.**

and, recalling *Goldfinger*, spins Fiona at just the right moment so she catches the bullet in the back. Naturally, he's got a nice parting shot: "Mind if my friend sits this one out? She's just dead!"

Bond and Felix finally uncover the Vulcan and the corpses and set their sights on the Disco Volante, which means Bond now requires Domino's help. If any other spy were in this predicament, he'd tell Domino about her brother alone somewhere and explain the stakes in this potential world crisis. Not Bond — he mixes pleasure with pain in the only way he knows how: First, he has underwater sex with Domino among the pretty coral (we see bubbles climbing to the surface). Then, walking among the rocks, she gets a poisonous spine stuck in her foot from a sea anemone, so Bond carefully removes the spine with his teeth. It reminds Domino of her protective brother when they were children and how Bond makes her cry like him. Now they quietly sit down and Bond gently breaks the news about her brother, Largo, and the bombs. She's confused and angry, but there's no time to think, so she agrees to help. But when Bond starts to explain how to use the camera with the Geiger counter, she spots Vargas, who followed them. Bond instantly kills him with a speargun. Domino regrets it wasn't Largo, and asks Bond to kill him for her; then she remembers a secret cove on the other side of Palmyra that might be important.

That's an understatement: Bond joins Largo's men at the cove and slips among them in the cave, where the bombs are being transported back to the Disco Volante by underwater saucer. But Largo spots Bond and signals for a frogman to kill him. After tangling with him, however, Bond becomes trapped in the cave while Largo and his men leave with the bombs. Aboard the cruiser headed for Miami, Largo catches Domino with the Geiger counter and tortures her with a lit cigar and ice cubes until interrupted by his timid nuclear physicist (George Pravda). But Bond finds a way out of the cave to a coral reef; he swallows his radioactive pill and waits for Felix to come to his rescue in a helicopter so he can signal the Navy to mount an attack in Miami.

A team of aqua-paras drops from a plane into the emerald green ocean below to battle SPECTRE (orange vs. black) and prevent Largo from depositing a bomb. Wearing his self-propelling scuba gear, Bond joins the fray and takes charge. He sweeps through the water, killing one baddie after another with spear and knife and causing other destruction with his weaponry. He even lures two frogmen into a trap by abandoning his pack inside a wreck and exploding a grenade inside the hatch. The underwater mayhem is like an orgy of death in slow motion, with sharks and rays lured by blood, interspersed with beautiful inserts of fish and plant life. This was before Sam Peckinpah ushered in his more graphic brand of stylistic violence in *The Wild Bunch* (1969).

Bond goes after Largo and separates him from the bomb, but he gets away when Bond loses his mask and stops to get another while using the re-breather. Largo returns to the Disco Volante, where the other bomb remains, and manages to elude the Navy, but Bond sneaks onboard and they fight while the cruiser swings out control, threatening to crash. Yet, as in *FRWL*, a woman comes to Bond's rescue when Domino harpoons Largo right before he shoots him. Like Tatiana, Domino has grown more comfortable in her own skin with the help of Bond. Then, with Largo's corpse locked to the steering wheel, Bond and Domino jump overboard into an inflatable raft and watch the Disco Volante explode. But since they've already had their highly-anticipated sea sex, a sky-hook merely hoists Bond and Domino aboard a Navy plane and they vanish.

Sensing that Bond had reached critical mass, Connery warned *Playboy*, "But we have to be careful where we go next, because I think with *Thunderball* we've reached the limit as far as size and gimmicks are concerned....What is needed now is a change of course — more attention to character and better dialogue."

Easier said than done, which is why, along with several other factors, Connery was on a collision course with Bond in Japan.

# YOU ONLY LIVE TWICE

If Broccoli and Saltzman had proceeded to make Fleming's so-called "Blofeld Trilogy" in succession — *Thunderball, On Her Majesty's Secret Service* (1963), and *You Only Live Twice* (1964) — there certainly would've been "a change of course" and "more attention to character." But they didn't, which is a shame, because it deprived Bond of the same emotional arc on screen. In *OHMSS*, Bond finds true love and faces off with Blofeld for the first time, only to be crushed after the wedding when Blofeld kills his bride. Then, in *YOLT*, Bond exacts revenge by killing Blofeld in Japan, only to be left with amnesia and the prophetic title: "You only live twice — once when you're born and once when you look death in the face."

But when production of *Thunderball* ran long and they lost their window of opportunity in Switzerland for *OHMSS*, the producers skipped over to *YOLT* to make Bond's fifth adventure in Japan. However, the lapse in continuity necessitated a complete rewrite, so they abandoned Fleming for the first time and came up with a more spectacular version of *Dr. No*. They also infused the franchise with some fresh blood: director Lewis Gilbert (*Alfie*, 1964), who had previous experience shooting in Asia, and proficiently orchestrates all of the necessary elements; famed children's author and Fleming's friend, Roald Dahl (*Charlie and the Chocolate Factory*, 1964), who provides his sly wit with the script; and the masterful cinematographer Freddie Young (*Lawrence of Arabia*, 1962), who conveys the exotic beauty of Japan.

Of course, venturing into outer space was the next logical step after the underwater exploits of *Thunderball*. The film opens above Earth with a giant squid-like craft (Bird 1) swallowing up a much smaller U.S. capsule, proving that Bond had not yet "reached the limit as far as size and gimmicks are concerned."

But Connery had reached his limit as Bond, which was swallowing him up, so he called it quits

with *YOLT* (especially after failing to become a producing partner). "*Thunderball* started to become a problem," he told me, "not because of the film per se, but because they committed before they ever had the script ready. They were always looking for the next picture coming out, which is rather like the studios do now. And it's very expensive because you have to get a date for an opening and it's working ass-backwards. And I found that a demand on my time — the films got longer, like 18 weeks or 20. But a great deal of this stuff like on *You Only Live Twice* where we were in Japan for months was ridiculous. We had the wrong time of the year when we got there; it was stormy....[And] we kept moving the goal posts because they couldn't commit to a definite date, and I was having to turn down work because I was contractually committed to doing the movies. And eventually I just wanted out. But I was already getting disenchanted. Apart from the payment, which was puerile, they were bringing in a lot of science-fiction stuff."

That's because the franchise had become a victim of its own success with the need to create more extraordinary situations for Bond to get out of. "They had to get more extraordinary," asserted Craig, who's managed to avoid the same trap, "because when you have somebody who seems to know all the answers, what do you do with him?"

They also made Bond a fish out of water so he doesn't have all the answers in stopping Blofeld from turning the space race into World War III. Then, for good measure, they thwarted our expectations at every turn to prevent the formula from becoming too predictable, beginning with another "death of Bond" episode after hostilities break out between the U.S. and Soviet Union during a conference in some frozen wasteland.

We find Bond in Hong Kong, in bed, kissing a woman named Ling (Tsai Chin, who returns in a poker-playing cameo in *Casino Royale*). He asks, "Why do Chinese girls taste different from all other girls?" She tantalizes him, but Bond has no intention of eating only Chinese. Then Ling gets up and presses a button and the bed pulls up against the wall with Bond still inside. She lets in two assassins with machine guns, who fire into the bed. They leave ahead of the cops, who uncover Bond's bloody corpse. But it's all an elaborate hoax: Bond fakes his own death to better elude SPECTRE — a marvelous reversal of the death/rebirth theme at the end of the novel.

But there are more twists: We finally learn that he's Commander Bond as a result of his "burial" at sea and subsequent "resurrection" aboard the MI6 submarine in his Royal Navy uniform. He even tosses his cap onto the stand and greets Moneypenny as Penny. And he's on his best behavior with Admiral M, who informs him about a preemptive space launch by the Soviets prior to the next one by the U.S., and that his contact in Tokyo is named Henderson. On his way out, Moneypenny supplies the password ("I love you"), which Bond refuses to repeat. But we also learn that he studied Asian languages at Cambridge because he throws back the book on instant Japanese that she offers.

After being "torpedoed" back into the water, Bond makes his way through the crowded, neon streets of Tokyo, but definitely looks out of place. He's followed by a mysterious woman and soon met by her at a sumo wrestling match — her name is Aki (Akiko Wakabayashi). She drives Bond in her convertible Toyota 2000 GT to Dikko Henderson, a droll expatriate and MI6 field agent with a wooden leg (which Bond whacks to identify him). He's wonderfully played by Charles Gray (who will reappear with far less restraint as Blofeld in *Diamonds Are Forever*, 1971). Henderson refuses to go completely native, though, living in an apartment with an odd mixture of English and Japanese styles (courtesy of Adam). He hands Bond a martini (stirred, not shaken), and tells him to contact Tiger Tanaka, head of the Japanese Secret Service. But just as things are getting interesting, Henderson's stabbed to death in the back in a throwback to the good old days of espionage, when it was standard to expect the unexpected.

Bond follows the assassin to the front lawn and kills him with the knife during their struggle; then, in a continual escalation of events, Bond impersonates the assassin in the getaway car and pretends to be injured. The driver takes them to Osato Chemicals and carries Bond inside to the president's luxurious office, where 007 attacks the large assailant in a fight that's reminiscent of the ones with Oddjob and Bouvar: hitting him with a couch and sword when unable to hurt him, yet, oddly, knocking him out with a statue, breaking the head off. Like *Thunderball*, this early skirmish winds up being the best fight of the film.

But he's not finished yet. After hiding the body in a hidden bar, Bond pours a drink, which turns out to be horrible Siamese vodka. Nothing is what it seems, which Bond eventually realizes is the key to finding Blofeld. Then, noticing a safe behind a dislodged wall panel, Bond cracks it with a handy electronic device (he will use a more elaborate one in *OHMSS*), but triggers the alarm. Bond manages to steal some documents before leaving the building pursued by two security guards.

Bond fires at a guard outside and Aki pulls up in her car to rescue him in another twist. Bond doesn't trust her as she drives to a secluded subway station. She stops and gets out and enters a building. Bond follows her inside, falls through a trapdoor, and slides through a stainless steel chute recalling Orson Welles in *The Lady from Shanghai* (1947), landing upright in a comfortable lounge chair. But instead of entering the villain's lair, Bond unexpectedly finds himself in the underground office of Tanaka (Tetsuro Tamba): curved, spare, full of wood, and highlighted by two spherical monitors in copper that replay a video of Bond's capture. "Welcome to Japan, Mr. Bond," greets Tanaka, who marvels at how easily 007 falls for women.

Tanaka is the Japanese counterpart to M, well-cultivated like Bond, and lives in comfortable seclusion like Blofeld. He has his own private train and a lovely house and garden all to himself. But he's attained a state of grace, and enjoys Bond's company, graciously hosting him at his home and introducing him to his culture while aiding in the investigation.

That night they take a soothing Japanese-style bath assisted by a bevy of well-trained girls. Afterward, during his massage, Bond is pleasantly surprised again by Aki, who not only finishes the massage but also wants to have sex with him. No wonder he tells Tanaka, "I just might retire to here."

The following morning, Bond returns to Osato Chemicals with the name of a cargo ship as his only lead, and is amused to find that the statue he broke the previous night has already been replaced. Bond pretends to be a dull subcontractor named Fisher, wishing to buy Osato's MSG. The acerbic Osato (Teru Shimada) and his attractive secretary, Helga Brandt (Karin Dor), a redhead resembling Fiona, offer Bond champagne, but he resists. That is, until learning that it's a Dom Perignon '59. Bond also can't resist making up a morbid story about his predecessor falling into a pulverizer. Osato surreptitiously observes Bond's hidden Walther PPK through an X-ray machine behind his desk, and teases him that he should stop smoking (the surgeon general warning started appearing on American cigarette packs in 1965). After Bond leaves, Osato orders Helga to kill him.

It's Aki to the rescue again when Bond is fired at in front of Osato's headquarters. She alerts Tanaka on her videophone and the car following them is picked up by Tanaka's men in a helicopter with an electromagnet and dropped into the bay. Aki proceeds to the Kobe docks, where the cargo ship they've been looking for has been located. Bond realizes that it contains liquid oxygen for rocket fuel. But they are spotted by Osato's men and move to a higher level to trade gunfire. Aki escapes by rope and Bond fights them off before gracefully jumping down two levels and landing on some cardboard boxes. However, he's whacked from behind and taken prisoner by Osato.

After being hemmed in for most of the film, Bond is now strapped to a chair aboard the cargo ship. It's a familiar position: trying to seduce a femme fatale over to his side. He's interrogated by Helga, who is SPECTRE's Number 11. She tries intimidating him with a shiny scalpel; he pretends to be an industrial spy and offers $300,000 for Osato's secret MSG recipe. It appears to work: she cuts his rope and he retrieves the scalpel and cuts her dress straps as she kisses him ("Oh, the things I do for England"). But while flying back to Tokyo in her Cessna, Helga turns out to be another Fiona: she drops an exploding lipstick compact and pins him down with a bar that shoots out of the wall, and then parachutes to safety. Bond manages to free his hands at the last moment and pull the plane down to the ground and flee as it explodes.

In a first, Bond actually summons Q to bring a gyrocopter named "Little Nellie," which functions as an airborne Aston Martin. This will better help him locate the launch site. The "wonderful girl," as Bond calls her with plenty of sexual innuendo, is quickly assembled by four assistants. Then a rather beleaguered Q briefs Bond on some new firepower: two machine guns, two rocket launchers, air-to-air missiles, two flame throwers, two smoke ejectors, and aerial mines. Tanaka begs Bond to reconsider flying "Little Nellie" — it's too dangerous.

But that sense of daring is what defines Bond — and it's the first time he takes charge in Japan. In fact, he enjoys "Little Nellie" in action almost as much as his Aston Martin, disposing of four enemy helicopters with the flame throwers, aerial mines, rocket, and the air-to-air missiles, respectively. It's exhilarating fun and he senses that he must be getting close to the launch site.

We finally enter Blofeld's lair — an extinct volcanic crater — after his ravenous Bird 1 returns with the Soviet space capsule, bringing the two superpowers closer to war like Siamese fighting fish. Constructed on the back lot of Pinewood for a record $1 million, the circular set (400 feet in diameter and 120 feet high) was the largest and most magnificent of its time. It boasted a helicopter pad, full-scale rocket, a retractable metal crater lake, and a working monorail system. It required 700 tons of steel, 200 tons of plasterwork, 500,000 tubular couplings, 8,000 railway ties, and more than 250,000 square yards of canvas. It's Blofeld's kitschiest hideout, to be sure, and Adam's crowning achievement of the Connery era.

Meanwhile, we glimpse Blofeld in the command

center, still hidden but wearing the SPECTRE ring and petting his cat. He's played by Donald Pleasence, a sensitive character actor best-known for nervy nerds (*Look Back in Anger*, *The Great Escape*, *Halloween*). And this Blofeld's pretty nervy despite how well the mission's going (even his cat gets agitated). Back in his lounge, an all-purpose room divided by a two-piece bridge above a moat filled with piranhas, Blofeld extorts $100 million in advance from his Chinese benefactors (forced to deal with SPECTRE after striking out with Goldfinger), and we soon learn why: he's upset that Bond is still alive. Then he scolds Osato and Helga for not killing Bond, and, in a variation of his old routine, throws Helga to the piranhas by pulling a lever and collapsing the bridge, giving Osato one last chance ("Kill Bond…Now!").

But Tanaka takes Bond to his own hidden fortress, a ninja training camp (filmed at the exquisite Himeji Castle in Hyōgo), where, in the film's most remarkable sequence, Bond becomes Japanese to complete the mission. As a result, Bond gives himself over completely: he gets a cosmetic makeover on his eyelids and hair (performed by girls in bikinis, no less); and learns martial arts by fighting with swords and sticks and throwing metal stars. Tanaka even gives Q a run for his money by showing off a nifty rocket gun disguised as a cigarette, which he demonstrates by exploding a straw dummy.

However, the hideout is not impregnable: there are two attempts on Bond's life. First, an assassin sneaks into the camp in the middle of the night and slips onto the roof of Bond's guest house. He unwinds a string and lowers it to Bond's mouth and pours poison down the string. But Bond rolls over and Aki snuggles up against him and swallows the poison instead (a bitter irony after all she's done for him). She gasps, Bond awakens, and he shoots the assassin dead. Bond then rushes to her side as she dies. It's a poignant moment, an odd precursor to the tragic climax of *OHMSS* (sans Connery). But even though Bond has grown quite fond of Aki, he remains unflappable in his desire to get on with the mission.

Then, on the last day of training, Bond is directly attacked. While fighting with sticks, Bond is disarmed and raises his hands in defeat. But a knife suddenly appears at the end of his opponent's stick and he tries to kill Bond, who struggles, grabs the stick, and stabs the assassin to death. The execution is a ruthless reminder of Bond's "live and let die" credo.

In order to provide special cover as a fisherman, Bond takes a bride in a mock Japanese wedding ceremony, another precursor to *OHMSS*. But despite the formality, it's an occasion laced with humor. Bond sits with other grooms and cringes when two old and unattractive brides walk by (Tanaka teased him that his bride would be ugly). The third, Kissy Suzuki (Mie Hama), is very young and pretty. She's an Ama diving girl and Tanaka's agent, and Bond is relieved when she approaches; they solemnly walk to the temple and kneel as a priest marries the three couples and they conclude with the tea ritual. Given the circumstances and setting — lyrically lensed by Young and enhanced by Barry's lovely score — it's an enchanting moment for Bond.

But there's no honeymoon for Bond — this is strictly business for the traditional Kissy. They stay at her house on the Ama Island, where she insists they sleep in separate beds, so Bond pushes away his oysters ("I won't need these"). It's just as well because Tanaka interrupts Bond in the middle of the night to inform him that the U.S. has pushed up its next rocket launch. They have only a day to find the launch site. But since one of the local diving girls died mysteriously near a cave, Bond and Kissy check it out in the morning and discover that it contains poison gas to keep visitors away and that it leads to their destination in the distance. They spend the rest of the day hiking to the volcano and spot a helicopter going inside. They climb to the top and Bond smartly throws a rock and discovers that the lake is a metal façade. He observes how to get inside and sends Kissy back for Tanaka and the ninjas.

Having also learned the art of concealment and surprise from his ninja training, Bond enters the crater, climbs down using suction cups on his knees and elbows, and snoops around unnoticed. He observes the SPECTRE astronauts climbing aboard the monorail and follows the trail. He finds the American and Soviet astronauts being held prisoner in a cell and helps them escape; then he suits up as a SPECTRE astronaut and tries to join the mission, but is recognized by Blofeld on a monitor for carrying his air conditioner (one of 007's few mistakes). Bond is brought to the command center for their long-awaited meeting: "James Bond. Allow me to introduce myself…"

The bald Blofeld sticks his head out, revealing a hideous scar running down the right side of his face and around his eye with a severely drooping lid. He wears a tan Nehru suit, which somehow looks vulgar on him. "I am Ernst Stavro Blofeld," he proudly proclaims. "They told me you were assassinated in Hong Kong." "Yes, this is my second life," Bond quips without further comment on meeting his nemesis. "You only live twice, Mr. Bond," Blofeld counters in full megalomania mode.

But Bond quickly outwits Blofeld: he gets permission to smoke and explodes one of Tanaka's special cigarettes so he can open the crater and let the others inside. Tanaka and Kissy are accompanied by 100 ninjas: they throw down ropes and descend before the crater closes. Yet Blofeld remains undeterred and closes the shutters as they engage in an all-out war with SPECTRE. That is, until a ninja fires a rocket gun that blows through the shutters, causing Bond to sneer ("Impregnable?").

It's the beginning of the end: Blofeld escorts Bond and Osato to his lounge, where he takes a gun from his blond bodyguard, Hans (who resembles Red Grant). But instead of shooting Bond, he kills Osato to demonstrate the price of failure. Blofeld forces Bond through a secret door and they emerge from a tunnel beside the monorail. Blofeld points his gun at Bond and says goodbye, but, continuing a tradition since *FRWL*, Bond's life is spared — this time by Tanaka, who hurls a metal star that strikes Blofeld on the wrist. He misfires, drops the gun, and escapes in the monorail.

Emboldened, Bond picks up the gun and convinces the suddenly skeptical Tanaka that there's still a chance to prevent World War III. He tells him that there's a detonator button for Bird 1 in the command center, and so Bond makes a daring run for it. But he first must tangle with Hans in the lounge. Yet Hans is no Grant, and Bond easily throws him to the piranhas ("Bon appétit").

Bond then reaches the command center, and initially has trouble opening the case around the button (shades of *Goldfinger*). But he pries it loose and presses the button to destroy Bird 1 with a few seconds to spare. Blofeld isn't through yet, though: he hops off the monorail and detonates a self-destruct mechanism before resuming his escape. But Bond and the others escape through the tunnel, emerge out of the cave, and get in rafts to watch the mountain explode.

Now about that honeymoon," Bond seductively suggests to Kissy. They begin kissing, both thinking they're safe at last, but the raft is suddenly lifted up by the MI6 submarine in what turns out to be the best instance of coitus interruptus. M instructs Monepenny to tell Bond to come aboard, which she's thrilled to do. And we end on the submarine heading out to sea.

Thus, when *YOLT* opened in the summer of 1967 (breaking with fall/holiday tradition), we presumed that this was the last of Connery as Bond. Little did we realize that the unpredictable Scot would return after a one-film absence to usher Bond into the 1970s with his last official curtain call.

# DIAMONDS ARE FOREVER

Bond certainly has a score to settle with Blofeld after killing his wife in *On Her Majesty's Secret Service*. But with Lazenby out of the picture, they lured Connery out of retirement for *Diamonds Are Forever* in 1971 with a record $1.25 million and 10% of the gross (with the upfront money donated to his Scottish International Educational Trust for distinguished students, while the back end money Connery kept).

Connery called it "an enriching exorcism," but instead of maintaining the continuity of *OHMSS*, he reverted to a much lighter Bond for his last official appearance. After all, Connery was nearly 41 and looked it (paunchy and grayer with bushy eyebrows), so there was nowhere left to go but camp.

In fact, Connery's reemergence almost gives the impression that Bond has amnesia about Tracy or it was a nightmare with an imposter, which is ironic since *DAF* is all about imposters.

"I suppose I'm a bit slower, not quite as fit," Connery told the BBC about his Bond reboot. "Coming back in it to do this one, the wicket was better for me to make the conditions: of not being so much a pawn in the circumstances."

And with Blofeld back for the conclusion of this film trilogy, the circumstances required another departure from Fleming. Director Guy Hamilton was back to provide the *Goldfinger* touch along with screenwriter Richard Maibaum and most of the familiar crew. However, when the script didn't hook Connery, they took a chance on the young and promising Tom Mankiewicz. His pedigree was perfect — he was the son of Oscar-winning screenwriter-director Joseph Mankiewicz (*All About Eve*). He also demonstrated that he could handle English dialogue in the book for the short-lived Broadway musical *Georgy* (1970), based on the movie *Georgy Girl* (1966).

It worked — Connery liked the snappy rewrite. Mankiewicz not only applied the sharp wit that he inherited from his father to an ever-quipping Bond, but he also armed Blofeld and his gay assassins, Mr. Wint and Mr. Kidd, with an arsenal of lethal bons mots. Why should Bond have all the fun?

Not with Blofeld in a more jovial mood and willing to engage in verbal warfare with Bond. He comes off as a variation of George Sanders' Addison DeWitt from *Eve*, complete with cigarette holder, thanks to the urbane Mankiewicz and Charles Gray's flamboyant portrayal (a jump start in leading us through "The Time Warp" in *The Rocky Horror Picture Show*). But then Blofeld has reason to brag as a result of his clever sleight of hand (fooling Bond with one imposter trick after another): "As La Rochefoucauld observed, 'Humility is the worst form of conceit.' I do hold the winning hand."

But Bond appears to have all the fun in the pre-credit sequence. A faceless 007 hurls an Asian thug through the paper-thin walls of a Japanese-looking room, seemingly picking up where we left off with Connery in *YOLT*. "Where is Blofeld?" he demands. Then, he slugs a gambler in Cairo wearing a fez, which leads him to a sunbathing femme fatale. After making his signature entrance, Bond throttles her with her bikini top ("There's something I'd like you to get off your chest") to find the whereabouts of Ernst Stavro Blofeld.

Bond finally hunts him down in his latest lair (more stainless steel and copper from Ken Adam), where Blofeld's rushing to surgically create a look-alike to throw off Bond. Again, it's a fitting use of doppelgangers, considering the revolving actors. Here Blofeld boasts a full head of silver hair and has switched to the Mao-style Nehru jacket. But Bond foils the operation by killing the intended look-alike, who first pulls a gun on him from inside a mud bath. Bond deftly tumbles out of the way, releases a chord, and drowns the poor fellow with the rest of the superheated mud.

"Making mud pies, 007?" Blofeld sneers. Bond quickly disposes of his two guards with the help of a mousetrap-like finger clamp in his holster and some scalpels (there's more blood as well as more skin in *DAF*). He then thrashes Blofeld, ties him to a stretcher, and joyously sends him to his death in the mud bath ("Welcome to Hell, Blofeld"). Or so it seems.

Back in London, Bond has the inevitable letdown. He's irritable and takes it out on M when assigned a simple diamond smuggling case that's beneath him. The government's South African mining operation has been threatened by the smuggling and stockpiling of gems, only now the smugglers are being systematically wiped out.

Enter Wint and Kidd, who litter their killing spree with enough gallows humor to launch a Vegas lounge act. Bruce Glover plays the neatly dressed, more dominant Wint, while jazz musician Putter Smith portrays the funkier-looking, soft spoken Kidd. But they're quite the sadists. "Curious how everyone who touches those diamonds seems to die," Wint observes after slipping a scorpion down the back of a dentist. Then after blowing up the next courier in his helicopter, they conclude: "If God had wanted man to fly, Mr. Kidd…" "He would have given him wings, Mr. Wint." And the two walk off hand in hand.

But for the moment, the only thing that interests Bond is the fine '51 Solera offered by his host, diamond expert Sir Donald Munger (Laurence Naismith). He teases M about missing out on the exceptional sherry because of his liver ailment, but M snickers that there is no vintage for sherry, to which Bond snobbishly replies, "I was referring to the original vintage on which the sherry is based, sir — 1851, unmistakable." It's the opposite of their argument about Col. Smithers' disappointing brandy in *Goldfinger*, but the dick-swinging never ceases.

Bond's mission is to follow the chain from Holland to the U.S., posing as smuggler Peter Franks. In a cute scene, Franks (Joe Robinson) is detained at the Dutch port, and Moneypenny (posing as a customs official) greets Bond in Franks' car to facilitate the switch. When Bond inquires what he can bring her back from Holland, she asks for a diamond ring, but will settle for a tulip. He

drives off to catch the Hovercraft and she looks on longingly. It's a tender farewell to their flirty routine.

Meanwhile, Bond initiates a flirty routine with his sexy and kooky contact in Amsterdam, Tiffany Case (Jill St. John, the Ring-A-Ding-Ding girl from Frank Sinatra's *Come Blow Your Horn* and *Tony Rome*). Bond definitely likes what he sees when catching her in bra and panties ("That's a nice little nothing you're almost wearing"). But she plays hard to get at first, offering him a drink and changing clothes and wigs while explaining how she was born on the first floor of the famous jewelry store when her mother was looking for a wedding ring. It's like a scene out of a light caper: "Which do you prefer?" she asks in reference to her hair color. "Well, as long as the collar and cuffs match," he counters. She winds up being a redhead, retrieving Bond's fingerprints from the glass to make sure they're authentic. But he's one-step ahead of her, thanks to Q, who's provided latex covers with Franks' prints.

Speaking of Q, Bond thanks him over the phone in his hotel room for his latest innovation — another Connery-era closure. But while loading the Aston Martin with a set of rockets (no doubt inspired by his success with "Little Nellie"), Q warns Bond that Franks has escaped British custody.

Bond rushes back to Tiffany's apartment, where he intercepts Franks just in time outside the entrance. However, the ensuing fight in the elevator — the last great one of the Connery era — is buttressed by broad humor. This goes way beyond the witty exit line, and is a harbinger of more outrageous things to come with Roger Moore. In essence, Connery has set the kitschy tone for Moore.

A chatty Bond leads Franks into the lobby and elevator with a horrible Dutch accent. They begin the ride up and Bond sizes him up apprehensively; he looks at his watch and actually misses with the first punch when his elbow shatters the window behind him. Then they bash each other around, reminding us that Connery's aging 007 can still do the dance. But not without every bit of strength and cunning: he hits the stop button with his foot while being strangled, and slams the door on his arm to knock a shard of glass loose. Even so, it takes a fire extinguisher to finish Franks off outside the elevator. First, the foam slows him down, and then a shot to the back sends him hurling to his death down below. Bond then alertly slips his gold Playboy Club membership card into Franks' wallet to fool Tiffany: "My God, you just killed James Bond!" she shrieks. "Is that who it was?" cracks Bond. "Well, just goes to show, no one's indestructible."

That's funny coming from the soon departing Connery: After 50 years, nobody's more indestructible than Bond. But, again, it's another instance of a more self-deprecating 007, who's just looked death in the face once more and laughed.

There's also a lighter and chummier relationship with Felix Leiter (played here by Norman Burton a la Cec Linder). Franks' corpse comes in handy for transporting the diamonds back to LA, where Bond is greeted by Felix at LAX (posing as a customs official). But when Felix gives up trying to find the diamonds in the body, Bond can't resist a playful nod to Holmes and Watson at Felix's expense: "Alimentary, Dr. Leiter."

Next stop, Vegas, to drop off the diamonds at a mortuary called Slumber, escorted in a limo by the kind of anachronistic gangsters last seen in *Goldfinger*. It's a far cry from Bond's more exotic destinations, with its sleazy charm and neon-lit mirages. Then again, it's the last outpost where dreams are made of, so what better place to take over the world without arousing suspicion?

From here, the plot gets very complicated, with Bond outsmarting the smugglers and surviving various attempts on his life by Wint and Kidd. In fact, Bond only avoids being cremated alive at the last instant when the next smuggler in the chain, Shady Tree (comic Leonard Barr), realizes that he switched the diamonds for fakes. But that just makes them even since Bond's $50,000 fee is counterfeit.

Bond then follows Shady to the Whyte House, the hotel/casino owned by the reclusive Howard Hughes-like owner, where he performs standup. But he's too late — Wint and Kidd have already been there. Bond then decides to collect his real $50,000 by shooting rigged craps with the permission of casino manager Saxby (Bruce Cabot).

And since he likes to mix gambling with sex, Bond doesn't mind being picked up by gold digger Plenty O'Toole ("Named after your father, no doubt"); he generously slips her $5,000 for providing such pretty eye candy. Plenty's played by Natalie Wood's voluptuous younger sister, Lana, and eagerly escorts him back to his hotel room. However, just when Bond unzips her down to her transparent pink panties and purple high heels, they're interrupted by the Slumber mobsters, who promptly throw Tiffany out the window. Fortunately, she lands in the swimming pool directly below, which is purely unintentional ("I didn't know there was a pool down there").

And who should Bond find in his bed? Why, Tiffany, of course, who now wants to partner with Bond and escape to Hong Kong if he'll give her the diamonds. He agrees, hoping somehow she'll lead him further up the smuggling chain. So, with the help of Felix and his agents, Bond arranges for Tiffany to retrieve the diamonds in a stuffed bear at Circus Circus. She promptly ditches them in the crowd, but finds Bond waiting for her at her residence. No more games: he explains the situation and wants the diamonds back. With Plenty floating dead in Tiffany's pool and wearing one of her wigs in a case of mistaken identity, she has no alternative.

Tiffany leads him to a locker at the airport but they're too late: Saxby's already retrieved them. They follow him to a gas station, where Saxby hands them over to refraction specialist Dr. Metz (Joseph Furst), who takes them to Whyte's remote research lab outside of Vegas. With the help of Tiffany's diversion, though, Bond infiltrates the lab and impersonates a German technician. But his obnoxious presence immediately irritates Dr. Metz, who's trying to put the finishing touches on the secret satellite project. But before Bond can figure out how the diamonds are involved, the real technician shows up, and he's forced to flee in a moon buggy, pursued by Whyte's men on dirt trikes.

It's the most surreal Bond chase ever and doesn't make any sense, but, as critic Roger Ebert noted, it's all about reveling in the wild moment. Indeed, the sight of 007 in the desert and out of control

in this bizarre vehicle, mechanical arms flailing, is a hilarious commentary on just how far Bond has descended. He's no longer graceful or effortless, but with Connery at the helm, he's still a commanding presence. He's much more relaxed when hopping onto a dirt trike to finish his escape.

This is topped by the hilarious chase through downtown Vegas in a Mustang Mach 1 with a terrified Tiffany by Bond's side. Running circles around the local police, smashing two-dozen cars, and creating lots of mayhem, the sequence amazingly culminates in Bond turning the car on its side in an alley. Even Connery thought they went too far with this stunt. But, like the "Little Nellie" action sequence in *YOLT*, it's the first time that Bond is truly in control. Interestingly, there's even a forerunner to *Live and Let Die's* Sheriff J.W. Pepper in the form of a flustered police chief.

Bond then trades up to the bridal suite at the Whyte House "in order to form a more perfect union" with Tiffany in a kitschy waterbed full of fish. She's anxious to cooperate with Felix to avoid prison, and he's anxious to confront Whyte to discover what this is all about. So Bond sneaks into Whyte's penthouse, riding on top of the elevator and looking magnificent on top of the world. He then scales the walls, using a bolt gun and harness straps like Batman to fly through the air and climb inside. He lands in a gadget-filled bathroom and is greeted on the intercom by the voice of his hospitable, Southern host.

But when Bond enters the immense glass and steel penthouse (Adam having another field day), he shockingly finds himself face to face with not one but two Blofelds ("Double jeopardy, Mr. Bond"). It's an impersonation nightmare inspired by a dream Broccoli had about his friend, Howard Hughes. One Blofeld sits behind a desk and the other reclines on a sofa; then the first Blofeld demonstrates a voice algorithm recorder that reproduces Whyte's voice during a business call. Bond is clearly impressed and enervated by the challenge. But which one is the real Blofeld?

When a cat creeps and leaps onto Blofeld's lap on the couch, Bond fires a bolt at his forehead.

But then another cat proudly slinks and joins its master. "Right idea, Mr. Bond," Blofeld beams. "But wrong pussy," Bond bemoans. The cat-and-mouse continues with Bond trying to find out what he's plotting while somehow surviving the night. It's uncannily *Sleuth*-like, which Mankiewicz's father was concurrently adapting as his final film for production and release in 1972.

But Blofeld's gotten smarter: he knows from experience that it's best not to show your hand too soon. So he says goodnight and instructs Bond to take the elevator, which immediately arouses his suspicion: "Well go on, go on, it's merely a lift," Blofeld implores. "Or should I say elevator? In any event, I'm sure you'll find it far more convenient than mountaineering about outside the Whyte House."

But there's simply no way out, so score one for Blofeld: Bond enters the elevator, where he's gassed unconscious and then buried alive by Wint and Kidd — this time in a new irrigation pipe. When he awakens, he smells "like a tart's handkerchief," thanks to Wint's aftershave, and makes company with a rat. He later escapes in the morning by shorting out the automatic welder inside the pipe, and cheerfully exits when the workers arrive to fix it.

Now the power suddenly shifts to Bond. With the help of Q, who creates his own version of the voice recorder, he impersonates a scared Saxby intimidated by 007 to fool Blofeld into divulging the whereabouts of Whyte. He's being held captive at his summer home outside of Vegas (in reality the landmark Elrod house in Palm Springs, made of concrete and glass and built on top of giant boulders — tailor made for Adam).

Bond enters the futuristic-looking living room, where he encounters Bambi (Lola Larson) and Thumper (Trina Parks), a wily duo standing guard. Bond is not sure what to make of them, except as a ménage a trios fantasy. But he mistakenly underestimates the deadly gymnasts, who toss him around like a plaything. It's like the *FRWL* gypsy fight turned against him. However, in luring the girls into the swimming pool, Bond overpowers them (looking very sexy, by the way, in a soaking white shirt and pink tie), and rescues the eccentric Whyte (singer/actor/sausage king Jimmy Dean).

In retaliation, Blofeld (in drag!) abducts Tiffany while Q tests his latest electronic ring toy that helps him clean up at the slot machines. Then Blofeld tests his sparkling diamond laser satellite by blowing up U.S., Soviet, and Chinese nuclear weapons (he plans auctioning off global nuclear supremacy to the highest bidder).

With Whyte's help, Bond locates Blofeld on an offshore oil rig in Baja, and makes a grand entrance to play his own game of fakery by switching the computer cassette with the satellite codes in the control room. It's not easy at first: Blofeld has Bond searched and confiscates the phony cassette. But Blofeld reverts to careless form by escorting Bond to the control room and announcing his intention to destroy Washington. This allows Bond another opportunity to switch cassettes with the help of Tiffany (he slips the phony one in her bikini bottom). Then before being locked up, Bond signals Felix to mount the helicopter attack by releasing a weather balloon. Unfortunately, Tiffany turns into a "twit" (the first Bond bimbo) by inadvertently switching them back again and gets caught by Blofeld trying to fix her mistake ("We're showing a bit more cheek than usual, aren't we?").

But Bond easily breaks out to join the fight. Only the final confrontation with his rival turns into a farce when Blofeld tries to escape in his bathosub: Bond takes over the crane controlling the vehicle and bashes the control room with it, destroying the computer, saving Washington, and killing Blofeld. Or so it seems.

In fact, in a tip of the hat to *DAF*, Steven Spielberg's *The Adventure of Tintin* contains a dueling crane climax in which Daniel Craig voices the villainous Sakharine.

As usual, Bond finds himself back at sea: this time on a cruise with Tiffany. She has an important question to ask about their future, but they're interrupted by Wint and Kidd posing as stewards with a feast and a Bombe Surprise for dessert. Bond's snobbery saves the day, though, when he gets another whiff of Wint's pungent aftershave and

catches him in a goof about a Mouton Rothschild '55. While Wint tries to strangle Bond with a chain, Kidd prepares to impale him with flaming skewers. But Bond sets Kidd on fire with a splash of Courvoisier, and he jumps overboard. Then the resourceful Tiffany redeems herself by throwing the cake at Wint, exposing the bomb and allowing Bond to overtake him. He straps the bomb to Wint's rear with the chain (talk about pleasure and pain), and hurls him overboard where he explodes on impact ("He certainly left with his tails between his legs").

Tiffany finally asks her question: "James, how the hell do we get those diamonds down again?" They look up at the sky — and just like that, goodbye Connery and hello Moore in a pretty smooth handoff. A variation of this will take place in Brosnan's last scene as Bond with Halle Berry's Jinx in *Die Another Day*.

But, of course, Connery would return as Bond one *final* time 11 years later in *Never Say Never Again*, the non-Eon remake of *Thunderball*, thanks to the persistence of producer Kevin McClory. For those fans disappointed by the campy *DAF*, the reboot offered a more dignified conclusion: allowing Connery to believably play up the aging (too many free radicals in his system) and the exhausting nature of the fights (relying more on brains than brawn).

Yes, there's self-deprecating humor, but it's character-driven, as Bond is forced to redeem himself when a new and younger M (Edward Fox) wants to retire him and the entire Double-0 section. Director Irvin Kirshner (*The Empire Strikes Back*) also restores a more proper balance between danger and wit, and Bond's clash with Klaus Maria Brandauer's anxious Largo lends a hint of melancholy: two Cold War relics struggling to find their place in a dumbed down world.

For Connery's rehabilitated Bond, however, he's truly had enough and wants to retire to the Bahamas with Kim Basinger's Domino, leaving us with a sly wink and some exhilarating memories.

# GEORGE LAZENBY: ODD MAN OUT

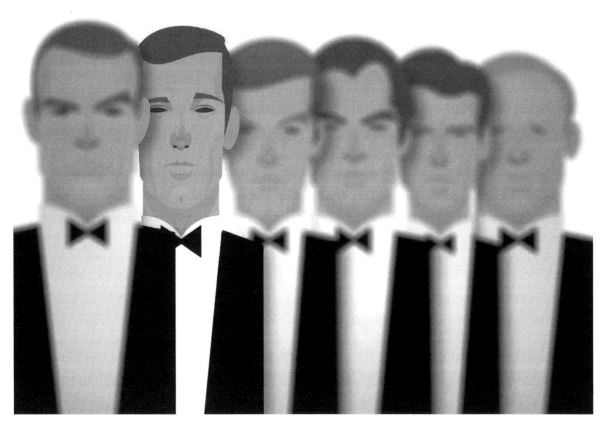

If Connery was an unlikely Bond, then George Lazenby was the unlikeliest. The Australian car salesman and male model (born Sept. 5, 1939) had no previous acting experience, and his only modest claim to fame was promoting Big Fry chocolate bars on TV. But when nobody else dared to follow Connery, Lazenby bluffed his way into Bond with nothing to lose.

"I think, first of all, I was very capable physically — I was a natural athlete," Lazenby suggested. "When I was in school, I never had any lessons or training. I just did it, and I would come in second or third. And Peter Hunt [as first-time director] liked the idea of having someone outside of the acting world, so he could not only get him to do what he wanted, but also to have a lot of praise for being able to pull it off with an unknown."

Like Connery, Lazenby came from a tough working class family: he was brought up in a small town, carved out his own future, and landed Bond with a conceited self-determination. That worked to his advantage when the producers decided they wanted another Connery. But Lazenby not only lacked Connery's talent and charisma, he was also too young and inexperienced to play a burned out Bond ready for marriage and retirement. To most fans and observers, he just couldn't live up to the daunting task — he was Connery lite. But despite his shortcomings, there was something endearing about Lazenby: he was the first actor to reveal Bond's emotional side, and his awkwardness fit the circumstances, particularly when Bond is at his most uncertain. The fact that he had never acted before brought a refreshing rawness to the role.

"I didn't know how to deal with the deeper aspects of acting," Lazenby confided. "It's not just saying the words, but how you feel. And so you're like an instrument. I had never seen myself on screen before, except in commercials where I didn't speak."

> **Everyone I worked with were seasoned pros....I didn't realize at the time that it would show my shallowness as an actor.**
>
> *George Lazenby*

Lazenby's journey with Bond began when he heard about the casing opportunity from a talent agent he once dated, Maggie Abbott. As Charles Helfenstein (my publisher) relates in his authoritative *The Making of On Her Majesty's Secret Service,* "Abbott thought that Lazenby's arrogance would make him ideal for the part. Lazenby was living in Paris at the time, a move made because of his concern that he was getting overexposed in Britain....The idea of playing James Bond got Lazenby back on a plane to England."

To increase his chances, Lazenby snuck into the Eon office in London, sporting a Connery-style haircut from Connery's barber at the Dorchester Hotel, a Conduit Cut suit intended for Connery from tailor Anthony Sinclair, and a Rolex. He simply waited for the receptionist to step away. "Up the stairs I went and walked right into [casting director] Dyson Lovell's office," Lazenby recounted during a Q&A with John Cork in Santa Monica at a screening of *OHMSS* in 2010. "He's on the phone and he said, 'Who are you?' I said, 'I heard you're looking for James Bond.' He was talking to Harry Saltzman on the phone. He said, 'Harry, I've got someone here,' and he said, 'Bring him over.' If Dyson wasn't on the phone and had talked to me for five minutes, he would have realized I was a fake.

"We're walking across the road to Harry Saltzman's office and he said, 'Tell me your life story.' I'd never heard a question like that in my life so I made it up and said, 'Well, I've been making movies in Russia, in Germany, in Hong Kong.' Just spinning off these lines. I couldn't remember what I said because when I got into Harry's office, he says, 'Tell me your life story' and I was like, 'Fuck, I can't remember what I said.' I just told him, 'Let *him* tell you.' [Lovell] said, 'Oh, he's played roles in Russia and Germany....' Anyway, he said, 'I want him to meet the director. Bring him back here: four o'clock tomorrow.' By this time, I was shitting myself — I'm way over my head.

"That night I went looking for an acting coach and I found one. His name was Ronan O'Rahilly. He made Radio Caroline, the pirate radio ship. I go in the next day — and I don't know what made me do it — but Peter said, 'Tell me about yourself.' I said, 'Well, the first thing is, I've never been an actor before.' He's just come from Switzerland; he's pissed off. All of a sudden, he just falls on the floor laughing. He says, 'They brought me back from Switzerland to see you!' I said, 'Well, I'm not an actor. I've never spoken in front of a camera in my life.' He said, 'Stick to your story and I'll make you the next James Bond. You fooled two of the most ruthless guys I've ever met in my life. You're an actor.''

Lazenby told me what clinched it was when he decked stuntman and former wrestler Yuri Borienko during a screen test. "I didn't mean to, but energy starts to flow and boom! When I came through a room, I practically broke the door down. They had me tone it down a bit because I was coming on too strong. And a lot of that was bluffing. I think that's what got me the part— being over the top."

After four months of rigorous testing, training, and grooming (with Hunt reprising the role of Svengali after Young's great success with Connery), Lazenby was still understandably nervous about his acting abilities. During the crucial love scene with co-star Diana Rigg, for instance, "they yelled cut 15 times." But Lazenby contends he had a falling out with Hunt after only three days of shooting, the result of a misunderstanding in which the actor threw some noisy visitors off the set while the director was away and after the crew refused, unaware they were Hunt's friends. According to Lazenby, he tried to apologize but Hunt avoided him and used assistant director Frank Ernst as a go-between to relay instructions. Hunt and other members of the cast dispute Lazenby's account (and Helfenstein's photographic evidence suggests the two talked throughout filming).

"I think it's a measure of the man's personality," Hunt told *Retrovision* in 1989. "He changed about all over the place, when it all went to his head. You must remember that he was an ordinary little guy from the backwoods of Australia and he was suddenly thrust into a very sophisticated area of filmmaking, and it was very difficult for him. I had to do certain [unpleasant] things that directors have to do… to get emotions out of him, but he didn't seem to think that that was fair."

So perhaps it wasn't such a surprise that Lazenby announced before the end of production that he would not return as Bond. "The late sixties was a rough time for Bond because of the hippies," he offered. "When *On Her Majesty's Secret Service* came out, *Easy Rider* was a hit movie. People were wearing bell bottoms and growing their hair and singing love songs against killing. And Bond wasn't about that at all. So it was a rough time for me in that sense as well. I thought the title song should be done by Blood, Sweat & Tears. That shows you where my head was at. But I gambled and walked away from a seven-picture Bond contract that was offered before the end of shooting the film. To be honest, it wasn't my thinking. I was convinced of that by Ronan. He said you're a movie star now, go and do whatever you want. And I had never signed a contract. I just said, 'No, I've gotta walk.' That's when United Artists offered me money under the table — any movie I wanted to do in between Bonds trying to keep me to sign the contract. And Ronan said Bond is too conservative and it's Connery's gig anyway. He promised to get me movies. But he couldn't because everyone was afraid to touch me. They either thought I was still tied up to Bond or was damaged goods."

Still, despite any regrets, Lazenby fondly looks back at his lone appearance as 007: "There are a few moments where we catch Bond when he's more vulnerable that I'm quite proud of," he proclaimed. These include the sequence in the village when Tracy rescues him, his subsequent proposal in the barn, and, of course, her brutal slaying after the wedding.

"The feelings weren't always there," Lazenby admitted. "But I was never one to walk away from a risk and this was the biggest professional one I ever had."

# ON HER MAJESTY'S SECRET SERVICE

*Something old, something new,*
*Something borrowed, something blue…*

If you think about it, the wedding rhyme's the perfect metaphor for the first Bond film without Connery and the one with bloodstained wedding bells for 007. It's all about moving forward with someone new and trying something completely different while still being Bond, which has since become the goal of every post-Connery portrayal.

Of course, it would've been more meaningful watching Connery's Bond experience love and loss with the shocking wedding-day murder of his bride by Blofeld. But, again, it wasn't meant to be with *On Her Majesty's Secret Service* yielding to both *Thunderball* and *You Only Live Twice*. Yet even screenwriter Maibaum admitted that they hadn't earned the right to be serious during the Connery era. That required a new Bond, the most faithful Fleming adaptation, and a more realistic approach.

Although the outcome was critically and commercially disappointing, *OHMSS* still marked an important step in the evolution of Bond: the actor switch provided the first opportunity to put a more human face on the world's most famous superspy. And time has certainly been kind to the orphan now considered one of the franchise's greatest films. You can even see its imprint on such serious successors as *For Your Eyes Only*, *The Living Daylights*, *Licence to Kill*, *The World Is Not Enough*, *Casino Royale*, *Quantum of Solace*, and the upcoming *Skyfall*. Christopher Nolan paid homage to his favorite Bond film in *Inception* (2010) with both the ski chase sequence and central theme of love and loss.

"It's a wonderful movie — a good movie," suggested Dalton. "You see in that one event of marrying somebody and having her killed, a psychological basis for, if you like, his attitude towards women. You can't fall in love; otherwise, they're a target. You don't want to get too serious for these movies, but this one comes closest."

Nobody understood this better than editor-turned director Peter Hunt, who threw away the gadgets and stripped the franchise down to its essence. He also found in Lazenby the right physicality to carry on the Bond legacy. But with some important surprises along the way, beginning with the gun barrel sequence. The walk is a combination of Connery's cat-like stride and Lazenby's swagger. He drops to one knee before firing and his image is completely erased by the descending blood. It's a harbinger of things to come, considering Bond's marriage, the violent climax, and Lazenby's one-off as 007.

Hunt returned to *Dr. No* for inspiration. Hidden in darkness, Bond drives a conventional Aston Martin DBS on a coastal highway in Portugal to John Barry's synthesized strains of the familiar theme. A woman in a red Cougar XR-7 convertible hurriedly overtakes him and he lights a cigarette, revealing the hint of the "rather cruel mouth," but with a dimpled chin. He follows the mysterious lady to the beach, spies her through his telescopic sight, and sees her trying to drown herself in the sea. He gallantly rescues her as dawn breaks, and, after reviving her, we finally view him close up with his cheerful greeting: "Good morning, my name's Bond, James Bond."

As *Jeeves* author P.G. Wodehouse observed, "It is never difficult to distinguish between a Scotsman with a grievance and a ray of sunshine." In other words, it's apparent from the start that this fresh-faced Bond lacks his predecessor's worldliness and ironic detachment. But what he does possess is sincerity, which is important for this story, and he proves a very capable fighter when immediately held at gunpoint by two thugs. A fast and furious scuffle ensues as Bond efficiently dispatches the attackers with the help of an oar, a boat, and a net. Hunt accelerates the speed and intensifies the crash cut in all the action scenes with new editor and future Bond director John Glen. This has the effect of lending gravitas to Lazenby's performance as well as minimizing the extreme running time (140 minutes: the longest until *Casino Royale's* 144 minutes).

Then something extraordinary happens: Bond

notices that the lady has jumped into his Aston Martin, intercepted her Cougar, and sped away. Like a rejected Prince Charming, he picks up her shoes, looks just off camera, and observes, "This never happened to the other fella."

Indeed. It's a wonderful ice breaker, and the only acknowledgment of a change in Bonds. But more important, it signals that nothing's going to be as easy for this 007. Lazenby said it was also part of a running gag on set: "Everything I did, whether it was doing a lot of press interviews or a fight scene [without a stunt double], whatever, I kept saying, 'I bet the other guy didn't have to do this,'" he revealed. "Finally, Peter said I could use the line in the opening scene, though they polished it slightly."

There's even danger in Maurice Binder's title sequence. A nostalgic montage from the previous films bumps up against several silhouettes associated with time, including the new Bond hanging precariously from a clock. This foreshadows the sad love theme, "We Have All the Time in the World," which John Barry underscores throughout.

Bond rescues the lady again, this time at their hotel casino when she can't cover her bet (production designer Syd Cain invokes a more Mod look overall, including the use of purple). Her name is Contessa Teresa di Vicenzo, better known as Tracy. She's played by the Shakespearean-trained Diana Rigg, another graduate from *The Avengers* (1965-68). And there's a lot of the sexy and feisty Mrs. Peel in the free-spirited and self-destructive Tracy, who proves to be the perfect match for Bond.

Tracy tosses Bond the key to her suite as reward for bailing her out. But Bond must endure another physical test when he finds a more formidable foe waiting for him in her suite. This rough-and-tumble fight results in a bloodied lip for Bond, who grabs a handful of caviar on his way out, impressing us with his knowledge of its northern Caspian origin.

The confusion continues when Bond finds Tracy in his suite wearing a hotel robe over lingerie and pointing his gun at him. He angrily grabs her wrist to force the gun loose, applies more pressure to stop the game-playing, and slaps her across the face when he thinks she's lying. "I can be a lot more persuasive," he threatens. "I'm sure you can," she

counters. "Whatever else I may be, I am not a liar."

He pushes her away and tells her to get dressed, but she sits on the bed, lost in thought. After softly taking her hand and an aborted kiss, Bond forgets about sexual conquest and tries to be more understanding. "Look, you don't owe me a thing," he concedes. "I think you're in some sort of trouble. Would you like to talk about it?" But for the moment, Tracy resists getting closer: "No, Mister Bond. The only thing you need know about me is that I pay my debts." She certainly does: Bond wakes up blissfully in the morning to discover Tracy gone and "paid in full, as well." This never happened to the other fella, either.

Lazenby has often been referred to as the "hippie Bond" as a result of his gentler characterization of 007. This image was dramatically reinforced when a long-haired and bearded Lazenby admitted in a 1970 TV interview that he longed to play a "more humane" Bond, but was met with a lot of resistance. Yet this token of affection with Tracy — and what follows between them — is precisely the kind of sensitive Bond Lazenby aspired to.

Bond soon learns all about Tracy when he's abducted, in a further twist, by the assailants for a meeting with their boss, Marc-Ange Draco (Gabriele Ferzetti, *L'Avventura*, 1960). Draco is not only head of the European crime syndicate Unione Corse, but also Tracy's father. Like *FRWL's* Bey, Draco's an easygoing charmer, and even has a similar secretary/mistress for his amusement. He tells Bond in his lavish office tucked away in a Lisbon backstreet about her troubled life: a burned out jet-setter who's lived "too greedily." As Draco remarks, "I gave her too much, and it brought her nothing."

If Lazenby appears out of his depth during this long, expositional scene, he explained it was because "everyone I worked with were seasoned pros, and, of course, I didn't realize at the time that it would show my shallowness as an actor."

But Lazenby has a much easier time conveying Bond's resistance to seeing more of Tracy. It's the last thing he needs, considering her emotional frailty and his hedonistic lifestyle and dangerous profession. But Draco persists, offering Bond £1 million pounds in gold as inducement to marry her. He refuses, of course, and suddenly realizes that Draco might be of assistance in finding the elusive Blofeld. But the price of compromise still seems high.

The ritualistic visit to MI6 headquarters offers Bond no choice. After eagerly tossing his hat onto the stand, he stuns Moneypenny by flirting more aggressively: calling her "darling," kissing her on the cheek, and pinching her. He even asks her over to his place for drinks, but she's the one to hesitate: "If only I could trust myself."

However, M has quite a shock for Bond: he's lost confidence in his ability to find Blofeld after two years and dismisses him from Operation Bedlam. What appears to be an inside joke about the changing of the guard turns out to be some sort of strategy to shake Bond of his boredom. But Bond leaves in a huff and hastily dictates a resignation letter to Moneypenny before heading to his office.

With his future as 007 now in jeopardy, Bond sits and reflects about the past, taking out such souvenirs as Grant's watch garrote, Honey's knife, and the re-breather from *Thunderball*. Remember Fleming's line from *Casino Royale*? "Like all cruel, harsh men, he was easily tipped over into sentimentality." Of course, this Bond is neither cruel nor harsh. But he sneaks a drink and apologizes to the Annigoni portrait of the Queen. What Draco said earlier about something eating away at Tracy's soul, might apply to Bond as well: it's the first crack in his armor. But Moneypenny rescues him when she changes the resignation letter to two weeks' leave, prompting a sweet thank you from Bond and a rare admission of gratitude from M: "What would *I* do without you, Miss Moneypenny? Thank you."

Bond's professional/personal tug-of-war comes to a head at Draco's birthday party. Overlooking a bullfight on Draco's estate, which intensifies the encounter, Tracy forces her father to stop using her as a pawn and tell Bond what he wants to know (there's a connection between Blofeld and a lawyer in Switzerland). She runs off in tears, but Blofeld can wait: Bond catches up and tenderly dries her eyes and holds her.

We then witness something very privileged: an intimate, glam montage of Bond and Tracy's whirlwind courtship, accompanied by Louis Armstrong gently singing "We Have All the Time in the World." They hold hands on the beach, ride horses, and sit in their secret garden stroking, of all things, a black cat. Apparently she's tapped a longing deep inside him and their romance becomes therapeutic for him as well.

But, alas, Bond must return to Her Majesty's Secret Service and find Blofeld. He sneaks into the lawyer's office and grabs info about his whereabouts using a combo safe-cracking/photo copier (the film's only real gadget). He also snatches a *Playboy* centerfold, tucking it inside his jacket and looking like a nervous school boy as he walks out, but at the same time reaffirming his bad boy image.

Bond then visits M at his stately 18th century home, Quarterdeck, near the Thames: a franchise first, where we're introduced to a more human side to M as he tends to his butterfly collection. Bond first can't resist impressing M with his knowledge of lepidoptery before briefing him on his breakthrough: Blofeld has contacted the College of Arms in London claiming to be heir to the title Count Balthazar de Bleuchamp (the French derivation of his surname). Bond further reveals that he's already met with genealogist Sir Hilary Bray (George Baker) at the college using his own family tree as cover (the Bond motto is "The World Is Not Enough"). In fact, Bond's arranged to impersonate Bray to ostensibly authenticate Blofeld's claim.

Looking, sounding, and acting sufficiently nerdy, a bespectacled Bond (dubbed by Baker) is escorted to Blofeld's hideaway in the Swiss Alps by henchwoman Irma Bunt (Ilse Steppat), a more obedient Rosa Klebb. Nestled 6,000 feet above a small village, Piz Gloria (an actual revolving alpine restaurant retrofitted with a helipad by the production) serves as Blofeld's ingenious cover: an exclusive institute for allergy research, where a dozen gorgeous girls have been recruited internationally for testing. Cain designed an elegant Piz Gloria set in keeping with the more refined Blofeld, featuring the plush Alpine Room dining area, attractive rotunda with a 360-degree view of the mountains, and separate underground lab with purple-glowing antisepsis entrance.

Indeed, Blofeld's aristocratic masquerade as de

**Director Peter Hunt watches George Lazenby and Lois Maxwell perform the office scene.**

Bleuchamp turns out to be a personal obsession: he's ditched the SPECTRE ring, and lopped off his earlobes, but he's still bald and can't resist the flashy Nehru garb. What's more, he's a lot more active, attractive, and athletic. Surprisingly, he's played by Telly Savalas, who specialized in psychopaths (*The Dirty Dozen*, 1967) before gaining fame as *Kojak*. Still, he wouldn't be Blofeld without a nefarious plot for world domination and this one's his most inventive: he's developed a toxic virus that will sterilize the food supply. But even masquerading as the timid Bray (wearing filly shirt and kilt, no less), Bond has no trouble bedding two of the patients to learn just enough to cause trouble. Ironically, the expert at everything is betrayed by a genealogical slip up and his lasciviousness: he's captured by Bunt after sneaking a second time into the room of the kooky English girl (Angela Scoular) allergic to chickens. Before locking Bond up, though, Blofeld arrogantly boasts that he's trained his "angels of death" to dispense the omega virus around the globe and that nothing can stop him.

Bond's inevitable getaway offers a lot more than physical peril: it reveals a man desperately trying to remain in command. First, Bond narrowly escapes on a cable-car wire (tearing out his pockets as gloves); then skis down Piz Gloria pursued by Blofeld and his men in what still remains the franchise's most spectacular set piece (courtesy of ski stuntman/cameraman Willy Bogner Jr.). Machine gun fire knocks Bond down, forcing him to continue with one ski until he falls near the edge of the precipice. He luckily ambushes a would-be attacker with his ski, but another thug overtakes him, and Bond struggles to keep him quiet when a group of Blofeld's men approaches. However, after they pass, Bond has a definite look of concern. Is he suddenly worried about his survival? He barely fights off the thug: hurling him off the precipice and skiing into the village below.

But Bond immediately spots Bunt and hides in a shed. Big mistake: it's full of bells and a nervous Bond attracts another assailant. He smartly uses the bells as a weapon and sneaks out a high window. Bond grabs a jacket and tries to lose himself in the crowded Christmas Eve celebration. But he's unnerved by every sudden sight and sound, especially the fireworks. It's the exact opposite of a more poised Bond being chased through Nassau's Junkanoo festival in *Thunderball*. Yet this is an entirely different situation, with much more at stake for Bond, and Lazenby is so natural, so emotionally naked, in conveying a man frightened and trapped.

It's no wonder that he finds a quiet spot to sit and bury his head. Then he's approached by a skater: he looks up and, miraculously, it's Tracy, who's come to his rescue. They dash away in her Cougar pursued by Bunt and Blofeld's men, and, when Tracy asks why they're after him, the old Bond returns with the quip: "I suspect they're trying to kill me."

Bond quickly gathers himself and tries to keep Tracy focused ("Just keep my mind on your driving") as they attempt to reach a post office so he can phone London. He gently kisses her a couple of times when she eludes their pursuers. But the call is aborted when Bond is nearly shot and they're off again. This time, they duck into a car rally and Tracy takes charge during this funny and exciting chase, which ends with Bunt's Mercedes tumbling over and exploding ("We didn't even stop for the prize!").

They scuttle into a snow storm and are forced to spend the night in a barn. Safely alone together, Bond is deep in thought and Tracy wants to talk about it. Yet it's not Blofeld that's on his mind but their future. Bond tries to explain his conflict between professional obligation and personal desire, and Tracy offers to maintain the status quo. But, to her surprise, he confesses his love for her and proposes marriage — he's ready to give up his license to kill.

Despite how difficult it was for Lazenby, it's a sublime moment: "I don't think he ever chased a girl before," he recalled. "But I understood that he was falling in love and he had to decide what to do. Like many men, even if they're killers, they have that gene that compels them to mate with the opposite sex. And when you find that special one, you want to be with her."

In a joyful exchange, they consider possibilities for their residence: Tunbridge Wells, Belgrave Square, Via Veneto, Paris, and Monaco ("I wonder how much they're asking for this place?"). Bond even tries sexual abstinence until their honeymoon, but, no, that's going too far.

They leave the barn just ahead of Blofeld and his men in the morning, and Bond and Tracy look lovely together on the slopes. Bond regains his confidence and gallows humor after a baddie falls into a snow machine and his blood spurts out ("He had a lot of guts"). But Blofeld cunningly causes an avalanche and puts an end to their escape. He kidnaps Tracy while Bond lies helpless under a pile of snow. There's a reflection of a worried Bond back in London that seems as though he's aged 10 years. However, M won't allow him to intercede since the UN has decided to meet Blofeld's incredulous demands: total amnesty for all past crimes and official recognition as Count de Bleuchamp. Meanwhile, Blofeld foolishly tries coercing Tracy into marrying him in a blatant competition with Bond.

So Bond goes rogue for the first time by engineering an aerial raid of Piz Gloria with Draco and his men, while Tracy does her part to distract Blofeld with poetic jousting: "Thy Dawn, O Master of the World" to his "The Arms of Mighty Helen." Bond makes his entrance sliding down the ice with a machine gun, and Tracy even dispatches a henchman (Borienko), which brings back fond memories of Mrs. Peel. Only her father knocks her out after refusing to leave without Bond when they rig the place to explode.

Blofeld gasps at the destruction of Piz Gloria: it's like an artist watching the death of his creation. His first instinct is to run, which results in a thrilling bobsled chase down the mountain. Yet Blofeld nearly gets the best of Bond: first with a grenade that explodes in front of Bond's sled and causes it to overturn, and then in a fistfight in his sled (their one and only dance) until a tree branch ensnares him.

"Your Royal Highnesses, my lords, ladies and gentlemen, the toast is the bride and bridegroom, Mr. and Mrs. James Bond." The wedding in Portugal is beautiful yet surreal. It's so strange seeing Bond getting married, wondering what's to become of 007. It's like a dream: M and Draco talk shop; Q awkwardly apologizes to Bond for being so rough on him and Bond obliquely thanks him for all he's done; Bond proudly refuses Draco's £ 1 million; and Moneypenny catches Bond's hat and cries while he wistfully waves goodbye, confirming her unrequited love once and for all.

Bond and Tracy are finally alone together in his Aston Martin on the same coastal highway where she overtook him. But to have more privacy, they stop and Bond gets out and removes the floral arrangement. He apologizes for not giving her a wedding present, and she thanks him for giving her the greatest gift: "a future." And like children, they play "He Loves Me, He Loves Me Not" with some flower petals.

But the dream is shattered when Blofeld (wearing a neck brace) and Bunt drive by and she sprays the car with bullets from an M16. Bond jumps back into the car to pursue Blofeld, but he can wait: the arch-nemesis has exacted his revenge. It's a devastating moment, unforgettable, and movingly captured by Lazenby, as Bond cradles his murdered bride.

Hunt told *Retrovision* that he forced Lazenby to rehearse all day on set in the car in an effort to break him down "until he was absolutely exhausted, and by the time we shot it at five o'clock, he *was* exhausted, and that's how I got the performance."

For Lazenby, it was the emotional high-point of his fleeting career. "At the time, I didn't understand that part of life — the dark side of what killing does," he admitted. "It was the last scene we shot. I had the book with me and I read it right before the scene and cried, and the assistant director told me that Peter said James Bond doesn't cry. So I read the scene again and did it once more without the tears. Diana Rigg was lying on my lap and biting me on the leg. I don't know why — probably to get me to emote or something. And I got the feeling. Wherever you can get it, you know?"

A patrolman approaches and stops, but Bond tells him everything's fine. "There's no hurry, you see. We have all the time in the world." Then he buries his face in her hair and loses it, and the camera pulls back for a close-up of Tracy through the shattered windshield, blood streaming down her face. Robert Towne sums up his legendary *Chinatown* as "the futility of good intentions." The same applies to *OHMSS*, which ends with Bond's painful comeuppance and the stark realization that there's no escape from 007.

# ROGER MOORE: JOKERS WILD

If George Lazenby was the broken-hearted Bond, then Roger Moore was the party Bond. He was Errol Flynn to Connery's Cary Grant: the sweet distraction that got us through the turbulent seventies and the first half of the Go-Go eighties. "Roger comes in the humor door, and I go out it," Connery told *Time* in comparing their two approaches.

Or, as Dalton flamboyantly suggested, "Roger was very, very experienced and skilled in carrying off that sort of flippant onion ball — lovely, lighthearted, but it had nothing to do with spy movies or *From Russia with Love*."

Maybe so, but Moore's devil may care Bond wasn't in it for the spying — he was in it for the high life: the girls, the drinks, the food, the cigars, the clothes, and the sport. Moore (born Oct. 14, 1927), the first Bond from London, says he was primed for the role of a lifetime after a string of debonair TV heroes: *Ivanhoe* (1958), *Maverick* (as cardsharp cousin Beau, 1960-61), *The Saint* (which turned him into an international star as the raffish Simon Templar), and *The Persuaders* (paired with Tony Curtis as crime-fighting playboys, 1971-72).

In fact, Moore was apparently in the running for Bond at every opportunity, and his time finally came with *Live and Let Die* — the perfect fit. "Well, the way I play it, I make everybody look the same, I think," Moore noted. "Rather like that wonderful character actor George Arliss many years ago, who played all those famous historical characters [*Disraeli*, 1929]: He made them all look like George. As Spencer Tracy said, 'Say the lines and hit the marks.' As Lee Marvin said, 'Say the marks and hit the lines.' I carried somewhere in between. I played it for more humor."

As a result, Moore took Bond to a whole new level of absurdity. For one thing, he found the whole spy game ridiculous since there's no pretense in hiding Bond's exploits. For another, Moore knew he couldn't get away with being a cold-blooded assassin anyway, so he needed another tactic.

"My conception of Bond is not of a man who enjoys killing," he explained in *Roger Moore's James Bond Diary*. "I shan't be a Sam Peckinpah character, getting obvious enjoyment out of killing, but when the time comes to squeeze the trigger, Bond does it quicker and with greater accuracy. He enjoys the good things in life, a good attractive woman, and he will combine business with pleasure. He is not averse to taking a lady to bed, and then giving her a sharp clip around the ear to find out why she went to bed with him — was it the enormous size of his Hampton or for information?"

In other words, Moore's Bond is more Kiss Kiss than Bang Bang. Moore even pretended the baddies had halitosis to work up a proper look of disgust during the fights. Then there were those incredulous looks in the face of danger when he arched his eyebrows."It was the villains that had all the fun and got to say, "You've really gone too far this time, Mr. Bond,'" Moore laughed. "I loved them all....They have characters to come in, but Bond is just Bond."

Even so, Moore tried to make Bond his own right from the start with *Live and Let Die*. He smokes cigars, orders bourbon instead of a martini, Bollinger champagne instead of Dom Perignon, plays gin, and sports a navy blue chesterfield coat and powder blue denim suit (progressing later on, of course, to safari jackets, leisure suits, and flared pants). Because he's less physically threatening than Connery, he's also more reliant on gadgets. And yet he displays extraordinary strength and athleticism when necessary.

Moore maintains that it was all about being

> As Spencer Tracy said, 'Say the lines and hit the marks.' As Lee Marvin said, 'Say the marks and hit the lines.' I carried somewhere in between. I played it for more humor.
>
> *Roger Moore*

casual both on and off screen. "[We] had a wonderful atmosphere on the set. Cubby had this running backgammon game, which we never settled up until the last day of shooting," he added. "And we just had a lot of laughs doing them. Maybe sometimes it got a bit hairy. But I find it much easier to work this way. I remember the last day of shooting [*The Man with the Golden Gun*], and I saw Cubby's head peering out from one of the sets, and a bucket of paste came flying down at me on one of those wonderful silk suits I was looking forward to stealing."

But it was a rough transition. For *Live and Let Die*, Moore had to cut his long hair, dye his hair brown, (making Craig the only onscreen blond Bond), lose 20 pounds, and whip himself into shape. Guy Hamilton even tried to toughen him up in *The Man with the Golden Gun*."I think it's most evident in the scenes I had with Maud Adams, where I twisted her arm and threatened — rather coldly — to break it unless she told me what I wanted to know," Moore recounted in his memoir, *My Word is My Bond*. However, he tried to resist such bullying before deferring to his director, suggesting that his Bond would've charmed the information out of her in bed. "My Bond was a lover and a giggler."

Not surprisingly, it wasn't until Moore's third film, *The Spy Who Loved Me*, when Bond really clicked for him. It remains his favorite, best suiting his style and persona, thanks in large part to the return of director Lewis Gilbert (*YOLT*), who was a kindred spirit and gave him freedom to be himself.

Moore also enjoyed the great location shoots on *Spy*, particularly among the wondrous Egyptian pyramids. "After the scene where I fight Jaws on the Temple of Karnak, which comes down, I had this great line, 'Egyptian builders,'" Moore recounted. "But we were worried about the censor [who was on set] so I just mouthed the line. But the sound man wasn't in on the gag, so he yelled, 'I didn't hear him — we'll have to do it again!' But they dubbed it in later in London. Friends in Egypt said it was the biggest laugh in Cairo."

For someone who jokes that he was surprised he lasted longer than seven days, let alone a franchise record seven films in 12 years (1973-85), Moore wound up having the last laugh as 007.

# LIVE AND LET DIE

The shot of Moore's Bond hang gliding at night with a long cigar in his mouth probably best sums up his casual image. In contrast to Connery's ride atop the elevator preparing for danger in *DAF*, his Bond just enjoys the relaxing moment.

And yet Moore was worried from the start that he wouldn't be able to distance himself from his good friend, Connery, so he voiced his concerns with director Hamilton. "We met at Scott's in Mayfair, in true Bond-style, over a dozen oysters and martinis," Moore wrote in the *James Bond Diary*. "I confessed to Guy that in reading the script I could only ever hear Sean's voice saying: 'My name is Bond.' In fact, as I vocalized to myself I found I was giving it a Scottish accent!'"

But Hamilton reassured Moore that he would quickly find his own style, and helped him out wherever he could, including taking away the martinis and having M and Moneypenny brief Bond at his apartment. In addition, George Martin replaced John Barry as composer for the first time (coming along for the rock 'n' roll ride with Paul McCartney and Wings), and de-emphasized the "Bond Theme" in favor of an instrumental version of the title song more directly linked to the new Bond.

Meanwhile, Mankiewicz was back to keep it light (though the puns aren't as good as the physical humor). He significantly riffs on the popular Blaxploitation genre (*Shaft*, 1971, *Super Fly*, 1972): conjuring a drug dealing plot that traverses Harlem, the Caribbean, and New Orleans. This actually marks the start of Bond following trends more than setting them.

Hamilton also returned to the obstacle course formula of *Goldfinger* — only more so. Here Moore's Bond cleverly survives one perilous situation after another by outfoxing his adversaries. Again, that's because Moore's more gentlemanly Bond prefers to use his license to kill as a last resort, and his dance with the baddies is an occupational hazard, not a dangerous thrill.

The first hint of Moore's casual Bond is apparent in his hatless gun barrel opening (but this film is not shot in Panavision). Yet he grips the gun with both hands, emphasizing that "Bond does it quicker and with greater accuracy."

But Bond doesn't appear in the pre-credit sequence, which is all about ceremonial death, as three MI6 agents are mysteriously disposed of. The first at the UN (by a blaring audio tone during a session), the second in New Orleans (knifed during a mock funeral procession), and the third in a Caribbean island called San Monique (bitten by a green serpent during a frenzied voodoo ritual).

Fittingly, our introduction to Moore's Bond is in bed with the curvaceous Italian agent Miss Caruso (Madeline Smith). But he's awakened in the early morning by M, who makes a rare visit to his home to brief him on the situation, and send him packing to New York to investigate the smooth Dr. Kananga (Yaphet Kotto), ambassador to San Monique. But it's played like farce, with Bond trying to hide her from M. While Bond lures his boss into the kitchen to make him coffee with his espresso machine (the first gadget of the Moore era), she sneaks into the closet. Then Moneypenny arrives with Bond's plane ticket, and immediately figures out what's going on and assists in the charade.

As this is only the second glimpse of Bond's home, production designer Syd Cain takes the opportunity to visually introduce the new 007 while reinforcing his iconic image as a lover and a connoisseur: the split-level bedroom is the centerpiece, the reception area is traditionally furnished, and the small kitchen is modern and techno.

Bond appears less confrontational with M, although when trying out his new magnetic Rolex from Q (who doesn't appear in the film), he mischievously irritates his boss by snatching his spoon. Then before departing for New York, he can't resist unzipping Miss Caruso's dress with the watch to make sure it really works.

In New York, Bond gets into trouble immediately. While driving from the airport to meet with Felix

Leiter, his driver is killed and he crashes the car, causing the CIA agent to clean up the mess. Here Felix is played by good-natured David Hedison (*Voyage to the Bottom of the Sea*, 1964-68), who's either wiretapping Kananga or running interference for Bond.

Bond goes to Harlem and immediately figures out that Kananga is connected to badass gangster, Mr. Big, who runs a drug operation through his Fillet of Soul restaurant franchise. His reach is ubiquitous and Bond gets snatched by his amiable thugs where ever he goes. He steps into the first trap when entering the local Fillet of Soul, where he definitely looks like a fish out of water. But he doesn't care — he knows he's going to somehow prevail and so do we. It's part of Moore's charm. Even when ordering his bourbon "neat," he flaunts his superiority. However, when he sits down in a booth and spins around into Mr. Big's headquarters on the other side, it's the only time he's taken aback.

Bond quickly recovers, though, at the sight of the beautiful clairvoyant Solitaire (Jane Seymour) reading Tarot cards. He plays along and charmingly introduces himself ("My name's Bond, James Bond") with a much longer pause for emphasis. But she's already been following him through the cards. Then Henchman Tee Hee (Julius Harris) intercedes by smashing Bond's gun with his pincer. He lost his right arm to the crocodile, Old Albert, at his farm in New Orleans. But he's no Captain Hook and has a wicked laugh. Bond just sneers while tossing his gun into the trash can ("Funny how the least little thing amuses him"). This is ironic considering how much Moore detests firearms as a result of being grazed by a bb gun as a child.

Solitaire draws "The Fool" for Bond. No matter: he continues charming her until Mr. Big emerges from a meeting and barks at his henchmen to "waste him." But on Bond's way out, Solitaire shockingly draws "The Lovers" card, and Bond grins at the optimistic game-changer.

Outside, Bond easily disposes of his captors, slamming a metal staircase into them. Thus, unlike his predecessor, he avoids a fight whenever possible. Then, when CIA agent Strutter shows up to brief Bond about Mr. Big's nefarious activities, Bond

arguably summons the best quip of the film: "Where were you when I didn't need you?" After conversing with Felix through a hidden radio transmitter inside the agent's car ("a genuine Felix lighter"), Bond follows Kananga to San Monique.

Filmed in Jamaica, the fictional Caribbean island certainly echoes *Dr. No*, including the participation of Quarrel's son (Roy Stewart), while going further with prettier settings and the introduction of voodoo and the occult. But Bond gets a surprise when checking into his hotel and being informed that "Mrs. Bond" has already checked in. Unlike his predecessors, however, the new Bond inspects the room for bugs by using a hairbrush that serves as both a bug detector and Morse code transmitter. Then while taking a bath, he's greeted by a serpent, which he cleverly kills with his cigar and aftershave. And so it goes: this Bond opportunistically uses whatever's handy to survive.

"Mrs. Bond" finally shows up and turns out to be neurotic CIA agent Rosie Carver (Gloria Hendry), the first African-American Bond girl. She initially resists Bond's seduction until getting freaked out by the dead snake in the bathroom and an ominous voodoo hat, courtesy of the charismatic Baron Samedi (Geoffrey Holder), who scares the locals into submission so Kananga can operate without fear of discovery.

The following morning Quarrel Jr. takes them on his boat to the spot where Bond's colleague was murdered in the pre-credit sequence. But there's another trap set for Bond and Rosie is the bait as a double-agent working for Kananga. Yet he's already on to her after being tipped off with a treacherous Queen of Cups card (when turned upside down), and threatens to kill her after having sex if she doesn't tell him everything.

It's the first important test for Moore's Bond, but it backfires because Rosie's more frightened of Kananga than him (which never would've happened with Connery). She makes a run for it and is killed by a poison dart from a voodoo scarecrow intended for Bond. His only hope now is to seduce Solitaire. She's actually Kananga's ward, and he relies on her psychic powers to plan his operation. But now she's conflicted because of being sexually linked to Bond

and can't read the cards. So Kananga threatens to kill her if she doesn't regain her touch. His brutishness has no limit, since he disposed of her mother when she was no longer useful to him, but it's a weakness that Bond quickly learns to exploit.

To be on the safe side, though, Bond literally stacks the deck with the virginal Solitaire to make sure they become lovers. Afterward, he discovers just how frightened and child-like she is, so Bond confesses that he cheated with the Tarot cards and promises to protect her from Kananga in exchange for her help. He's become a much better persuader the second time around. No wonder Moore succeeded Audrey Hepburn as UNICEF's Goodwill Ambassador.

Solitaire leads Bond to the secret poppy field revealing Kananga's heroin smuggling operation with Mr. Big. But they luckily elude Kananga's thugs by escaping in a double-decker London tourist bus, further demonstrating Bond's resourcefulness. It's a slapstick chase and Bond proves an adept driver (even when losing the top deck). Next, they follow the trail to Mr. Big in New Orleans. But an even more ridiculous chase ensues after they're apprehended at the airport and Solitaire distracts the baddies long enough for Bond to flee. He spots a Cessna and gets in, only there's an elderly lady waiting for her first flying lesson. So Bond makes the best of it by running circles around his pursuers, ripping off the wings when racing through the hanger, and leaving Felix to clean up another mess with the authorities.

Felix isn't taking any chances and accompanies Bond to the Fillet of Soul in the French Quarter (where CIA agent Strutter is knifed in another mock funeral death trap). Even though Bond avoids a booth this time, Felix is lured away and Bond is set up once again. But not before being serenaded with the title song: a marvelous self-reflexive musical moment that prompts a smile of appreciation from 007.

Just then, Bond disappears underneath the floor and is confronted by Mr. Big, with Solitaire and Tee Heel by his side, demanding to know if he deflowered her. But Bond is too much of a gentleman to kiss and tell, and demands to see Kananga. So he's hardly surprised when Kananga removes the mask to reveal his Jekyll/Hyde existence like a comic book villain, and the game continues.

Kananga explains his welfare junkie plan to give away the heroin, put the Mafia out of business, and then jack up the price after monopolizing the multi-billion dollar drug trade. But Bond remains unflappable, so Kananga puts the pressure on Solitaire by forcing her to tell them the registration number on Bond's Rolex. At first, Tee Hee fumbles getting the watch off Bond's wrist ("Butterhook"). But for every wrong answer, Kananga instructs him to torture Bond, beginning with snapping his right pinky and then proceeding with "more vital areas." Fortunately, Solitaire passes the test.

Bond is taken prisoner at Tee Hee's crocodile farm, where they distribute the heroin, and is left to be gobbled up by dozens of hungry crocs. At first, he tries the Rolex to bring a boat closer to him, but it's tied up, so when he's cornered by Old Albert and his buddies, the quick-thinking Bond makes a mad dash to the other side by stepping over the heads of the crocs. He sets fire to the farm and escapes in a Glastron speedboat, demonstrating his skill with another vehicle. This results in the film's most spectacular chase through the Louisiana bayou, pursued by Kananga's men as well as the local police, who wind up in a highway pile up.

It's basically a more elaborate and funnier version of the Vegas chase in *DAF*, with Bond outmaneuvering everyone and frustrating the hell out of Sheriff J.W. Pepper (Clifton James), a Southern-fried blowhard who refuses to admit he's in way over his head ("You picked the wrong parish to haul ass through boy"). Not even when Bond soars over him. Then when Bond's fuel tank gets shot up, he merely steals another speedboat from a resident, disrupting a wedding in the process, and eventually gets caught in a showdown. So he smartly grabs a pale of gasoline, double backs and tosses it in his attacker's face, sends his boat out of control, and knocks him into a ship's hull where he explodes. Of course, there's another fine mess for Felix to clean up, and Pepper nearly has a coronary when learning about Bond: "Secret agent? On whose side?"

Bond then glides his way back to San Monique. While the CIA blows up the poppy field, he rescues

Solitaire from a sacrificial voodoo ceremony, and tangles with Baron Samedi and his cronies (finally requiring fine marksmanship with a .44 Magnum, Dirty Harry's weapon of choice, and sealing the Baron in a coffin filled with snakes).

From there Bond and Solitaire infiltrate Kananga's underground refining plant, where the super baddie is more confident than ever and invites Bond to join him in a glass of champagne. He's also amused by Bond's shark gun, and laughs uproariously after firing a compressed air bullet into an inflatable couch, getting a jolt out of quiet henchman, Whisper (Earl Jolly Brown).

But this just plays into Bond's hand: Tied to Solitaire above a shark tank and dripping blood from his wrist, Bond turns the Rolex into a buzzsaw and escapes for a fight with Kananga. They wind up in the water and Bond stuffs a bullet he snatched into Kananga's mouth, forcing him to blow up and explode on top of the cave ("He always did have an inflated opinion of himself").

As with *DAF*, though, there's some unfinished business. Bond and Solitaire take the train, and proving that he's got more than sex on his mind, Bond continues to play the good tutor, teaching her how to beat him at gin rummy. This inspires Solitaire to thank him for making her a "complete woman."

But lo and behold, Tee Hee pays a surprise visit and Bond finds himself in the toughest scuffle of the film. They thrash each other around, recalling *FRWL*, but, again, Bond opportunistically gets out of another jam: He grabs tweezers and snaps the wires on the henchman's artificial arm, rendering the pincer useless and Tee Hee helpless. Bond then takes a moment to catch his breath before tossing him out the window and continuing his tryst with Solitaire ("Just being disarming, darling"). But in a final twist, *Live and Let Die* closes on a close-up of the Baron laughing his head off on the front of the speeding train.

It's a reminder that the party never ends with this new Bond.

# THE MAN WITH THE GOLDEN GUN

*Live and Let Die* proved a modest success for Moore's first Bond outing (faring better than *DAF* internationally yet lagging behind domestically). But given the premise in which Bond is pitted against the world's best hit man — a sort of alter ego — with his reputation and survival at stake, the response was to make Moore a bit more ruthless like Connery. The result was awkward for Moore, who was still in search of his comfort zone. (In fact, when he became Bond, his son Geoffrey actually asked if he was going to be as tough as the real 007 — Sean Connery). But that would get resolved soon enough.

Originally, *The Man with the Golden Gun* was slated after *YOLT* as a Far East follow-up to be shot in Cambodia, and Moore was approached to succeed Connery. But the project was pushed back when war broke out in the country, paving the way finally for *OHMSS*.

When it was ultimately made, *TMWTGG* was exquisitely shot by Ted Moore and Oswald Morris (Oscar winner for *Fiddler on the Roof*, 1971) in Macau, Hong Kong, Bangkok, Phang Nga Province in Thailand, and Beirut. But it marked the last Bond film produced by Saltzman, who subsequently sold his Danjaq interest to United Artists. And once again they had to abandon Fleming and make it relevant for the times, capitalizing on the 1973 energy crisis. However, like *YOLT*, this was another missed opportunity. Fleming's final novel (published posthumously in 1965) picks up where *YOLT* left off: Bond struggles to regain his memory, is brainwashed by the KGB, and assigned to kill M (what a great pre-credit sequence that would've made). His assassination attempt fails and after a full recovery and debriefing, Bond goes after an assassin who uses a trademark gold plated gun that fires golden bullets.

Hamilton was back for his fourth and final outing, and Mankiewicz and Maibaum each took turns tailoring the script. "I think what Guy was trying to do is make my persona a little sharper and a little tougher," Moore remarked in the audio commentary for *TMWTGG* MGM Ultimate Edition. In light of the more over-the-top Moore films later on, it remains a fascinating experiment.

Once again, Moore does not appear in the pre-credit sequence (at least not literally). But we're introduced to the legendary "man with the golden gun," Francisco Scaramanga, on his remote island surrounded by uprooted rock formations. He's played by Christopher Lee, Fleming's step-cousin, and Hammer Horror icon, originally considered for Dr. No. He's relaxed, aesthete, and supremely confident; and joined on the beach by bored girlfriend Andrea Anders (Maud Adams). They are served champagne by diminutive servant, Nick Nack (Herve Villechaize).

But looks are deceiving in this film, which weighs heavily on the outcome. Nick Nack actually plays a little game with Scaramanga, hiring assassins to keep him sharp, and the latest victim is an American gangster (ubiquitous Marc Lawrence, who goes back to the early thirties and played a similar role in *DAF*). He's lured inside a funhouse with a hall of mirrors, where he's easily stalked and killed by Scaramanga. Like the *FRWL* pre-credit, it's a warm-up and Scaramanga concludes the exhibition by shooting the fingers off a Bond mannequin.

A golden bullet etched with 007 is subsequently sent to MI6, which presumes that Bond is Scaramanga's next intended target. Bond regales M and Chief of Staff Colthorpe (James Cossins) with his knowledge of Scaramanga: A trick-shot artist born in a circus, KGB-trained, who charges $1 million a hit. His one distinguishing feature is a third nipple.

"Who would pay a million dollars to have me killed?" Bond cracks."Jealous husbands, outraged chefs, humiliated tailors. The list is endless," M barks. The political heat from 10 Downing Street is so intense because of the energy crisis that he orders Bond to resign or go on sabbatical. But Bond refuses: He's currently on the trail of a missing

British scientist, Gibson (Gordon Everett), who's working on a way of harnessing the sun's power to solve the crisis. It's "kill or be killed," as the saying goes, so Bond offers to find Scaramanga first. Thus, the film becomes a personal duel to prove his worth (and symbolically justify Moore's casting as 007).

Even Moneypenny gets testy with Bond when he asks for help in tracking down Scaramanga. In divulging that agent 002 was killed in a Beirut cabaret with a belly dancer named Saida, her anger is a veiled concern for his safety. Ironically, Moore and Maxwell studied together at the Royal Academy of Dramatic Art and become good friends, and this enhances their rapport. Maxwell once even opined that Moneypenny would've settled down with Moore's Bond but have a fling with Connery's.

Saida (Carmen du Sautoy) has kept the golden bullet as a good luck charm, and, with some difficulty, Bond manages to snatch it from her belly button while kissing her abdomen. But the price of the golden bullet is a brutal fight with the local thugs.

Back at Q Branch, Bond impatiently watches Q and Colthorpe analyze the bullet in the hope of tracing its maker. It's a rare moment when Bond must rely on their expertise to guide him. They figure out that the bullet is the handiwork of a Portuguese gunsmith in Macau named Lazar.

Meeting Bond is an honor for Lazar (Marne Maitland), who wants to build a special gun for him. But when Bond quickly brings up Scaramanga, Lazar insists on showing off his latest achievement: a rifle for a client missing two fingers. Bond humors Lazar but then fires a warning shot when he refuses to lead him to Scaramanga ("You're quite right… an inch too low"). It's the first instance of a tougher Bond from Moore, but fully justified given the circumstances.

Lazar leads Bond to Andrea, who acts as Scaramanga's courier, and he follows her to Hong Kong. But while 007 is in hot pursuit of her, he's inadvertently cut off at the ferry terminal by a nice but ineffective field agent with a crush on him, Mary Goodnight (sex symbol Britt Ekland, *The Wicker Man*, 1973). No matter: Bond locates Andrea and sneaks into her hotel bathroom and spies her in the shower, recalling the way Bond surprised Fiona in the bathtub in *Thunderball*.

But the brutal treatment of Andrea to get to Scaramanga seems extreme for Moore's Bond, since it's unprovoked. He slaps her face and twists her arm and humiliates her; and the harder edge serves as a barometer of this Bond's mettle. At first, she admits that Scaramanga only has sex with her before the kill, caressing her face with his gun. Then, after telling Bond that he can find Scaramanga at the Bottoms Up club, he pressures her into providing a useful description of him, and threatens her with further harm if Scaramanga doesn't show up.

As Moore reiterated, however, he'd much rather break her heart than her arm. "The characters I play aren't physically violent to women or children, and I'm afraid this Bond was," he explained in the audio commentary.

The good news is that Bond isn't a target after all; the bad news is that he can't prevent Scaramanga from killing Gibson, the missing solar energy expert, outside the strip club. Even worse, Bond gets apprehended by a local cop, Lt. Hip (Soon-Taik Oh). But instead of hauling him off to the station, Hip, who's really an MI6 operative, takes him to a naval intelligence base aboard the half-submerged Queen Elizabeth in Victoria Harbor, where Bond finds M ready to throw him to Scaramanga for jeopardizing the mission. It's a nightmarishly off-kilter set (designed by Peter Murton and constructed by co-art director Peter Lamont) that perfectly captures the tense mood. "Good dialogue stems from a fault and dialogue is verbalization of that fault," Moore explained in describing the cross-purposes of the scene.

Bond's now tasked with finding the gadget that caused Gibson's demise: a solex agitator, which converts radiation from the sun into electricity, thus solving the energy crisis. After being berated by M, Bond redeems himself by suggesting that Gibson's employer, Thai businessman Hai Fat (Richard Loo), put the hit on him. At least Q obliges Bond when he has a kinky solution for meeting Fat at his Bangkok estate: a third nipple.

However, Bond miscalculates in presuming that Fat has never met Scaramanga, who is now his partner in the solex scheme. After going to the trouble of impersonating Scaramanga and trying to intimidate Fat about the threat that he poses (a variation of the Saxby voice impersonation in *DAF*), Bond is captured later that night in a trap and taken prisoner at Fat's karate training center, where the fighters are instructed to kill him.

But Moore's Bond is more of a tactician than a fighter, so at the first opportunity, he roundhouse kicks a youngster in the face while bowing. This, of course, recalls Butch Cassidy's classic kick to the groin in *Butch Cassidy and the Sundance Kid* (1969), and also anticipates Indy's marketplace surprise in *Raiders of the Lost Ark* (1981) when he shoots the overzealous swordsman.

But all this manages to do is make the next bout a particularly brutal one, which Bond realizes he can't win so he crashes his way out of the school, and is joined by Lt. Hip and his two nieces, who deftly take on the entire school (again, looks are deceiving). This allows Bond to escape by boat on a canal (where none other than Sheriff J.W. Pepper and his wife are part of a tour). Also out of character, Bond nastily tosses a souvenir-hawking kid overboard after getting him to make the boat go faster (very unbecoming of the future UNICEF Goodwill Ambassador).

Scaramanga seizes the opportunity to kill Fat and steal the solex, and Bond kills the time with Goodnight and finally gets her into bed. However, Andrea sneaks into Bond's hotel room, and he's forced into another farcical hide the girl in the closet routine. Andrea senses that she's now disposable and comes to Bond for help, admitting that she sent the golden bullet. After Andrea leaves two hours later, Bond apologizes to a very upset Goodnight and promises to make it up to her (Moore's Bond at his most sincere).

Good thing, too, because Goodnight finally comes in handy: Bond meets Scaramanga for the first time at a boxing tournament, where he's already killed Andrea. He gives Bond a chance to walk away alive, but Bond grabs the solex and slips it to Goodnight, who then gets nabbed by Nick Nack and locked in the trunk of Scaramanga's car. Bond gives wild chase in an AMC Hornet with Sheriff Pepper inadvertently along for the ride (echoing the boat chase in *Live and Let Die*), resulting in one of the most spectacular car stunts ever — a 360 jump off a bridge ("Ever heard of Evel Knieval?"). Even so, Scaramanga tops Bond at his own gadget game by transforming his car into a plane and flying to his island near Thailand with Goodnight as prisoner.

Thanks to her homing device, however, Bond figures out Scaramanga's location on the South China Sea and is greeted by his suave host. Like Mr. Big, though, Scaramanga is a fraud — he enjoys the good life but his refinement is manufactured. This becomes apparent during the tour of the lab, where he confesses his plot to sell global solar power to the highest bidder, yet Bond must fill in the scientific details for him. Then, at lunch, Scaramanga scribbles down Bond's '34 Mouton wine reference so he can add it to his collection. When you get right down to it, he's still just a trick-shooter. But when Scaramanga asserts that they are basically the same, artistic-minded killers, Bond slams him for his delusion ("There's a useful four-letter word, and you're full of it"). In a clear departure from his predecessor, Bond declares that he normally gets no satisfaction from killing, but that disposing of Scaramanga would be a distinct pleasure.

Scaramanga then proposes "a duel between titans," which Bond accepts as a gentleman, but only after proclaiming that Scaramanga is nothing of the sort and insisting that they finish Nick Nack's delicious lunch. There's an elegance to Roger Moore's Bond, which serves him well: a sense of pride that never really seems snobbish.

They begin back-to-back and walk 20 paces, with Nick Nack as referee: Bond's six shots to Scaramanga's one. But as soon as Bond turns around to fire, he finds himself in the more elaborate cat-and-mouse in the funhouse.

As with everything else, Moore's Bond relies on the best tactical advantage to prevail. Here he uses the element of surprise to deviate from the playbook that has been shrewdly devised by Scaramanga, ruining his "indisputable masterpiece." And what is his surprise? Why, Bond masquerades as the 007 mannequin to get the jump on his arrogant opponent and shoots him dead.

But that's only half the battle: Goodnight pulls a Tiffany Case by inadvertently upsetting the delicate balance of the solar plant (knocking a baddie into a pool of liquid helium). Bond must then retrieve the solex under pressure before a laser strikes him and before the island explodes. The unflappable Bond does so without any gadgets, proving that the legacy is intact after this trial by fire.

For the third consecutive film, however, the henchman gets one last crack at Bond, though this time it's played entirely for laughs aboard Scaramanga's Chinese junk ship, as Nick Nack hurls wine bottles at Bond, but he eventually stuffs him into a wicker cage and straps him to the mast. For good measure, Bond gets to say "goodnight" to M and hang up the phone while finishing sex with Goodnight. It's the first time that Bond gets the last word with his boss, which is only fitting after the abuse he's taken from M throughout the film.

It's a lighter touch that substantially carries over into Moore's next outing, which will turn out to be the pinnacle of his tenure.

# THE SPY WHO LOVED ME

The third time was definitely the charm for Moore, and the 10th Bond film became the biggest grosser to date ($185.4 million worldwide). The result was a liberating experience for Moore, who cemented his lighter portrayal, immediately exemplified by the free-wheeling gymnastics of the pre-credit and credit sequences.

"[Lewis Gilbert] and I had more or less the same sense of humor, which is slightly off-the-wall," Moore told me. "We had a marvelous rapport: 'What are you going to say in this scene?' We would try something fun and Cubby would decide which one he liked best. So he played with the lines. John Glen came on the scene later and he was happy to go along with the way I was doing it, which was obviously successful."

But it didn't start out that way. Fleming stipulated that only the 1962 novel's title could be used since he was dissatisfied with his radical departure (told from a young woman's point of view "through the wrong end of the telescope"). As a result, the adaptation proved exceedingly difficult for Broccoli's first solo producing effort. No less than 12 screenwriters were hired (including *A Clockwork Orange* author Anthony Burgess and *Animal House's* John Landis) to figure out a credible Armageddon plot with a Soviet spy falling in love with Bond. The ever reliable Maibaum did most of the heavy lifting, but after working in Blofeld and SPECTRE, Kevin McClory (who was developing his own Bond film) threatened another lawsuit, so the return of the arch-rival was scrapped.

Ultimately, Gilbert succeeded Guy Hamilton and screenwriter Christopher Wood (*Seven Nights in Japan*, 1977) was recruited to reinvigorate the formula. He shared final screen credit with Maibaum (and Mankiewicz did a dialogue polish).

Ken Adam returned for his distinctive touch; cinematographer Claude Renoir (grandson of Pierre-Auguste Renoir) provided glam and grandeur to the Egyptian locales; and editor/second unit director John Glen (*OHMSS*) also returned to film the ski scenes and enliven the pace. John Barry was unavailable to score, so Marvin Hamlisch stepped in, fresh from the Broadway smash, *A Chorus Line* (1975).

We instantly notice during the gun barrel opening that *The Spy Who Loved Me* returns Bond to widescreen splendor, in keeping with Broccoli's glossier mandate. British and Soviet ballistic-missile subs mysteriously disappear in a throwback to *YOLT*. KGB head General Gogol (Walter Gotell, who played Morzeny in *FRWL*) summons agent XXX (in bed with a lover) on a beeper disguised as a music box that plays "Lara's Theme" from *Doctor Zhivago*. Only XXX isn't the Bondian-looking male, but the beautiful female, Major Anya Amasova (Barbara Bach).

In a similar vein, Bond is summoned by M via watch ticker tape while having sex with a Soviet spy in Austria. England needs him, so he "pulls out" and skis downhill to flee his pursuers in direct homage to *OHMSS*, using a handy ski pole gun and doing a spectacular 360 back flip (Willy Bogner returned as ski sequence photographer). Best of all, though, is his death-defying base-jump (performed by Rick Sylvester) off the ledge, culminating with the legendary Union Jack parachute opening. In fact, the flipping motif spills over into Maurice Binder's weightless credit sequence ("Nobody Does it Better," indeed).

But with its underwater MacGuffin, *Spy* melds *Thunderball* with *YOLT*. Anya is briefed by Gogol about the missing sub, a Cairo connection, and the death of her lover at the hands of a British agent in Austria, setting up a collision course with Bond. Commander Bond is then briefed aboard a naval base by the Minister of Defense (Geoffrey Keen), Q, Admiral Hargreaves (Robert Brown, who later replaces Lee as M), and Captain Benson (George Baker, who portrayed Hillary Bray in *OHMSS*). MI6 has obtained evidence of a tracer, which Bond demonstrates, that jeopardizes the secret route of the British Polaris submarine fleet. Q explains that such a device could simply track a submarine by its wake. They presume that the Soviets are to blame for their missing sub, and Bond is dispatched to Cairo by the Minister.

But, of course, this familiar Siamese fighting fish routine is instigated by the latest breed of megalomania: marine biologist Karl Stromberg. In casting the villain, Eon took the Goldfinger approach and tapped a German character actor, Curt Jurgens. Moore even jokingly referred to Stromberg as "Fishfinger" on the set. While there's obviously still a trace of Blofeld in Stromberg, he's really the second coming of *20,000 League's* Captain Nemo. He has forsaken humanity and lives aboard Atlantis: a giant, spider-like, submersible structure off the coast of Sardinia, Italy. Adam emerged from a creative funk on Kubrick's *Barry Lyndon* (1975) to design a curvaceous palace fit for this Renaissance man, containing a 60-foot refectory table and tapestry paintings of Piero della Francesca, Mantegna, and Botticelli that rise up and reveal the oceanic world in all its beauty and ugliness.

Stromberg has captured the British and Soviet subs with the help of a tracking device created by two scientists that he toys with and then disposes of in an exploding helicopter, but not before exposing his female assistant as a traitor. She's tried to sell the microfilm plans to a smuggling ring, so Stromberg sadistically feeds her to his shark while listening to Bach's *Air on the G String*, the first homage to Steven Spielberg's *Jaws* (1975). Stromberg then dispatches his two henchmen to Cairo to kill anyone who comes into contact with the microfilm plans: the baldheaded Sandor (Milton Reid) and Jaws, the quiet giant with steel teeth (Richard Kiel, the recurring henchman from the Bond-inspired *The Wild Wild West*, 1965-68).

Bond rides by camel in Egypt (evoking *Lawrence of Arabia*) to visit an old Cambridge chum who's now a Bedouin sheikh. He leads him to two smugglers in Cairo: Fekkesh and Max Kalba. But Bond isn't in such a hurry that he can turn down a night with a gorgeous Egyptian servant girl.

However, the layover impedes 007: He is met at Fekkesh's apartment by a seductive woman, who's supposed to lure him to his death, yet after a delicious kiss, she tips him off, and Bond uses her as a shield when Sandor tries to shoot him. A rooftop fight ensues and Sandor clutches Bond's tie for dear life. But after Sandor tells him that Fekkesh can be found at the pyramids, Bond knocks his hand away and watches the goon fall to his death ("What a helpful chap"). At least such ruthlessness is lighter and more convincing than abusing women.

But Bond's too late: Anya cozies up to Fekkesh at the Pyramids of Giza show. Then Bond gets a break when Fekkesh nervously runs off and follows him. Jaws also stalks Fekkesh: biting through a chain lock and killing him by literally going for the jugular. Bond watches in amazement, but loses Jaws when the lights dim from the pyramid show; however, Bond finds an appointment card in Fekkesh's pocket that leads him to Kalba.

But not before being jumped by two Soviet agents and dispatching them with ease in front of Anya. It's a delightful meet cute. He runs into Anya again at the Mujaba club, where they commence a rivalry. They try to impress each other with knowledge of their respective dossiers, and Anya even orders a martini for Bond. But then she goes too far by mentioning the death of Tracy, stopping at nothing to succeed yet hitting a sensitive nerve, which Bond acknowledges before excusing himself and resuming his search for Kalba. Dealing with Tracy has always been a delicate issue among the Bonds, but it's the perfect opportunity to introduce a softer side to Moore's portrayal, while drawing a parallel with Anya's own personal loss (which they both will have to confront eventually because of Bond's complicity).

Bond finds Kalba and tries to negotiate for the tracking device, when Anya shows up and they find themselves in a bidding war. Kalba is then called away by Jaws and killed (the two spies are too preoccupied with winning the prize that neither thinks to stop him). But after Bond discovers the body, the rivals hide out in Jaws' van, unaware that he's lured them into a trap. Again, Bond and Anya are too busy fighting over the tracking device.

Jaws drives them to some desert ruins in the morning and they immediately lose the giant. It's comical watching Bond and Anya back away from each other among the ruins, not wishing for the other to get an advantage. When Jaws re-emerges, Bond tries to take him on, which looks even more hilarious in the iconic surroundings. Better still is the shot of Anya aiming a gun at Jaws' crotch and saving Bond's life; but she grabs the microfilm in the confusion and ditches 007. Fortunately, he has the van key so she can't leave without him, and when the giant knocks over the scaffolding and is buried under a pile of masonry, Bond catches up with her. But Anya's unable to shift gears and drive away, which prompts Bond to poke fun at every misstep ("Can you play any other tune?"). Yet Jaws returns and nearly tears up the vehicle with his teeth.

Finally, she backs the giant into a wall and they flee until the van overheats and they're forced to wander through the desert (to Maurice Jarre's *Lawrence of Arabia* theme) before catching a boat back to Cairo. During a quiet moment, she discusses her survival tactics in Siberia, and the one Bond likes the most is "shared bodily warmth." Then, while Anya sleeps and snuggles up against him, Bond checks the microfilm and makes a copy with a camera. At last he has an advantage, and takes the opportunity to flirt and kiss once she awakens. But then she knocks him out with sleeping gas from a fake cigarette and retrieves the microfilm.

But just as the game of one-upmanship gets interesting, détente is forced on the rivals at a secret meeting with the British and Soviets. Bond surprises everyone with the revelation that vital data is missing from the microfilm. Q, meanwhile, has set up shop beneath the ruins and during his visual presentation, Bond points out a strange-looking anomaly, which Anya recognizes as Stromberg's corporate insignia. The two spies make eyes at one another; they obviously have the makings of a good team and are dispatched to Sardinia to meet Stromberg.

Aboard their train Bond loosens up and tries to seduce the icy Anya, but retreats to his adjoining cabin when she rejects him. There's a definite sense of Tee Hee déjà vu, though, when Jaws sneaks up on Anya from her closet and attacks her, giving Bond the opportunity for a rescue. Clearly overmatched, Bond cagily grabs the exposed filaments from a broken lamp to temporarily stun Jaws and toss him

out the window. Jaws merely dusts himself off. But that's all it takes for Anya to stop playing hard to get and bed down with Bond.

When they arrive in Sardinia, Bond picks up Q's latest creation, a tricked out white Lotus Esprit (which is Moore's answer to Connery's Aston Martin). Bond poses as jet setting marine biologist Robert Sterling with Anya as his wife, only Moneypenny books a hotel reservation with two beds, disappointing Bond, amusing Anya, and giving hope to the pretty receptionist. They are met by Stromberg's vivacious assistant, Naomi (Caroline Munroe, from 1967's *Casino Royale*), who escorts them by speedboat to Atlantis.

Bond prefers to meet Stromberg alone, which upsets Anya. But when Bond then tries to shake Stromberg's hand, he resists. It turns out that Stromberg shares an even stronger bond with his oceanic friends: his right hand is webbed, the latest in a long line of physical deformities for Bond baddies. Although Stromberg doesn't believe Bond's cover for a second, he can't resist showing off his lair while confessing his deepest desire to build an underwater paradise for all humanity. In fact, he tries to trap 007 by asking him to identity an exotic species in his aquarium. Bond teases before identifying the Pterois volitans, a venomous coral reef fish — how very Connery of him. Stromberg is impressed but concludes the meeting before Bond can discover anything useful. No matter: when Naomi shows Bond and Anya a scale model of Stromberg's Liparus supertanker, Bond notices something strange about the design of the bow.

Stromberg summons Jaws, who confirms the identities of Bond and Anya, and he orders Jaws to kill them both. A motorcyclist is immediately dispatched to blow up the Lotus, but Bond evades the oncoming missile from the sidecar and the cyclist flies off a cliff into a pile of feathers ("All those feathers and he still can't fly"). Jaws trails right behind in a car with other baddies. Bond sprays them with liquid concrete, which sends the car off a cliff and crashing through the roof of a man's house. But the indestructible villain walks away unscathed again.

A helicopter piloted by Naomi now gives

chase with machine gun fire, and Bond one-ups Scaramanga: he drives the Lotus into the ocean, where it turns into a fabulous mini-sub and Bond is able to blast Naomi with a missile (Mankiewicz believed this visual absurdity defined the Moore era). Bond and Anya drift back toward Stromberg's base and fend off some divers with harpoons, and are forced to land on the beach, to the amazement of sunbathers.

Back at the hotel, after Q helps Bond get a location fix on the Liparus, the rivals are both blindsided when Bond lights a cigarette for her with an Austrian lighter. He reminds her that it's part of the job ("It was either him or me"), but she vows to avenge her boyfriend's death after the mission.

It's the dramatic highlight of the film, when both must confront the unintended consequences of their profession, as well as a chilling reversal of their awkward encounter at the Mujaba club.

Time to stop Stromberg: Bond and Anya join the crew of an American sub in the vicinity of the Liparus. However, before they can board the supertanker, they are swallowed up a la *YOLT*.

The initial glimpse of the interior of the 400-foot-long supertanker with three nuclear subs in front is astonishing. Another of Adam's signature stainless steel constructs, it's made up of several compartments: the cavernous submarine pen, control room, prisoner quarters, missile storage, and armory. However, unlike Adam's historic volcanic

**Bernard Lee, Roger Moore, Walter Gotell, and Barbara Bach form an impromptu conga line on the Eygptian set of *The Spy Who Loved Me*.**

crater in *YOLT*, the enclosure for the Liparus set became a permanent fixture at Pinewood, the now famous 007 Stage, and remains one of the largest in the world. Of course, Adam still delights in describing how he snuck Kubrick onto the abandoned set one Sunday afternoon to figure out how to light it correctly. And after crawling around the stage for four hours, the director expertly advised him where to strategically place source lighting. No wonder the Liparus shines so brightly as another character in the movie.

Stromberg's use of the Liparus immediately becomes clear when he orders the crew of the U.S. sub to surrender or face death by cyanide gas: he intends to launch a missile attack against New York and Moscow, annihilate the world, and begin a new civilization beneath the sea. This goes beyond anything even Blofeld concocted, so there's greater urgency to defeat him. Stromberg spots Bond and Anya and separates them, taking her back to Atlantis with him by speedboat, and locking Bond up with the rest of the sailors. But Bond manages to get free and release the prisoners and lead a spectacular revolt against the guards to gain access to the control room. But getting through the thick armor shielding proves daunting, so Bond decides to get a nuclear weapon from the armory to blast through the operations room.

It appears that he's too late, though: the subs are only three minutes away from firing their missiles. But the quick-thinking Bond uses the tracking device to fool the subs into reprogramming the missiles and firing at themselves, resulting in them inadvertently destroying each other. Bond and the sailors escape in the U.S. sub using a torpedo to blow open the bows. They head for Atlantis as the Liparus explodes and sinks.

The bad news is that the U.S. captain has been ordered by his superiors to destroy Atlantis. But Bond persuades him to hold off for an hour while he tries to rescue Anya. Fortunately, Q has sent a wet bike that Bond uses to board Atlantis. Stromberg attempts to force Bond into the shark tank through the elevator's trap door, but Bond outsmarts him and pulls a gun on him. The two then face off on the long dining table as Bond demands that Stromberg release Anya. But Stromberg shoots an explosive gun harpoon through a tube under the table, which Bond narrowly avoids. Then Bond does something he hasn't done since murdering Dent in *Dr. No*: he tells Stromberg that he's had his shot and plugs him several times with his gun. It doesn't have the same impact, but it'll do.

Lo and behold, Jaws enters and they tangle in the chamber housing the shark tank. Reprising his dance with Oddjob, Bond realizes he's outmatched and uses an electro magnet to throw Jaws into the tank with the shark ("How does that grab you?"). Of course, the indestructible giant comes out on top in a wrestling match with the shark after putting his teeth into it.

Bond finds Anya and they escape in a mini-sub just as the torpedoes destroy Atlantis. But her instinct is to kill Bond and pulls a gun on him. Unflappable as ever, Bond turns on the charm and seduces her, offering champagne as a truce: "Maybe I misjudged Stromberg. Any man who drinks Dom Perignon '52 can't be all bad." Meanwhile, Jaws resurfaces and lives to fight another day.

Then, in his most embarrassing rescue, Bond and Anya are discovered making love through the porthole of their mini-sub when it surfaces and is picked up by a naval vessel with their superiors. But when asked by the incredulous Minister what he's doing, Bond has the best comeback of the film, which also serves as a summary statement for the Moore era: "Keeping the British end up, sir!"

Although the tag states that "James Bond Will Return in *For Your Eyes Only*," Broccoli couldn't resist substituting a more appropriate outer space adventure, given the blockbuster success of *Star Wars*.

Bond has always struggled creatively with success, which is a nice position to be in as the most enduring franchise: Find a tone that works, take it to extremes, pull back and try something different, and then repeat the cycle all over again.

With *Moonraker*, they obviously ramped up the absurdity and hardware while venturing into sci-fi. In fact, *Moonraker's* both a reworking of *The Spy Who Loved Me* as well as a follow-up, but with enough distance from Connery for the return of some classic touches: Shirley Bassey singing the theme song, the Moneypenny greet and flirt in the office (with a delayed surprise when Bond tosses his gondolier's hat into a vacant gondola in Venice), Bond drinking a martini, his anachronistic sexism, and a super villain wearing Nehru suits.

Moore was fine with it: "Some people prefer Olivier's Hamlet, and some Gielgud's," he told *People* in 1979. Nor did he mind a brainier Bond girl in the form of Lois Chiles' astronaut/spy even if 007 did: "I'm a little older and more experienced, so I think I can push the actresses around a little," Moore quipped. "The trouble is: they push back, most of them. Bloody women's lib!"

Gilbert was back at the helm one last time along with scribes Mankiewicz and Wood (who got final screen credit for crafting a variation on a very familiar theme). Instead of a billionaire industrialist obsessed with repopulating humanity undersea, this one wants to do the same in outer space and also enlists Jaws as his henchman; instead of Bond engaged in a rivalry with an enemy spy, he matches wits with an ally; and instead of saving the world in a super tanker, Bond stops Armageddon aboard a space station.

But *Moonraker's* just different enough to provide a few surprises here and there. An American space shuttle on loan to the British is hijacked without a trace and the carrier plane that transported it is destroyed along with its crew. Meanwhile, Bond is double-crossed by a cute flight attendant he's seduced and fights with the pilot before being pushed out of the plane by Jaws without a parachute. But Bond manages to wrestle the chut away from the pilot in another spectacular opening with Jaws in pursuit. Bond pulls his ripcord to elude the giant, whose ripcord breaks. Yet his fall is miraculously broken by a circus tent. Their amusing routine is like watching Road Runner and Wile E. Coyote.

Indeed, when Moneypenny asks Bond why he's late, she refuses to believe that he fell out of an airplane without a parachute. No matter his mild frustration: Bond's reputation precedes him. The same goes for the irascible Q, who started harping again about Bond's mistreatment of his equipment in *Spy* and continues harassing him in *Moonraker*.

Still, Bond's in an agreeable mood during his briefing with the Minister, M, and Q until he tries to excuse himself and Q detains him by showing off his latest gadget: a wrist dart gun activated by nerve impulses. It contains five poison tipped and five armor piercing tipped darts. Bond straps it onto his right wrist and tests it out by firing one at M's wall painting, hitting the butt of a horse. Like the mischievous snatching of the spoon with the magnetic Rolex, it gets a rise out of M and then Bond condescendingly remarks to Q, "You must get them in the stores for Christmas."

The lovely helicopter pilot Corinne Dufour (Corinne Clery) flies Bond to Drax's exquisite French chateau/headquarters in California. It was actually filmed in France, of course, but the story allows them to joke about Drax importing it stone by stone.

Bond enters the magnificent drawing room of this 18th century home and finds Hugo Drax (Michael Lonsdale, *The Day of the Jackal*) playing Frédéric Chopin's "Raindrop" *Prelude* in D-flat on his grand piano. The tall, dark-haired Frenchman wears a black Nehru suit and demonstrates more wit and refinement than the previous super baddies of the Moore era. But Bond isn't fooled: he knows how to spot a control freak with a streak of Nietzsche, and Drax turns out to be the worst tyrant Bond has ever faced. One almost longs for the contrarian Connery: suggesting a preference for an alternate Chopin to tweak his opponent. But that's not Moore's style — he's usually diplomatic until provoked.

In fact, the cunning industrialist politely tells Bond that his reputation precedes him while at the same time asking for an apology for the loss of his shuttle: "How would Oscar Wilde put it? To lose one aircraft may be regarded as a misfortune. To lose two seems like carelessness."

But Bond isn't about to concede: "An apology will be made to the American government when we've discovered why the Moonraker wasn't in that wreckage." For once, his loyalty "commands respect," yet Drax sneaks in another English put-down when he invites him to his country's lone contribution to Western civilization: afternoon tea. But Bond politely declines his offer of tea and cucumber sandwiches, preferring to find out more about his multi-national operation and desire to conquer space for the future of the human race.

As Bond is escorted to the training center overseen by Dr. Holly Goodhead (Chiles), Drax drolly tells henchman Chang (Toshiro Suga), "Look after Mr. Bond. See that some harm comes to him." But like his predecessors, Drax underestimates 007 at his own peril.

Yet it's disconcerting when Bond reacts with surprise to Goodhead's gender and that she's a trained astronaut. Maintaining continuity is one thing, but the sexism seems misplaced a decade after Connery. Of course, Goodhead is suitably insulted, but takes pleasure in strapping Bond inside a centrifuge trainer after briefing him on the Moonraker. It's the *Thunderball* near fatality on the spinal traction machine all over again: Goodhead leaves and Chang almost kills Bond when turning it to full G-force. Fortunately, before succumbing, Bond flashes back to the wrist dart gun demonstration and disables the machine. But when Dr. Goodhead arrives in a total state of confusion and tries to help him up, Bond resists. He's shaken and doesn't trust her and hasn't been this vulnerable since *OHMSS*.

But then dressed smartly in black like Cary Grant's John Robie in *To Catch a Thief* (1955), Bond attempts to seduce the friendlier Corinne. "My mother gave me a list of things not to do on a first date," she coyly suggests. But Bond tells her that he only wants information about Drax's secret operations. It works like a charm and Corinne doesn't even mind when she catches Bond snooping around Drax's study in the middle of the night. She points him to a safe, which he easily opens with a cigarette case safecracker that uses x-rays to reveal the tumblers, and he finds blueprints for a glass vial made in Venice.

But Bond is detained again; this time by Drax, who invites him to shoot pheasant on his beautiful estate. As with Largo, Bond pretends to be an ordinary shot, missing the pheasant with his shotgun but hitting Drax's sniper in a tree. It's probably the most fun Bond has with him.

Drax exacts his revenge on Corrine, the latest in a long line of sacrificial lambs, dating all the way back to Quarrel in *Dr. No*. But this instance is particularly brutal. First he fires Corrine and then instructs Chang to unleash his two Dobermans on her. Cinematographer Jean Tournier (*The Day of the Jackal*) shoots from Drax's twisted point of view, emphasizing the gorgeous surroundings as Corrine is viciously stalked and mauled (off screen) by the beasts.

In Venice, Bond checks out a glassblowing factory owned by Drax and matches containers with the blueprints while being shown several valuable works by a pretty assistant, including a bowl, a dish with aquamarine medallion, and glass-handled sword. But before he can investigate further, Bond runs into Goodhead at a museum glass exhibition. She's in Venice to address the European Space Commission. Bond eases up on the sexism but they continue their verbal jousting. For instance, when he asks if she can think of a reason for not having drinks, she responds: "Not immediately. But I'm sure I shall."

Then, in the latest example of his signature water

chase, Bond transforms a gondola into a hovercraft when pursued through the canals by Drax's henchmen on speedboats. He manages to stay ahead of the machine gun fire, though, and escapes across St. Mark's Square when a skirt inflates on the hovercraft, causing double-takes from bystanders and a pigeon that goes beyond self-parody.

Bond then stumbles onto a secret biological lab, in which the entry code ironically is the opening five notes to composer John Williams' *Close Encounters of the Third Kind*, 1977. (Spielberg gave permission despite continually being turned down by Broccoli to direct a Bond film.) Inside the lab, Bond finds a chemical being placed in globes, but, in his haste, he leaves out a vial of the chemical, which one of the scientists knocks over, releasing a deadly nerve gas. Bond helplessly watches both of them die (but the lab animals and plants are unaffected).

Bond finally tangles with Chang (dressed in full Kendo armor) in the museum glass exhibition. It's arguably Moore's best fight scene, displaying adept swordsmanship and physical prowess in combating Chang, as they recklessly destroy shelves of expensive antique glass objects. When Chang realizes that he's overmatched, he throws his protective mask at Bond and flees. They wind up in a clock tower and Bond prevails when hurling him through a glass window and into a grand piano down below ("Play it again, Sam").

However, during the fight Bond spots evidence of Drax moving his operation to Rio de Janeiro and sneaks into Goodhead's hotel room to confirm his suspicions about her identity. He deduces that she's with the CIA after pointing out standard gadgetry in her room, including a deadly diary (and admitting that he has "friends in low places"). He then proposes that they join forces and the flirting heats up before having sex. Yet the rivals can't wait to ditch each other in the morning.

But Bond blunders by dragging the Minister and M to the secret lab (insisting that they all wear gas masks), only to find that it's been cleared out by Drax and turned into a palatial room ("Not being English, I sometimes find your sense of humor difficult to follow"). He even gets his apology from the Minister. Alone together outside, Bond is promptly given two weeks' leave by M, but hands him a sample to give to Q; M unofficially sends him off to Rio. Meanwhile, Drax hires Jaws to replace Chang.

Bond is met in his hotel suite by a charming Brazilian contact, Manuela (Emily Bolton), who's more than willing to kill five hours with him until nightfall. She then takes him during the carnival to a warehouse owned by Drax. But while he sneaks inside and finds an air-freight sticker, Manuela is nearly killed by Jaws. It's an eerie encounter, in which the giant wears a clown costume and slowly creeps up on her. He takes off his mask and tries to sink his teeth into her like a vampire, but she's saved by the mingling carnival crowd that sweeps him away.

Bond then reunites with Goodhead at the top of Sugarloaf while monitoring Drax's air freight planes, and they put aside their rivalry just in time to combat Jaws in an exciting cable-car fight sequence. "Do you know him?" she asks. "Not socially. His name's Jaws. He kills people," he answers wryly. But with a chain and teamwork, Bond and Goodhead escape Jaws by leaping from their cable-car while sending his crashing. Yet this time Jaws is saved in the rubble by a petite blond with pig tails and fantastic strength named Dolly (Blanche Ravalec) — and it is love at first sight. However, Bond is provided with another rescue opportunity when he escapes and Goodhead is captured by Drax's henchmen disguised as hospital workers.

We next glimpse Bond dressed in gaucho garb, galloping on a horse up to a 16th century Benedictine monastery (accompanied by Elmer Bernstein's rousing theme to *The Magnificent Seven*). It turns out to be the MI6 branch in Brazil. When Q tells him that the toxin comes from a rare black orchid, Bond corrects him about the location of its origin in the Amazon. But the ever-reliable Q has a new vehicle for Bond: a tricked out hydrofoil, which Bond uses to navigate the rough rivers of the Amazon.

Indeed, while searching for Drax, Bond is attacked by a fleet of speedboats led by Jaws and armed with mortars. But Bond counters with heat-sinking torpedoes and rear-launching mines. Yet when encountering the Iguacu Falls, he escapes in a hang glider, leaving the hydrofoil and Jaws to plummet down the waterfall. This is just the kind of earth-bound defiance that Drax craves. Bond then follows a beautiful girl into Drax's ancient temple lair in the jungle. But first Bond must overcome another obstacle when wrestling with a python in a pool. He adeptly stabs it with deadly toxin from a ballpoint pen with hypodermic needle.

"Mr. Bond, you defy all my attempts to plan an amusing death for you," Drax complains. "You're no sportsman. Why did you break off the encounter with my pet python?" "I discovered he had a crush on me," Bond retorts.

While witnessing four Moonrakers lifting off, Drax proudly describes how he's gone beyond sterility in genetically altering the rare orchid's pollen to induce death in humans. It's even more gruesome than Blofeld's sterility plot in *OHMSS* and, as Bond soon discovers, exceeds Stromberg' human destruction in *Spy*. Drax adds that he stole his own Moonraker to replace a faulty one.

Drax then orders Jaws to place Bond in the blast chamber of Moonraker 5, where he is reunited with Goodhead. They escape through an air vent, thanks to an explosive charge from Bond's Seiko, and commandeer Moonraker 6, docking with Drax's hidden space station (another futuristic design marvel from Adam). Inside Bond recognizes the Noah-like Ark metaphor in the way Drax has coupled the passengers.

In fact, Drax plans to destroy all human life by launching 50 globes containing the toxin into the Earth's atmosphere. He's additionally transported several dozen young men and women of varying races, which he deems as genetically perfect, to the space station. They would live there until Earth was safe again for his new "master race." Bond smartly uses this against Drax by turning Jaws against him, since he and Dolly don't measure up to the super villain's physical standards.

So, Jaws and Dolly join Bond and Goodhead, who disable the radar jammer hiding the station from Earth. A platoon of U.S. Marines arrives in a military shuttle, and a *Star Wars*-like laser battle ensues. After launching three of the globes, Drax attempts to flee but Bond corners him. Drax relishes the opportunity to kill Bond himself, but Bond surprises him with one of the darts from the wrist gun. He pushes Drax into the airlock and ejects him into space ("Take a giant leap for mankind").

Jaws helps Bond and Goodhead escape in Drax's space shuttle as the space station disintegrates (Jaws uses his teeth to open a champagne bottle and toasts Dolly: "Well, here's to us!"). Bond acts like Luke Skywalker in zapping the globes (though the third one he has to shoot manually when the automatic system overheats).

Bond and Goodhead then make love in space, prompting the Minister to once again wonder what Bond's doing. Q, who isn't watching the monitor, humorously blurts out that he's "attempting re-entry." But leave it to Goodhead to ask Bond to "take me around the world one more time." His blasé response: "Why not?"

It was surely time to ground Bond in reality once again for Moore's fifth entry.

# FOR YOUR EYES ONLY

Despite *Moonraker* raking in a record $202.7 million worldwide, it was apparent that Moore's Bond had gone as far as he could with humor and hardware. A fresh start was required as 007 entered his third decade, and *For Your Eyes Only* offered a more down-to-earth opportunity. In fact, Moore, who was no longer under contract, nearly called it quits during a prolonged salary renegotiation that dragged on into pre-production. But he returned for this lone attempt to humanize his Bond with more seriousness and sensitivity: settling an old score and struggling with vengeance.

Yet when I asked Moore about the theme of revenge, he shrugged it off by saying, "I remember Lewis Gilbert reading a review once and he said that it's quite extraordinary the way people read into things. There are things we don't even think about. I don't self analyze."

But Moore finally conceded the departure in *My Word is My Bond* after a shout out from so many admirers. As with *TMWTGG*, however, he was uncomfortable with being more ruthless, but deferred to new director John Glen's desire to return to Fleming (following in Peter Hunt's footsteps but helming a record five Bond films in the eighties).

Indeed, with the available novels exhausted, the more character-based espionage film was culled from two of Fleming's short stories published in a 1960 anthology: *FYEO* (about murder and revenge in Greece) and *Risico* (about two rival smugglers). Scripted by Broccoli's stepson, Michael Wilson (promoted to executive producer on *Moonraker*), and Maibaum, *FYEO* also crucially takes its cue from *OHMSS*. Meanwhile, *Moonraker* marked the last Bond for Ken Adam, so Peter Lamont was promoted to production designer and provided a grittier look for the Mediterranean setting in concert with new cinematographer, Alan Hume.

In the pre-credit sequence, Bond visits Tracy's gravesite with flowers, initially conceived as a way of maintaining continuity if Moore had bowed out,

but now picking up the emotional thread from *Spy* when the mere mention of Tracy by Anya touches a raw nerve. It's also an indirect lift from the opening of the *OHMSS* novel, in which Bond annually visits the gravesite of Vesper Lynd, his first love from *Casino Royale*, which also ends tragically. So this serves as a similar pilgrimage.

But Bond is quickly interrupted by a priest informing him that a helicopter is on the way from his office to pick him up. The helicopter arrives bearing the name Universal Exports (the MI6 cover for Bond alluded to periodically throughout the franchise). As Bond enters, though, the priest gives him the sign of the cross, signaling trouble.

And sure enough, his old nemesis, Blofeld, is back, confined to a wheel chair with the cat on his lap and wearing the neck brace from *OHMSS*. But, with Kevin McClory asserting sole creative control of Blofeld, he's only alluded to indirectly. He electrocutes the pilot and traps Bond via remote control. Blofeld (an uncredited John Hollis) then puts Bond through a rough ride in London, in a reversal of the bathosub climax from *DAF*, cackling all the way at his sweet revenge. But before he crashes, Bond adeptly climbs outside the rear of the plane and back into the pilot's seat to disable the cable and take control. The cat smartly abandons Blofeld, who turns into a coward when the tone turns silly ("I'll buy you a delicatessen in stainless steel"). But Bond picks up the wheel chair and drops Blofeld down a North Thames industrial chimney, bringing a smile to his face.

This sets up the theme of vengeance, which will reverberate subsequently throughout the franchise. The electronic surveillance ship, the St. Georges, which holds the Automatic Targeting Attack Communicator (ATAC) used by NATO to communicate with the allied Polaris subs, is subsequently sunk in the Ionian Sea by an ancient naval mine. Back in Cold War mode, General Gogol seizes the opportunity to retrieve the transmitter for the Soviets (a twist on *FRWL's* Lektor), hiring his contact in Greece. Then a marine archaeologist searching for the ATAC for the British is murdered on his yacht along with his wife by a Cuban hit man, Gonzales (Stefan Kalipha). Their daughter, Melina Havelock (Carole Bouquet, *That Obscure Object of Desire*), a slender, dark-haired beauty, reminiscent of Tracy, witnesses the execution and burns with anger.

While Moneypenny pretties her face, she notices in her mirror a hat being tossed onto the stand, bringing a smile to her face: "Moneypenny, a feast for my eyes," Bond announces. After a warm kiss and embrace, she asks, "What about the rest of you?" "Well, I was going to get around to that." But she cuts Bond off and sends him into his briefing, informing him that M's on leave (actually Bernard Lee passed away from stomach cancer, but they weren't prepared to replace him just yet). Bond cheerfully tosses her a flower.

Bond awkwardly finds Tanner (James Villiers), the chief of staff, sitting behind M's desk, smoking a pipe like his boss. There's a fitting look of displeasure on Bond's face. But Tanner's even more intolerant of 007's vices than M. They tell him about Operation Undertow and instruct him to fly to Madrid to interrogate hit man Gonzales and find out who hired him.

Bond drives up to the villa in a new white Lotus Esprit Turbo and surveys the female eye candy at the party and spots Gonzales being paid off by someone. Bond's captured and made fun of by Gonzales, who is unexpectedly killed by an arrow fired from Melina's crossbow. She's certainly a better shot than Tilly in *Goldfinger*. Bond takes the opportunity to fight his way out and escapes with Melina in her tiny car after his Lotus self-destructs when a thug tries tampering with it. They precariously navigate the narrow streets of Madrid in a comical variation of his previous automotive escapades.

Afterward, Melina makes clear her intention to kill the man that hired Gonzales. But Bond warns her about the dark path she's embarking on: "The Chinese have a saying: 'Before setting out on revenge, you first dig two graves.'" But Melina tells

Bond that he doesn't understand: she's Greek and they always avenge their loved ones. How little she knows about Bond.

Tanner berates Bond for messing up without a trace, but Bond advises that he observed the payoff, so he joins Q in a secret room with a new Identigraph machine (introduced in the *Goldfinger* novel). Ironically, the secret code for the room is the opening notes to "Nobody Does it Better," which Q initiates with a look of disgust and Bond completes with a grin. After accurately capturing a visual representation of the man with wavy blond hair and octagonal-shaped spectacles, Q identifies him as Emile Locque (Michael Gothard), an underworld enforcer from Brussels working for Greek smugglers, who's currently in Cortina, Italy.

Now driving a red Lotus, Bond makes contact with Ferrara (John Moreno), who arranges a meeting with local businessman Ari Kristatos (Julian Glover). Kristatos proudly introduces Bond to his latest ice skating protégé, Bibi Dahl (skater Lynn-Holly Johnson), who's training vigorously for the Winter Olympics. She instantly flirts with Bond, so Kristatos asks him to accompany her to the biathlon in his place. After Bond agrees, he tells him that Locque's connected to his erstwhile partner, Milos Columbo (Chaim Topol, *Fiddler on the Roof*), a notorious gangster sarcastically known as "The Dove," who fought in the Greek resistance with him during World War II.

Bond spots Melina and ducks into a florist so she won't see him. But after he saves Melina's life by fighting off attackers on motorcycles and discovering that she was lured by a fake telegram, Bond explains the severity of the situation and sends her back to Corfu, promising to return for her when he finds out more.

Back at his hotel, Bond finds the teenage Bibi in his bed. But feeling older than ever, he rebuffs her sexual invitation and they sneak out of his room. What has Bond come to? Then at the biathlon, she attempts to make her lover jealous: East German champion Erich Kriegler (John Wyman). But when Bond's followed by Locque and his goons, he eludes them by participating in the ski jump, magnificently flying over a contingent of baddies waiting below, which now includes Kriegler. Proving once again that he's a spectacular skier (courtesy of Bogner, once more), Bond outperforms and punishes them on the slopes, even paying homage to *OHMSS* by perilously skiing on a bobsled run.

However, Bond is further attacked by three men posing as hockey players at the ice rink after saying goodbye to Bibi. In another comical turn, he thrashes them with a stick, sending the first two into the net, and scoring a hat trick with the help of the Zamboni ice resurfacer. After leaving the rink, though, Bond finds Ferrara dead in his red Lotus, with a Dove pin calling card in his hand. He angrily keeps the pin as a souvenir.

In Corfu, Bond makes good on his promise to fill in Melina, who shows him the lovely view her father used to enjoy. Bond wonders if he left any clues on the yacht, but Melina admits that she's lacked the courage to enter his study. In an attempt to help Melina put the past behind her, he reassures her that there is still hope.

At Gastouri's Achillion Palace, Moore's Bond plays baccarat for the first time, impressing Kristatos and an attractive, middle-aged woman with his skill and daring. He then plays a little power game with Kristatos over dinner: Bond orders prawns, salad, and Bourdetto; and Kristatos orders the same. But when Kristatos recommends a white Ribolo from his home town of Catalonia, Bond snobbishly tells him that it's "a little too scented for my palette," and orders the Theotaki Aspro.

So Kristatos tests the extent of Bond's daring. He first inquires if Bond is from the British Narcotics Board, since Columbo runs heroin through the UK; Bond humors him. Kristatos then asks if he has the resolve to kill Columbo, and Bond tells Kristatos to just lead him to Columbo. That's easy: he's sitting nearby with his mistress, Countess Lisl von Schlaf, the woman with eyes for Bond at Gastouri's. She's played by Cassandra Harris, the late wife of eventual Bond actor Pierce Brosnan. In fact, she introduced Brosnan (co-star of the popular *Remington Steele*

series, 1982-87) to Broccoli at a dinner party in 1981 while working on the film, and he obviously made a favorable impression.

Only Kristatos and Bond don't realize that Columbo is recording their conversation, which he listens to after excusing himself. When Columbo returns, he has a drunken altercation with Lisl, paving the way for Bond to seduce her to get closer to him.

Then something unexpected happens: Bond takes a genuine liking to Lisl over a champagne nightcap at her beach house when both her nightie and Liverpool accent start to slip. She admits that Columbo asked her to spy on him and Bond lets his emotional guard down for the first time since Tracy. After all, they're both lonely, and she's unlike most of the superficial women he encounters. It's a rare dramatic display for Moore and Harris is refreshingly poignant as Lisl. The following morning, they enjoy a relaxing walk along the beach until they're ambushed by Locque and his cohorts on supercharged dune buggies. Lisl tries to flee but Bond can't protect her — she's struck dead by the henchman's vehicle. But Bond is saved by men donning clothes with white dove insignias.

He awakens at Columbo's headquarters and discovers that he's been tricked: Kristatos is really the super baddie hired by General Gogol to retrieve the ATAC. Despite being awarded the King's Medal after World War II, he was a double-agent who betrayed Columbo and Great Britain. So it turns out that Bond is more fallible in *FYEO*, a consequence of emotional involvement and poor judgment. Yet the signs of Kristatos' cunning were apparent all along, if only Bond had not played the odds with him. Columbo is actually a small time crook with a zest for life, a weakness for pistachios, and a fun sense of humor, recalling Bey, Tanaka, and Draco.

To prove his claim, Columbo organizes a raid on Kristatos' opium-processing warehouse in Albania, where Bond additionally discovers that Kristatos sunk the St. Georges. After the raid, however, Bond seizes the chance to hunt down and kill Locque, resulting in the film's most powerful and

controversial moment. After Locque speeds away in his car, Bond impressively catches him on the other side by running up a steep staircase; he fires a shot that sends the car teetering on the side of a cliff. Locque sits helplessly as Bond tosses him the dove pin, causing the vehicle to move more precariously over the edge. Then Bond angrily kicks the car and sends the henchman to his death, satisfying his thirst for vengeance.

Yet Moore explained in *My Word is My Bond* that he quarreled with Glen about the handling of the execution. While Glen insisted on a cold-blooded throwback to Fleming, Moore argued that it wasn't true to his Bond. He offered a compromise: a gentle push rather than a swift kick, but Glen held firm and Moore played the scene as instructed.

"I think the old Bond would've let the pin in and caused it to roll, and then just open my hands with a little shrug — just the weight of the pin, not the kick," Moore clarified in the *FYEO* audio commentary.

Given the film's harder edge, though, it's much more effective to witness a return to Bond's ruthless nature, especially considering how fond he was of Ferrara and Lisl. Having a ha-ha moment with Bond merely tossing the dove pin at the psycho killer seems misplaced. It was awkward enough the way he cheerfully tossed Blofeld down the chimney. But even Moore concluded in his memoir that perhaps Glen had the right instinct all along, and that it was indeed a turning point for his Bond.

With renewed vigor, Bond reunites with Melina on the yacht and explains that Kristatos killed her father and that they must locate his log, which she finds and deciphers. They recover the ATAC from the St. Georges wreckage, only to be attacked underwater and ambushed by Kristatos when they surface. The villain relieves Bond of the ATAC and keelhauls Bond and Melina. But they cut themselves free (no gadgets this time) and escape with the help of a spare diving tank. Thanks to her father's parrot, Max, they realize that the rendezvous point between Kristatos and the KGB is St. Cyril's in Greece.

MI6 might be flummoxed about the location, but Columbo knows exactly where Kristatos is headed: an abandoned monastery atop a mountain, where they used to hide from the Nazis. Columbo instructs them to split up and recommends that Bond climb the right face away from the building. Meanwhile, Kristatos knows it's only a matter of time before his rival leads Bond to him, so he anxiously makes plans to escape to Cuba, upsetting Bibi's Olympic hopes.

While climbing the treacherous mountain, Bond kills Kristatos' henchman and chauffeur, Apostis (Jack Klaff), and then lets a basket down when he reaches the top to assist the others. Bibi and her trainer (Jill Bennett) help Bond and his colleagues with the guards and he disposes of Kriegler, leaving Columbo to confront his nemesis. Bond retrieves the ATAC and Kristatos surrenders, but that's not good enough for Melina. She wants to kill him, yet Bond pleads with her not to go down that dark path; that it's better to turn him over to the Greek police.

Still she insists, so Bond tells her to be prepared "to dig those two graves," making us wonder again about his own grave beside Tracy's. However, Melina doesn't have the right to kill Kristatos, who pulls a hidden switchblade on Bond, but is disposed of by the swifter Columbo and his knife. His thirst for vengeance is finally quenched.

Gogol arrives by helicopter to take possession of the ATAC, but, in a nod to *Ice Station Zebra*, Bond destroys the transmitter: "That's détente, comrade. You don't have it; I don't have it."

Then when Bond and Melina try to enjoy a romantic evening aboard the yacht, they're interrupted by a call from Prime Minister Margaret Thatcher (Janet Brown), who wants to personally thank 007. But Melina wants a moonlit swim, and, so, in an aquatic throwback to Connery, they sneak away, and Max, the parrot, says, "Give us a kiss, give us a kiss," embarrassing the Prime Minister and humiliating Tanner, who arranged the call.

Watching Moore in *FYEO* might not be as much fun as his definitive turn in *Spy*, but it's a noble Bond performance when viewed as part of 007's evolution. In fact, *FYEO* will serve as a template for the two upcoming Dalton films, also directed by Glen.

# OCTOPUSSY

Once again, Moore considered retiring as Bond. He was 54 and concerned that he might be too old for the job. Plus he was forced out of his comfort zone in *FYEO*, and didn't have Gilbert to rely on anymore. But getting Moore back was important: UA nearly went bankrupt after the *Heaven's Gate* debacle of 1980, so after merging with MGM, it was vital that they deliver a hit Bond. Not only that, but Connery was lured back for *Never Say Never Again*, so they faced the "Battle of the Bonds," and it was the wrong time for a reboot. Thus, after considering several newcomers, (including American actor James Brolin), they retained Moore with a sweeter deal.

More important, they let Moore be Moore again for his penultimate film, arming him with gadgets and humor, and having him casually slip in and out of glam locales in Udaipur, India. He also displays incredible survival skills along the way in preventing a Cold War flare up in Berlin.

The 13th Bond film from 1983 is taken from two Fleming short stories: *Octopussy* and *The Property of a Lady*. A new writer, George MacDonald Fraser, was recruited to work with Michael Wilson. Fraser was the author of the flamboyant *Flashman* novels and screenwriter of Richard Lester's irreverent *The Three Musketeers*; however, Maibaum returned to pull it all together.

In fact, *Octopussy* is really a reworking of *Goldfinger*. In the pre-credit sequence, Bond goes undercover to blow up something once more in a Latin American country (presumably Cuba, given the dictator's close resemblance to Fidel Castro). Posing as Col. Toro, his mission is to plant a bomb in a high-security airbase and destroy a radar plane. He's assisted by the fetching Bianca (Tina Hudson), who uses her sex appeal to help Bond after he's discovered by the real Toro and taken prisoner in a truck. Driving alongside them, her distraction enables Bond to dispose of two guards by pulling their parachute chords and then join her. He then shoots the tires out of the truck and makes a getaway in the Acrostar mini-jet stored in the trailer. After

eluding a heat-sinking ATA missile, Bond maneuvers through the hangers and does a 90-degree roll (recalling the *DAF* car stunt) outside a very narrow exit, enticing the missile to destroy the radar plane inside the hangar. After landing, he instructs the owner of the local gas pump to "fill her up."

Then, in East Berlin, a man dressed as a clown is pursued in a forest by twin knife throwers from the circus: Mischka (David Meyer) and Grischka (Anthony Meyer). It's beautifully shot by Alan Hume and recalls the mauling of Corrine in *Moonraker*. Just when he thinks he's escaped, the clown is struck by a knife and falls into the river, but struggles through the bank and stumbles his way to the nearby British Embassy, where he crashes through the window and delivers an ornate Fabergé egg before dying.

Cut to Bond preparing to toss his hat onto the stand. But he notices a pretty young woman standing on a chair, so he dispenses with the ritual to flirt with her. But Moneypenny intercedes to explain that she's her new assistant, Penelope Smallbone (Michaela Clavell). Yet Bond has already come prepared with a bouquet of roses to bid her welcome, but the jealous Moneypenny holds her ground. And even though Bond does his best to flatter her, Moneypenny teases him about his fickle nature and warns her assistant to watch out for 007: "Take it, dear. That's all you'll ever get from him." Bond knows when he's outnumbered: "I can see you're going to fit in here very nicely."

During Bond's subsequent briefing, we're introduced to the new M (Robert Brown, who appeared with Moore in *Ivanhoe* and previously played Admiral Hargreaves in *Spy*). Not surprisingly, he's a no-nonsense chief like his predecessor, only a bit more sympathetic to Bond's shenanigans: cracking a smile during a private moment later on about his shrewd, if reckless, behavior.

Bond regales his superiors (which also include the Minister of Defense and art expert Jim Fanning, played by Douglas Wilmer) with his knowledge of the Carl Fabergé egg. It was a gift to the royal Russian family and the model contains the imperial state coach. However, Bond is informed that it's a fake and that 009 (the clown) was killed after stealing it. This raises an angry eyebrow from Bond. Of course, they suspect the Soviets. But since the real one's being auctioned at Sotheby's, Bond will accompany Fanning.

Meanwhile, the Soviet Union is imploding. During a contentious meeting at the Kremlin (featuring a revolving conference room made of marble), the fiery General Orlov (Steven Berkoff, *A Clockwork Orange*) attempts to halt the disarmament strategy spearheaded by General Gogol (it's nice to see someone giving props to Bond), and mount an aggressive assault against the West in the Eastern Bloc. But Gogol has the support of the Soviet Chairman (Paul Hardwick), and so Orlov goes rogue. Considering that the reform movements of *perestroika* (restructuring) and *glasnost* (openness) would be launched two years later in 1985 by Mikhail Gorbachev, the film's ideological backdrop was extremely timely. Then again, Bond continued as the West's symbolic problem solver amid political tensions between the Left and Right during the reign of Reagan and Thatcher.

It turns out that Orlov's military coup involves a scam to counterfeit the Fabergé egg. He's informed at the Kremlin Art Depository that the fake has been stolen and orders a new counterfeit to be made, so it's imperative that they retrieve the original once again.

At the auction, Bond shrewdly takes advantage of the situation by forcing the most aggressive bidder, Kamal Khan (Louis Jourdan), usually an unsavory seller, to pay £500,000 for "The Property of a Lady." Not only that, but Bond switches the real egg for the fake, allowing him to follow Khan back to his palace in Rajasthan, India.

Indeed, the exotic Indian setting (filmed in Udaipur) suits Moore's smooth Bond very well. If anything, he's more comfortable than usual. Unencumbered by rivalries or vendettas, Bond can indulge in the good life and slyly seduce his way into Khan's criminal world. Bond may look unassuming, but Khan quickly learns how lethal he can be.

Bond is met by snake charmer Vijay (tennis star Vijay Amritraj), who plays the "Bond Theme,"

which Bond acknowledges as a "charming tune." He escorts Bond to his local contact, Sadruddin (Albert Moses), who explains only that Khan is an exiled Afghan prince and sportsman. However, like Goldfinger, the affluent smuggler has set his sights on something much more lucrative and explosive.

Speaking of Goldfinger, Bond immediately finds Khan cheating at backgammon (naturally wearing a black Nehru suit). "It's all in the wrist," Khan tells the unsuspecting loser at the casino before throwing loaded dice. Jourdan (*Gigi*) is perfect casting: he made a career out of playing suave yet insincere opportunists. So Bond steps in to take the high-stakes bet using the real egg as bait and invoking player's privilege to use Khan's lucky dice. He out cheats the cheater ("It's all in the wrist") and wins 200,000 rupees, and Khan is just as much a sore loser as Goldfinger. In fact, his henchman, Gobinda (Kabir Bedi) crushes the dice in homage to Oddjob.

"I knew both Harry and Cubby, and we used to gamble during the bad days of the sixties and were seeing one another on a very regular basis," Moore told me. "We had Michael Caine and Ken Adam and his wife and Harry and his wife…whoever would survive on Saturday nights would play gin rummy on Sundays, and Cubby and I played backgammon."

Moreover, Moore suggested in the *Octopussy* DVD audio commentary that the whole scene was a rouse: "I don't think there was any reason for this backgammon game apart from the fact that we could give somebody the excuse to say, 'It's all in the wrist.'"

Bond and Vijay subsequently elude Gobinda in a comic car chase through the crowded streets of Delhi, using a Tuk Tuk taxi (three-wheeled but tricked out by Q for two-wheel driving). This allows Vijay to show off his fighting skill with a racket. But after Gobinda lands a shot with his rifle, Bond must fight his way through the market with his usual improvisational flair (making use of such props from the locals as fire and a sword). Vijay picks up Bond in another taxi and they hurl the "hard cash" at the crowd to make their final getaway. Only Bond would cavalierly throw away so much money ("Easy come, easy go"). Dalton's Bond would later do the same thing in an airplane in *Licence to Kill*.

They wind up visiting Q, who hates leaving his lab in London to help Bond in the field, yet Bond displays more juvenile humor than usual ("Having problems keeping it up, Q?"). Perhaps too much boredom has set in. This time Q equips 007 with a homing device and microphone in the egg along with an ultra-sensitive ear plug; a radio directional finder in his Seiko watch; and a Mont Blanc pen with nitric and hydrochloric acid. But Bond has adolescent fun testing the wrist-mounted TV monitor by zooming in on a woman's breasts.

It makes for a nice segue for Bond to hook up with Khan's lovely assistant, Magda (Kristina Wayborn), who wants the egg. She resisted his charm earlier at the casino, but now baits him with a surprise dinner. Bond's thrilled to play her game and have some fun at last.

Later, in bed, Magda's still insatiable: "I need refilling," she coos, causing Bond to raise an eyebrow at the double-entendre before offering to refill her glass. "Don't bother," she says, "We'll make yours a loving cup." When Bond inquires about the blue-ringed octopus tattoo on her back, she responds, "That's my little octopussy," resulting in the best double-take since Connery's intro to Pussy Galore. Bond activates the homing device and lets her escape in the morning with the egg. She seductively slithers down the balcony and is met by Khan. The rivals smile at one another before Gobinda knocks Bond out. Score one for Khan.

Khan takes a Roman-style barge rowed by several lovely ladies to the floating paradise of his partner in crime: the wealthy, mysterious, and exquisite Octopussy (Maud Adams). He's come to deliver the egg and walks indifferently past the bevy of ladies that inhabit the island. He finds her tenderly feeding her octopus in the aquarium. She's viewed from behind wearing a silk robe bearing the Octopussy insignia. The only thing that piques her curiosity is the mention of James Bond. Instead of killing him, she instructs Khan to bring Bond to her, which displeases Khan to no end.

As in *Goldfinger*, the second-half consists of Bond escaping from one jam after another. When he awakens, he finds himself prisoner at Khan's palace but joins Khan and Magda for dinner that evening. Khan wants to know everything Bond knows. And this piques Bond's curiosity. He's great at the game of concealment, too, of course. "Well, supposing for argument's sake," Bond says, "I don't feel like talking?" Khan assures him that he will after partaking of a "psychedelic compound" that causes brain damage. The stuffed sheep's head entrée, however, is enough of a turnoff for Bond. He returns to his room and then escapes with the aid of the acid pen just in time to eavesdrop on Khan and Orlov. Bond discovers that the jewelry smuggling is merely "the tip of the tentacle" in some larger plot that will take place in a week at Karl-Marx-Stadt.

After learning of Bond's escape in the jungle, Khan enjoys hunting him for sport with his rifle atop an elephant. But Bond cagily eludes his rival by surviving a tiger, spiders, leeches, crocodile, and gunfire. There's even a silly Tarzan pun with Bond swinging from vines. Incongruity never ceases during the Moore era. He luckily finds safe haven by swimming to an American tour boat ("I'm with the economy tour"). This prompts Khan to sneer, "Mr. Bond is indeed a very rare breed; soon to be made extinct."

After connecting Octopussy to the venomous Genus Hapalochlaena, and learning that men are forbidden from her island, Bond decides it's time to meet her. He sneaks in with a crocodile sub (a large step up from *Goldfinger's* seagull camouflage). But Bond surprisingly meets with little resistance. She claims she knew nothing about the death of 009, and then proceeds to question Bond about a Major Dexter Smythe. Bond explains that he was an ex-military officer working for MI6 caught smuggling Chinese gold. Bond confronted Smythe and gave

him 24 hours "to clear up his affairs" before taking him in. But Smythe committed suicide rather than facing a disgraceful court martial.

Octopussy discloses that she's Smythe's daughter, but that she's not after revenge. Quite the contrary: she thanks Bond for giving her father an honorable way out of his predicament. It's a refreshing reversal and indicative of this Bond's gentlemanly sense of fair play. Octopussy then divulges that she had a knack for jewelry smuggling at an early age, and that she's become an accomplished businesswoman. She owns several legitimate corporations, including the circus, and surrounds herself with a multi-talented female troupe that she's adopted and trained (including Magda). In that respect, she's like Pussy Galore and her Flying Circus.

Then when Khan pays a surprise visit and discovers that Octopussy is protecting Bond ("You have a nasty habit of surviving"), he plots to dispose of 007 by hiring local riffraff, including an imposing fellow sporting a spin saw (one-upping Oddjob).

It's a pleasure watching Adams in her second turn with Bond: As Octopussy, she's smart and sexy. Indeed, she's the most liberated woman of the Moore era. But, like most Bond girls, she's also volatile. Thus, when Octopussy invites Bond to become her partner and he politely refuses, she angrily berates him for his loyalty to Queen and Country. Bond follows her into the bedroom and forcefully seduces her. He not only gets a violent thrill but also elicits her help with Orlov.

But they are attacked in the morning by Khan's goons in her octopus-shaped bed. Recalling *YOLT*, though, Bond is saved by a drop of water before the spin saw beheads him. He deftly fights off the attackers (even the venomous octopus comes in handy when the aquarium shatters) and escapes in his crocodile sub.

After Q informs Bond that the assassins killed Vjay, he briefly meets with M at Checkpoint Charlie. It's certainly more respectful than their usual briefings, as M provides Bond with a cover and they ponder the connection between the smuggling operation and Orlov.

Bond finds out soon enough. He attends Octopussy's circus and surreptitiously follows Orlov to a rail carriage, where he overhears the plot to blow up the U.S. Air Force base in West Germany during a circus performance. By double-crossing Octopussy, they plan to switch the canister with the stolen jewels (to be smuggled by Khan) with one containing an atomic bomb.

Bond then sneaks aboard the circus train to disarm the bomb but finds Orlov and angrily confronts him about such wanton destruction of innocent lives. How could he possibly get away with it? But then Bond quickly realizes that there would be no way to trace the bomb, and Europe would seek disarmament in the false belief that the explosion was an accident. This would provide an opening for the Soviets to invade. (At the same time, Gogol figures out that Orlov has smuggled jewels out of Moscow and attempts to intercept him.)

A fight breaks out with Bond, who's forced to flee. But he steals Orlov's car (where the jewels are hidden) to catch the train by riding the rails. Orlov is shot by guards trying to cross the border and his dying words to Gogol are that he will become a martyr. Bond finally leaps onto the train and barely misses getting crushed by another oncoming train, and utilizes incredible strength and acrobatic skills just to hold on. He's eventually discovered by Gobinda and chased the length of the train by the henchman, and they wind up in a terrific rooftop fight before Grischka pitches Bond off the train and pursues him in the forest (Bond previously disposed of his brother, Mischka, on the train). He catches up and expertly traps Bond with his knives, but Bond alertly pushes through a barn door and hurls one of the henchman's own blades at him to avenge the death of 009.

Now Bond must somehow get to the base to disarm the bomb. But his famous charm betrays him when a car full of teenage girls teasingly stops to give him a lift and then drives off as they laugh at him. Maybe he is getting old after all. Then Bond is beat to a phone booth by a woman that refuses to give it up to him, forcing Bond to steal her car.

In a frenzied race against time, we have a reversal of the pre-credit sequence, only now Bond wishes to defuse a bomb rather than plant one. He breaks into the base with his car and then dresses up as a clown to elude the military police but they still catch him. Moore explained in the audio commentary that he was initially worried about looking too ridiculous but that it worked out just fine. Bond tries to explain the explosive situation to the commander, who merely laughs at him, and then pleads with Octopussy for help after explaining how she's been betrayed by Khan. She pulls a gun from a soldier's holster and blows the cover off the warhead. Having become an expert at this, Bond rushes in and calmly defuses the bomb just in time.

Octopussy turns to Magda and they return home to deal with Khan. Her female troupe mounts a surprise attack on Khan's palace, but she's taken prisoner by Khan after confronting him. So Bond comes to her rescue in a Union Jack hot air balloon commandeered by Q. Bond leaps into action and tries to locate Octopussy on his new wrist-watch monitor. Bond enters the mansion and slides down the banister, firing away, in a moment reminiscent of the Piz Gloria raid when he slid down the ice head first. Q is given a hero's welcome by the girls when he lands the balloon on top of a baddie.

Khan and Gobinda escape out the back with Octopussy, and Bond pursues them on horseback, somehow catching up to them after they board an aircraft and prepare to take-off. Bond jumps onto the plane and miraculously holds on for dear life, taking his amazing talent for survival to an outrageous extreme. No matter what aerial trick Khan attempts, he just can't shake him. So he sends Gobinda to kill Bond, but he tosses him off the plane. Finally frightened of Bond, Khan clumsily loses control; Bond and Octopussy leap out when he crash lands and then plummets over a cliff to a fiery death.

While M and Gogol makes peace with one another over drinks, Bond is laid up in traction inside Octopussy's barge at sea. Still, they struggle to fool around and she wishes he wasn't confined. And, just like that, Bond casts off his casts and they go at it. The prankster strikes again.

Good thing: because age will soon catch up to Moore's Bond.

# A VIEW TO A KILL

They had to make Moore a more lucrative offer he couldn't refuse to return as Bond one last time. Fittingly, they finally played up his aging. It was about time: he was 57 and no longer looked as credible as world savior. When I asked him what the downside was to playing Bond, he replied, "[The] leading ladies have become far too young. You have too many chins for them to look at." Indeed, Bond girl Tanya Roberts was 28 years his junior.

So it made sense for Bond to struggle sometimes in *A View to a Kill* (1985), but still manage to get the job done with considerable skill, luck, and assistance. Scripted by Wilson (promoted to co-producer) and Maibaum, the 14th Bond film is lifted from the *FYEO* anthology and represents yet another variation of *Goldfinger*.

But they made it very eighties hip by surrounding Moore with a younger generation of actors (Oscar winner Christopher Walken, disco diva Grace Jones, and the last of *Charlie's Angels*, Roberts), and by having Duran Duran perform the pulsating theme song that became the franchise's only number one hit single. On the other hand, Moore was paired with Patrick Macnee (John Steed from *The Avengers*) as a sidekick in the early going of his investigation.

We find Bond in Siberia during the pre-credit sequence. Using a miniature Geiger counter, he locates the dead body of 003 and grabs a microchip hidden in a locket around his neck. A surprise attack by Soviet troops puts Bond on edge and he flees; he's even forced to race on one ski again (thanks to Bogner, of course). Then he steals a ski mobile, but helicopter fire blows it up, so he ingeniously grabs a piece of wreckage and uses it as a snowboard to escape. But the helicopter continues its pursuit and Bond takes it out with a flare. Bond then makes his way to a submarine that's disguised as an iceberg and celebrates in style, as only he can, with the young and pretty agent, Kimberley Jones (Mary Stavin), despite the awkwardness of the age difference.

When he returns to MI6 headquarters, though,

Bond finds Moneypenny exquisitely dressed in a pink floral dress, and affectionately tosses her hat into her arms. This actually marked Maxwell's farewell as Moneypenny and the end of an era after 14 films, which was fitting considering her friendship with Moore.

Bond then gets briefed on the microchip and its significance to Zorin. But not before Q finishes testing his latest toy: a remote controlled Rover that will play a funny role in Moore's final scene. It's noteworthy that Bond displays a smarter instinct than his superiors about what's really going on with Zorin. There's been a security breach related to the development of a super microchip made by a British defense contractor now owned by Zorin. The microchip Bond retrieved in Siberia is an exact replica and so Bond naturally suspects Zorin, yet the Minister assures him that he's a French ally and staunch anti-Communist. However, Bond points out that the leak occurred after Zorin assumed control of the contractor.

So it's off to the races at Ascot to check out Max Zorin. The bleach blond Walken (*The Deer Hunter*) plays the baddie industrialist like a spoiled brat, strutting and smiling smugly. He's accompanied by his lover, dominatrix, and guard, May Day (Jones).

Moneypenny goes out displaying a feistier side, exuberantly cheering for the horse she's bet on, yet loses to Zorin's speedy Pegasus in a come from behind victory. To add final insult to injury, Bond bets on Pegasus and asks Moneypenny to claim his winnings, promising to take her out to dinner to celebrate. You really wish he would this time. Moore's Bond might not be a know-it-all like Connery's, but he certainly knows his way around a racetrack. It's another instance of letting Moore be Moore with his love of leisure activities.

After Pegasus suspiciously wins the race, however, Bond is introduced to Sir Godfrey Tibbett (Macnee), a renowned horse trainer and MI6 agent. He suspects that Zorin is cheating but can't prove it, so he's hired a French private detective to investigate further.

Bond meets the detective, Achille Aubergine (Jean Rougerie), at the Eiffel Tower's elegant Le Jules Verne restaurant, where they are entertained by a woman with paper butterfly marionettes. But Bond's impatient with the stereotypically brash Frenchman, who has nothing to offer in the way of good intel. Bond can't even enjoy his meal or the fine wine in trying to get a lead. When was the last time that's ever happened to this Bond? Aubergine merely tells Bond that Zorin's East German background is a mystery along with how he might be slipping drugs to Pegasus. But he intends to find out later in the month at Zorin's annual horse sale at his stable outside of Paris. Just then, Bond looks over at the cloaked puppeteer off stage, who is suddenly replaced by an assassin, who hooks the detective in the neck with a poisonous-barb-carrying papillon.

Bond pursues the assassin up the tower, who turns out to be May Day. But she escapes by parachute (a la Bond), forcing him to steal a taxi and give chase the hard way. He trashes the car and wreaks havoc along the streets of Paris, eventually losing the back half of the vehicle after driving along the top of a bus. He finally catches up to May Day by jumping onto a boat and crashing a wedding reception (shades of *Live and Let Die*). Yet she makes a final getaway by jumping onto a speedboat driven by Zorin. It's no longer so effortless for Moore's Bond.

Bond appropriately gets reprimanded by M in a car. Fortunately, Tibbett arranges for them to go undercover at Zorin's large estate in Chantilly, where Bond poses as horse dealer James St John Smythe, and Tibbett tags along as his chauffeur and valet. Only Bond abuses him in an attempt to throw Zorin and his staff off guard, much to the chagrin of Tibbett. He's not used to being treated so humiliatingly. Likewise, this Bond isn't used to playing such a cruel snob, so it's a nice opportunity for Moore to play against type. Then again, Bond can't resist feeding his sexual appetite when he insists on checking out a woman. But the envious Tibbett protests that they're on a mission, to which Bond lectures, "Sir Godfrey, on a mission, I'm expected to sacrifice myself."

But it doesn't take long for Bond to charm his

way around the chateau, the grounds, and stables to get a better fix on Zorin's nefarious activities. He notices Zorin greeting a lovely female guest (played by Roberts), who arrives by helicopter, but is later rebuffed by May Day when he tries to sneak into Zorin's study. However, Bond uses special polarized glasses to observe a payoff between Zorin and the mysterious female, and slips into the study through the back to photocopy a replica of the check worth $5 million. Later at a reception, Bond gets an inkling of what he's up against with the powerful Zorin. Although he gets nowhere with the suspicious Conley (Manning Redwood), who handles Zorin's oil interests in San Francisco, he gets indirect confirmation of the Pegasus cheating with the German horse breeding consultant, Dr. Carl Mortner (Willoughby Gray), who divulges that conditioning is more important than breeding. Bond then says hello to his host and congratulates him on his stables. They verbally spar (reminiscent of Bond's meeting with Largo) and Zorin excuses himself when Bond alludes to the Aubergine killing by asking if he likes fly casting.

But when Zorin spots Bond chatting with his mysterious female guest, he instructs May Day to separate them. No matter: she's in no mood to schmooze anyway and hastily departs in the helicopter. When Bond attempts a seductive farewell, he gets rebuffed once more by May Day, who insinuates that he will be taken care of: "You'll see to that personally, will you?" Bond replies.

That night, while Zorin and May Day toss each other around in an S&M martial arts display (picking up where Bond and Pussy left off), Bond and Tibbett discover an underground lab beneath the stables and uncover steroid-releasing microchips that boost Pegasus' performance. They are nearly caught by Zorin's security guards, though, but Bond beats off the attackers and smartly slips into May Day's bed to avoid capture. It's about time that Bond finally reverses the trend of being surprised by females in his bed. Pleasure and pain — just the way 007 likes his sex — only May Day insists on being the aggressor, which will recur when Brosnan's Bond beds Berry's Jinx in *Die Another Day*.

But now, of course, Zorin knows Bond poses

a threat and meets with him in the morning, confirming his real identity in his data base while pretending to find a suitable stallion for him. Then, while Tibbett is garroted in the Rolls Royce by May Day at a car wash, Zorin sets a trap for Bond: he challenges him to participate in a steeplechase against him and his stable hands. This turns out to be another cheat because the jumps are electronically modified for Bond. However, Bond spectacularly outperforms Zorin and his gang by overcoming every obstacle and then veers off the track into the woods, where he spots the Rolls Royce.

Ironically, he can't get out of this trap when he enters the car and discovers May Day in the driver's seat and Tibbett's corpse in the back. Zorin catches up and laughs at Bond's incompetence when threatened with reprisal. It seems Bond can't get any respect from Zorin. But here again, Bond is able to outfox a nemesis that's underestimated his cunning just because he looks way past his prime. Bond is

then knocked unconscious and stuffed into the Rolls and sent to his death in a nearby lake. But Bond regains consciousness and uses the air from the tires to stay underwater until Zorin and May Dave leave.

An angry Gogol confronts Zorin at a deserted track, telling him he had no authority to kill Bond. He demands that Zorin return to the KGB: his reckless behavior and risky commercial ventures have become intolerable. Zorin refuses so Gogol reminds him that the KGB trained and financed him. He's a biological freak. May Day arrives and gets rough with one of the agents and Gogol retreats but not without warning: "No one ever leaves the KGB."

Like Goldfinger, Zorin holds an ostentatious show and tell in a boardroom filled with guests that he blackmails into financing his venture: the destruction of Silicon Valley so he can monopolize the microchip industry. Yet Zorin has none of the

**Christopher Walken, Cubby Broccoli, and Roger Moore confer with director John Glen on the set of _A View To A Kill_.**

charm and theatricality of Goldfinger. Again, he's merely petulant. It's a wasted opportunity with the charismatic Walken. When one of the industrialists opts out, he's escorted out by May Day, pushed down a slide mid-air, and falls into San Francisco Bay. Thus, this elaborate meeting has been aboard Zorin's large airship. Zorin and May Day look down on the approaching San Francisco (from the Eiffel Tower to the Golden Gate Bridge) with a proverbial view to a kill.

Now presumed dead, Bond moves more freely to investigate Zorin. He meets CIA agent Chuck Lee (David Yip) at Fisherman's Wharf. Lee informs Bond that Zorin has been pumping sea water through his off-shore oil pumping station with the help of Conley, a disreputable geologist responsible for a mining accident in South Africa, and that Dr. Mortner is a former Nazi who experimented with steroids on pregnant women in concentration camps. Only a few offspring survived, developing extraordinary intelligence but becoming psychotic. Mortner later defected to the Soviets to avoid war crimes prosecution. Bond immediately hits on the secret that Zorin is one of "the steroid kids."

Lee then introduces Bond to a local fisherman, who tells him that Zorin's pumping station has obliterated the local crab trade. Bond infiltrates the station later that night and tries to inspect the pumping device, but is almost sucked into the propeller blades when the gates are opened, so he jams the propeller with his air tank and makes his escape to the surface as the pump breaks down. Coincidentally, explosive devices are discovered around the pump by Zorin's divers. As it turns out, a Soviet agent is responsible and has been recording Zorin's conservations with Conley about destroying Silicon Valley (code name: Project Main Strike). May Day even apprehends an intruder, who Zorin promptly throws into the blades.

After Bond comes ashore, however, he bumps into the real Soviet spy who's been monitoring Zorin: Pola Invanova (Fiona Fullerton). She's a tantalizing old adversary and Bond enjoys seducing her in a hot tub while switching cassettes more successfully than in *DAF*: "The bubbles… they tickle my… Tchaikovsky!" Pola purrs.

Believing she's gotten the best of Bond, Pola sneaks out while Bond showers, but when she joins Gogol in the car, they realize that Bond switched cassettes. Bond listens to the tape and learns of a strike against Silicon Valley in three days. Posing as a financial reporter, Bond meets with Howe (Daniel Benzali), an official from the Department of Conservation, and inquires about Zorin's dubious pumping station, but gets nowhere, so he suspects that Howe has been bought off.

Then Bond scores a coup when the mystery woman that was paid $5 million by Zorin meets with Howe. So Bond patiently waits for the young lady in reception and follows her home to a mansion along the San Andreas Lake Reservoir. But after breaking into the house, she confronts Bond with a shotgun and tries to phone the cops. Yet the lines have been cut and they are attacked by Zorin's goons. Bond grabs the shotgun, but it's loaded with rock salt, so he's forced to fend them off with his fists. Afterward, they get better acquainted and the film suddenly comes alive. We discover a more domestic side to Bond and he acts like a protective father to her. It's an appropriate send-off for Moore.

While still maintaining his cover as a journalist, Bond cooks them a quiche for dinner and she warms up to him. She tells him that her name is Stacey Sutton, she's a geologist working for Howe, and that Zorin has been pressuring her into selling him her interest in the oil company founded by her grandfather that he now owns. She even tears up the check, bringing a smile to Bond. Now that he's found that Stacey is the key to defeating Zorin, Bond's much more excited about the mission as well.

Indeed, it's wonderful seeing Bond reconnect the phone and falling asleep in a chair with the shotgun in his arms, watching over Stacey like a gallant knight. But the following morning he's awakened by a minor tremor. Stacey checks it out and discovers that the epicenter is near Zorin's oil field. She explains to Bond that pumping sea water into the oil fields could cause a major earthquake along the San Andreas Fault. However, it makes you long for a Bond who already knows the science and enjoys sparring with his young companion. No matter: the important thing is that Stacey is now on Bond's team. She tries to warn Howe but is fired.

They consult with CIA agent Lee at her home later that evening, but are they're still missing a valuable piece to the puzzle since pumping water into Zorin's mine would not be enough to start an earthquake. Lee is promptly killed in his car by May Day before he can investigate further, and Bond escorts Stacey to the Department of Conservation's file room, where they try to determine how many oil fields are affected. But Zorin and May Day burst in and take them to Howe's office. Zorin shoots Howe and sets up Stacey and Bond, leaving them in an elevator shaft while setting fire to the building.

With some difficulty, Bond manages to rescue Stacey and evacuate the burning building just as the fire department and police arrive. But they're fugitives, thanks to Zorin, so Bond and Stacey escape in a fire truck and are pursued by a dogged officer who's no more successful at catching Bond than Sheriff Pepper. It's pure slapstick with Bond trying to secure the out of control ladder as they race through the streets of San Francisco.

The following day, Bond and Stacey sneak into abandoned mine disguised as site workers, where tons of explosives are being shipped in by Zorin and primed for detonation with a special device. Bond deduces that a massive double earthquake will unlock the San Andreas and Hayward faults, destroying Silicon Valley.

But they are discovered by Zorin and flee deep into the mine, with May Day in pursuit. Zorin seals the mine, detonates the first explosion, and then viciously machine-guns Conley and the fleeing workers in a violent rampage inspired by Brian De Palma's *Scarface* (1983). It may have been in keeping with the times, but it wasn't to Moore's liking. In fact, he was "horrified" when he first glimpsed the footage: "I said, 'That wasn't Bond, those weren't Bond films.' It stopped being what they were all about. You didn't dwell on the blood and the brains spewing all over the place," he admitted in *Kiss Kiss Bang Bang: The Unofficial James Bond 007 Film Companion* by Alan Barnes & Marcus Hearn.

In any event, Bond and Stacey climb their way up a ventilation shaft. She escapes but May Day catches up with Bond and they struggle before they are washed away by the flood. But just when you think Bond and May Day are going to finally tangle, he winds up assisting her when she's crushed that Zorin abandoned her. Like Jaws, she's forced to join Bond rather than fight him. Still, it would've been fun to watch Bond figure out a way to kill May Day since she's not a Bond girl. But she gets even with Zorin by helping Bond remove the bomb and putting the device onto a handcar and pushing it out of the mine. She even sacrifices herself by staying on the car as the bomb explodes.

Zorin naturally abducts Stacey and escapes aboard the airship with Dr. Mortner, but Bond grasps the mooring rope. As in *Octopussy*, there's no shaking him, even when Zorin tries flying him into the Transamerica Pyramid and the Golden Gate Bridge. With his vaunted skill, though, Bond is able to lodge the airship with the rope. Stacey assists by attacking Zorin and his guard, causing him to lose control of the airship, which crashes into the bridge. She precariously jumps out of the airship and holds onto a pipe with Bond's help. Zorin attacks Bond with an axe in a hand-to-hand fight that anticipates the fiery *Quantum of Solace* climax, and Bond overtakes Zorin and causes him to plunge to his death. Like a vengeful father, Dr. Mortner then tries to hurl a bundle of explosives at Bond, who dislodges the airship and causes the doctor to drop it. As it drifts away, the airship explodes magnificently.

Once again, M and Gogol meet privately to repair détente. This time Gogol offers Bond the distinguished Order of Lenin medal, a first for a non-Russian citizen. After all, where would the Soviets be without Silicon Valley?

And, of course, Bond is nowhere to be found. That is, until Q's remote control Rover embarrassingly catches Bond and Stacey in her shower ("Just cleaning up a few details").

It just goes to show that the age difference between Moore and Roberts mattered enough that they didn't want to show them in bed together. But in a way, Moore's Bond has come full circle as a father figure, from the virginal Solitaire to the more girlish Stacey. He got out just in time.

The party's over: time for the metaphoric hangover.

# TIMOTHY DALTON:
# A NEW BREED OF BOND

With Moore's departure, came another opportunity to reinvent Bond. In fact, there was even first-time discussion of an origin story. As Cork and Scivally recount, Wilson and Maibaum toyed with the notion of a young orphan Bond raised by his grandfather after the deaths of his parents in a skiing accident (a link to *OHMSS*). The troubled lad would become a rebellious naval officer and, eventually, a promising sub-agent, redeeming himself and setting up his start as 007.

> **Every single person who works on a Bond movie…has their version of what a Bond movie should be: either because they love it or because they think it will be commercial.**
>
> *Timothy Dalton*

Alas, Broccoli didn't like the idea of exploring the roots of Bond, which would obviously have to wait until *Casino Royale*. He instead wanted to take a more serious look at the present-day Bond, and, for that, required a different kind of actor. Broccoli had his eye on the classically-skilled Welshman, Timothy Dalton (born March 21, 1946), who first came into prominence on screen as King Philip II of France in the Oscar-winning *The Lion in Winter* (1968), and as Prince Rupert of the Rhine in *Cromwell* (1970), before later becoming a distinguished member of the Royal Shakespeare Company.

This wasn't the first time that Dalton was considered for Bond. He was initially approached about *OHMSS*, but politely declined because he thought he was far too young, and then was earmarked as a possible replacement for Moore after his contract expired.

Dalton was definitely interested. The only problem was that he was unavailable because of prior commitments with the stage production of *Antony and Cleopatra* and the comic book film, *Brenda Starr*. Broccoli then turned to Pierce Brosnan (*Remington Steele*), who was screen-tested with several other rising stars from TV. But after accepting the role, NBC exercised a 60-day option to renew *Remington Steele* and Brosnan was suddenly out of the picture. After more delays, Broccoli approached Dalton again and they finally found a window of opportunity if they waited for him to complete *Brenda Starr*. Dalton finished on a Saturday, flew to London on Sunday, and started on Monday.

Fundamental to Dalton's interest in Bond, of course, was the idea of returning to Fleming. It would not only differentiate him from his predecessors, but also provide an opportunity to humanize Bond as a "lapsed idealist" in search of the truth.

"I read the novels and saw the first three movies," Dalton recalled. "You realize immediately that the films aren't really like the books. Or they had become completely unlike the books. By the time I came in to do the first one, Bond was sort of jokey, flippant. But people liked that. The books were tough. In [*The Living Daylights*] short story, he's popping pills — he's doing uppers — so he has to stay awake for like three days on the job. And, of course, he drinks and he does all the kinds of things that they did try to capture in the beginning."

As Dalton previously noted, however, the frustration of playing Bond (pre-Craig) is that there's no character arc. He's the catalyst that propels the narrative but remains unaltered by the life-threatening chain of events. So Dalton tried to get under his skin and reveal the internal struggle at every dramatic turn. As such, he was usually too engaged in the mission to enjoy the thrill and luxury like his predecessors.

"Whatever one says or whatever one would like to do, you have to deal with the concrete," Dalton revealed. "Every single person who works on a Bond movie, be they sitting in a production office in London or in Los Angeles with hands on responsibility, has their version of what a

Bond movie should be: either because they love it or because they think it will be commercial. So they're always applying a historical preconception onto something that you're doing now— me too. And that sort of hinders almost everybody in the process. For example, you know what a James Bond poster looks like, don't you? How many times has the poster changed? Why has it changed? Because ultimately there are a lot of commercial decisions made and there is a lot of molding."

At the time, most people found Dalton's Bond refreshingly realistic. He displays little humor, his green eyes burn with intensity, and he's not as promiscuous during the onset of AIDS. For the first time, Bond considers the consequences before taking action. He anxiously smokes, he makes mistakes, and he's uncertain. It helped that the situations were more relevant and the baddies more believable. This was a breakthrough, and a precursor to Craig's current portrayal (albeit with more panache and less brawn). The teaser poster for *The*

*Living Daylights* even proclaimed that Dalton was "the most dangerous Bond ever." Yet Dalton's Bond is underappreciated today: eclipsed by his more popular successors, who nonetheless acknowledge his impact.

"I think Bond had a lot of that [grittiness] in the beginning, then it sort of was lost, and then it came back again with Timothy Dalton," Craig suggested.

"Timothy played it right down the fucking line there," cheered Brosnan.

Ironically, Connery missed a sense of danger. "I think if anyone maybe Timothy made the mistake of thinking that it was going to be easier than it is."

"It's hard," Dalton reminisced. "Twenty weeks, 15-hour days. It was very tiring. You've got to mediate, you've got to concentrate. It's interesting, these long shoots. You see wonderful freshness for about six weeks, then there's an ease, and then you go on automatic pilot. There it is — for better or worse. But I do not regret for a single second doing the Bond films."

# THE LIVING DAYLIGHTS

To achieve a more Fleming-like, human Bond with Dalton, Wilson and Maibaum tapped *The Living Daylights* short story (1962), which contained a darker tone and promising political overtones. It would be the last Bond film to claim a Fleming title until *Casino Royale* (and contained Barry's final score). For topicality, they turned up the Cold War heat with the Soviet Union's quagmire in Afghanistan, and were inspired by a real-life incident of a Soviet spy defecting to the CIA and then re-defecting back to Russia. They added covert arms dealing for ideological shades of gray.

Meanwhile, director Glen ushered in the new Bond era by picking up the serious thread he began with *FYEO*. Also, Cubby's daughter and Wilson's step-sister, Barbara Broccoli, joined the team as associate producer, and her increasing involvement would definitely impact the future direction of Bond as franchise custodian with Wilson.

"There was little preparation for the first film," Dalton recounted. "I was just flung into it. I remember the press conference was the biggest I'd ever done. It was hell with 600 people all shouting at me and masses of cameras from all over the world. I just started doing it. You can't think of it as being different from any other job. You do it scene by scene."

While the gun barrel intro delivers a decisive Dalton as Bond, he's overwrought in our first glimpse of him in the pre-credit sequence. Bond's on a routine training mission on Gibraltar that immediately goes awry when a disguised assassin murders 004 by cutting his rappel. The discovery of the death and the scream of a monkey jolt Bond. But he's a man of instinct, which he will emphasize later during a disagreement with M, so he pursues 004's killer by jumping onto the imposter's Land Rover. After a furious fist fight, Bond parachutes out of the vehicle while it plunges over a cliff, resulting in a fiery death for the assassin. Bond lands on top of a boat, where he encounters a bored beauty in search of "a real man." When she asks who he is, he replies, "Bond, James Bond," matter-of-factly and informs the office he'll report in an hour. But when she invites him to join her, he smiles, and changes his mind ("Better make that two"). It's a nice touch that links him to Connery.

"I simply said don't write for me," Dalton revealed. "Write a wonderful Bond story where there's danger, where there's humor. And my job is to play it, to fill it out."

We pick up Bond in Bratislava, where he helps an old KGB rival defect to the West: General Georgi Koskov (Jeroen Krabbé, *Soldier of Orange*). This too appears on the surface to be straightforward. However, Bond's accomplice, Saunders (Thomas Wheatley), head of the Vienna section, has no regard for his irregular methods and keeps the escape route to himself. Bad idea. They wait for intermission at the concert hall, where a pretty blond cellist (Maryam d'Abo) catches Bond's eye. Sure enough, she turns out to be the sniper that Bond has been assigned to kill, but at the last instant, he spots something wrong — she's definitely not a pro. So he merely shoots the rifle out of her hands. Bond smells a trap and takes over the mission from Saunders, leaving him in the cold. He secures the nervous Koskov safely through the oil pipeline to Austria (literally in the scouring plug that cleans out the pipe). Afterward, Saunders threatens reprisal for disobeying orders. "Go ahead, tell M what you want. If he fires me, I'll thank him for it," Bond fumes. Dalton's Bond has seemingly reached the end of the line.

Back at headquarters, Bond has trouble tracking down the cellist with Q and Moneypenny (now played by the young and perky Caroline Bliss), who's still very smitten with 007 but in a school girlish way, offering to take him home to listen to her Barry Manilow collection. Still, Bond entices her to keep trying to find the cellist. Bond's first encounter with Q is more respectful though he doesn't think much of Q's "ghetto blaster."

Bond brings Koskov a tasty care package from Harrods during his debriefing at a safe house with the Minister and M. Koskov insists that Gogol's replacement, General Pushkin (John Rhys-Davies, *Raiders of the Lost Ark*), has renewed the "Smiert Spionam" policy in a dramatic departure from détente, and implores them to kill him to prevent nuclear war. With this revelation, the trio departs for London.

But then a blond assassin, Necros (Andreas Wisniewski), invades the safe house posing as a Cockney milkman and then a doctor and abducts Koskov. He tangles with an MI6 agent in the kitchen in a particularly brutal sequence. They thrash each other around and hurl pots and pans, and he burns the agent's face on the stove before knocking him out. The fight is noteworthy without Bond, but demonstrates what 007 will be up against.

Back in London, Bond refuses to believe that Pushkin's psychotic. It goes against his instincts. So M threatens to remove him from the mission in favor of someone who follows orders and not instincts, leaving Bond no choice but to accept the assignment. Q then equips Bond with a nifty key-ring finder containing sleeping gas and plastic explosives (dispensed when you whistle "Rule Britannia" or a wolf whistle), while Moneypenny resourcefully identifies the cellist, Kara Milovy, at the academy. So Bond takes the new Aston Martin V8 out for a spin and returns to Bratislava.

Bond admiringly observes Kara's rehearsal of the Alexander Borodin *String Quartet in D Major* and follows her on a bus, where she's apprehended by KGB agents, leaving her case behind. She's interrogated outside by Pushkin and Bond goes to a bathroom and opens the case and finds her rifle inside with blanks. Koskov's defection was obviously a setup. Bond goes to Kara's apartment, which has been ransacked by the KGB, to return the cello case and learn more. He's charming and casually dressed in leather jacket and sweater, and notices a picture of Koskov on the floor. Bond picks it up and compliments Kara on her musical talent, realizing that she's Koskov's girlfriend. Bond pretends to be his friend and that he's come to fetch her. Kara immediately warms to Bond and he suggests they look for Koskov in Vienna.

The Czech police pick up their trail immediately

when Kara insists that Bond return for her cello ("Why didn't you learn the violin?"), giving him an opportunity to show off the new features of the Aston Martin. He uses the hubcap laser to slice a car right off its chassis at the border; he blasts his way through a roadblock with a guided missile and speeds through the wreckage of a semi-trailer; then, on a frozen lake, he retracts the outrigger skis and cruises on the lake; and finally activates the rocket booster and jumps the car over the ramp of snow. But they're forced to flee, so he activates the self-destruct system and they slide down the hill on her cello case ("Glad I insisted you brought that cello").

In Tangier, Pushkin angrily confronts American arms dealer Brad Whitaker (Joe Don Baker, *Walking Tall*), an arrogant and vain ex-army cadet, disgraced for cheating at West Point, who insists on wearing his uniform. He recreates famous battles with high-tech toys in his war room and adorns the entrance with waxworks of himself as legendary military leaders. Pushkin threatens to shut Whitaker's operation down. Whitaker then meets at his home with Koskov and his henchman, Necros, and orders the elimination of Pushkin; Koskov assures him that Bond will do it for them. For insurance, Necros will kill another MI6 agent.

Ah, Vienna. Not like the bad old days of *The Third Man*, but a romantic sojourn. Being in Vienna with Kara reinvigorates Bond. They attend an opera and Bond informs Saunders of the ambiguous situation with Koskov and Pushkin and wears down his resistance. Saunders agrees to find out how Koskov could afford such an expensive Stradivarius cello for Kara.

While Bond waits for Saunders' intel report, he takes Kara to the Prater amusement park and an intimate ride on the famous Ferris Wheel used in *The Third Man*. Bond arranges for them to stop at the top to get a better view. "Is it real or just a dream?" she wonders. Kara's anxious to reunite with Koskov, yet she's nervously drawn to Bond, and he's put in the awkward position of seducing her further. It's analogous to the delicate relationship with Domino in *Thunderball*. But when Bond tenderly kisses her, it appears that he too gets caught up in the momentary refuge from danger. Has he once

again "easily tipped over into sentimentality"?

Reality resumes when Bond meets with Saunders at a café, and he informs him that Whitaker purchased the Stradivarius cello at an auction for Koskov and that he can be found in Tangier. Bond thanks Saunders for his cooperation and they part on better terms. But Saunders dies when he triggers an exploding device planted by Necros inside the sliding glass door. Bond furiously pops the balloon left as a calling card with "Smiert Spionom" scribbled on it and races after Necros, who vanishes in an instant. Bond even draws his gun, which scares the bystanders, so he puts it away and regains his composure. It's a rare public outburst by 007.

Bond confronts Pushkin at his hotel in Tangier, pointing his Walther with silencer at his face. Pushkin's girlfriend sits beside them in utter fear of Bond. But he claims to know nothing of Smiert Spionom, which was disbanded after Stalin, and offers condolences for the deaths of Bond's colleagues. Pushkin also insists that he's after Koskov for the misuse of state funds. "Involving Whitaker?" Bond asks. Pushkin refuses to answer and then signals his associate outside by pressing a silent alarm on his watch. Bond angrily hits him and tears off the girlfriend's dress, distracting the bodyguard long enough to knock him out. Bond then politely hands the girl back her dress and tells her to hide in the bathroom, and resumes his interrogation of Pushkin. Bond instructs him to get down on his knees and put his hands behind his back. He draws his Walther and this time he's prepared to shoot.

It's a crucial test for Bond, who again must rely on his instincts. Who does he trust: Koskov or Pushkin? It's a cunning replay of the good guy/bad guy reversal from *For Your Eyes Only* (inspired by Fleming's *Risico* story). Yet Pushkin is counting on Bond's sense of reason and fair play: "If I trusted Koskov, we wouldn't be talking," Bond admits. But as long as Pushkin's alive, they can't flush out Koskov. "Then I must die," Pushkin proclaims.

Bond and Pushkin then arrange a mock assassination, and Bond runs into Felix Leiter (now played by the youthful John Terry), who's been monitoring Whitaker. Bond apprises his old pal of the "put-up job" to calm him down, and Felix

tells him that Whitaker has yet to place a big arms deal order with the Soviets. Cut to Koskov, Necros, and Whitaker, who signal diamonds to be smuggled from Amsterdam.

Bond greets Kara at their hotel, who feverishly plays her cello. She stops and makes him a martini just the way he likes it. They are both tense. He tells her the truth about his identity and that Koskov intends to kill her, but she doesn't believe him. Kara angrily lashes out at him for pretending to fall in love with her so she would lead him to Koskov. Suddenly, Bond realizes that she's drugged him. Necros enters the room dressed as a doctor; Bond grabs Kara's arm and murmurs that he was the man sent to kill her but merely shot the rifle out of her arm. Kara grasps the truth as Bond draws his gun on Necros before losing consciousness. Koskov emerges also dressed as a doctor to reassure her. They sneak Bond aboard a plane as a heart transplant patient bound for Afghanistan.

While Necros joins Koskov in the front of the plane, Kara apologizes to Bond for being such a fool and he admits they were both fooled by Koskov. Such an admission of fallibility obviously separates Dalton's Bond from his predecessors. They quickly discover the diamonds in a container beside them. But after they land, Koskov turns Bond and Kara over to his comrades at the Afghan air base. However, with the help of his key-ring finder, Bond knocks the guard unconscious with the sleeping gas and they escape from the jail. But just as they leave, a grimy Afghan prisoner pleads with Bond to take him with them. Bond obliges and we know where his heart lies in this political struggle.

However, in a brilliant stroke of luck, the lowly peasant turns out to be Kamran Shah (Art Malik), the Oxford-educated leader in the Mujahideen resistance against the Soviets. Back at Shah's headquarters, Bond asks for help in getting him back to the air base, but Shah complains that it's too risky, even after Bond explains that the Soviets are purchasing American high-tech weapons to be used against the resistance. Fine, Bond will do it alone.

But Kara refuses to be left behind, so Bond tries his best to calm her down, calling her beautiful in Afghan ("Kheista") and assuring her that he'll come back for at the Khyber Pass. That only angers her more because she thinks she'll never see Bond again if he goes after Koskov. Yet in the film's warmest and most lighthearted moment, they have a pillow fight, and she tries to call him a horse's arse in her broken English, which causes Bond to laugh and brings a smile to his weary face.

The following day, disguised as Afghans (what a sight!), Bond and Kara join Shah and his freedom fighters and observe Koskov trading the diamonds for opium. The Mujahideen will then exchange the diamonds for arms, and Koskov will sell the opium in America before concluding his arms deal.

When Bond protests, Shah insists it's the only way to arm the resistance. But Bond points out that the deal will ultimately lend a crushing blow to their cause when the Soviets get a hold of Whitaker's superior arms, so he strikes a bargain with Shah: In exchange for his help, Bond will prevent the opium from reaching its destination. Shah agrees as long as it doesn't interfere with their transaction.

Bond then sneaks into the air base and plants a bomb inside the cargo plane with the opium. But he's spotted and barricades himself in the plane while chased by a Soviet convoy. Kara shames Shah into mounting an attack on the base to assist Bond, and she tries to catch Bond in a jeep, fending off a baddie in the process. Koskov miraculously survives an explosive collision with his jeep.

Kara manages to board the plane before taking off, but so does Necros, who surprises Bond when he tries to disarm the bomb. It's a déjà vu *Goldfinger* entanglement, as Necros tries to strangle Bond with a rope. But Bond lures Necros outside the plane as they both hold onto the cargo for dear life. Kara helps Bond by veering the plane up and down. During the struggle, though, most of the cargo flies away, and Necros hangs precariously to Bond's boot, which he cuts loose, sending the assassin to his death, leaving Bond with a ruthless smile.

Bond then informs Kara that Necros "got the boot," and disarms the bomb with only a few seconds to spare, but decides to deactivate it and hurls the bomb at the bridge below to save Shah and his men from the advancing Soviets. They cheer Bond on as the plane flies away. But Bond and Kara are soon forced to crash land when they run out of fuel, using Kara's jeep as a slingshot with a parachute before the plane explodes. But only Bond would think of food after such a harrowing experience ("I know a great restaurant in Karachi — we can just make dinner").

With Felix's help, Bond sneaks into Whitaker's place and confronts him while he's replaying the battle of Gettysburg with his war room toys. "I'm replaying the battle as I would've fought it," Whitaker says. Bond tells him he's come for Koskov, but when Whitaker finds out that his opium went up in smoke, he smacks Bond with a desk drawer and knocks him down.

They engage in a cat-and-mouse shootout, but it's not a fair fight with Whitaker wearing protective armor and using an assault rifle. In fact, he even echoes Bond's admonition to Dent in *Dr. No*: "You've had your eight, now I'll have my 80." But Bond outsmarts him by luring him into a trap and using the wolf whistle to detonate the explosive device in the key-ring finder, forcing a bust of "that British vulture, Wellington," to crush him. It's a further reminder that the simplest gadgets often work best for Bond.

Just then Pushkin enters and saves Bond's life by shooting Whitaker's bodyguard. Koskov rushes in and tries his innocent act on Pushkin, but Pushkin gets even by ordering him back to Moscow in a diplomatic bag. Once again, Bond has saved both sides of the Cold War.

Indeed, Gogol, who now heads foreign-service, accompanies M at a reception following Kara's recital. She's on a world tour, thanks to Gogol's diplomatic intervention, who invites her to play in Moscow. Shah arrives late and apologizes for being detained at the airport (causing M to tease Gogol), but happily joins the celebration. Yet there's no sign of Bond, who's away on another mission, according to M. Kara's clearly disappointed.

Not to worry: This Bond romantically surprises Kara in her dressing room with their own private celebration: "You didn't think I'd miss this performance, did you?" he smiles. "Oh, James," she swoons.

Unfortunately, it's the calm before the storm for 007.

Dalton's second and final outing as Bond takes him to his darkest place yet: a personal vendetta to kill the vindictive drug lord responsible for the mutilation of Felix and the death of his bride Della on their wedding day. Thus, *Licence to Kill* represents the most serious and violent departure until the coming of Craig, as Bond quits MI6 and goes rogue.

"I thought it had a good story but it was too dour," confided Dalton, who prefers *The Living Daylights*. "Of course, it was first called *Licence Revoked*, but MGM didn't think anyone would understand it… It had that one theme of revenge. And it had a go at establishing a different kind of Bond. But it dragged it away completely. Why can't you have both — seriousness and droll, cynical wit?"

And yet with Bond totally on his own for the first time, he's better able to appreciate the people closest to him, particularly Q, who comes to his aid as a more caring father figure. Plus there's a vital connection to *OHMSS* when Bond is reminded of Tracy right before terror strikes, serving as a motivating factor to do right by Felix. It's a code of honor that must be obeyed. At the same time, it allows Bond to make up for the fact that he didn't hunt down Blofeld with the same fervor. In this respect, *Licence to Kill* anticipates the similarly revenge-minded *Quantum of Solace*.

The 16th Bond film also marked a fond farewell for director Glen, screenwriter Maibaum (who again collaborated with Wilson), title designer Binder, cinematographer Alec Mills (who shot the grittier Dalton films after serving as camera operator on *OHMSS*, *Spy* and *Moonraker*), Robert Brown as M, Caroline Bliss as Moneypenny, and, most especially, Broccoli (who relinquished the reins for *GoldenEye* because of failing health).

*Licence to Kill* significantly strove for more American appeal, partly out of financial necessity (a heavier tax burden forced the production out of the UK for the first time, so they shot in Mexico and Florida), and partly to keep up with the latest action/adventures. After all, this was the era of *Miami Vice*, *Beverly Hills Cop II*, *RoboCop*, *Indiana Jones and the Last Crusade*, and *Batman*.

In the pre-credit sequence, Felix (reprised by David Hedison) rushes to his wedding in Key West with best man Bond and friend Sharkey (Frank McRae), a latter day Quarrel. Only Felix now works for the DEA and is suddenly whisked away by the Coast Guard in a helicopter to apprehend Sanchez with Bond tagging along as an "observer." The drug lord rarely leaves Isthmus City, but has come out of hiding to retrieve unfaithful girlfriend Lupe Lamora (Talisa Sota) in Cray Key.

Sanchez, played by the suave, pot-marked Robert Davi (best-known for TV roles in *Charlie's Angels* and *The A-Team*), is a new breed of Bond baddie, more grounded in reality, yet still obsessed with power and loyalty like all the rest. He tortures Lupe with his special sea spine and shark's teeth whip. But before he can take her back home, Felix's men and Bond break in and a gunfight ensues with 007 locating Lupe and Sanchez escaping in the confusion in a light aircraft. However, Bond orchestrates Sanchez's capture, hooking the plane to the helicopter and hauling Sanchez away. Naturally Bond and Felix parachute directly down to the church below to make the wedding.

Then, while DEA agent Ed Killifer (Everett McGill) taunts Sanchez a little too conspicuously about his million dollar bribes, Bond plays the dutiful best man at the reception. He assists flirty bride Della (Priscilla Barnes), who steals a kiss, and snatches Felix away from a clandestine meeting with pretty Pam Bouvier (Carey Lowell) to cut the cake. Killifer even manages to show up to congratulate the newlyweds, but Bond finds him too obnoxious to even acknowledge.

As the reception winds down, Felix and Della surprise Bond with an engraved lighter that's lovingly inscribed, and he's deeply touched. It's a genuine Felix lighter, but it's no joke. In fact, the flame proves extremely strong when Bond tests it out.

The joyous occasion concludes with Della trying to throw Bond her garter, but the tradition hits him like a hard slap in the face. He graciously declines and starts to turn away, but Della tosses the garter at him anyway. Bond catches it, acknowledging that he's not stuck in the past. After he drives off, Felix explains to his bride that Bond was "married once but it was a long time ago."

But history tragically repeats itself. For $2,000,000, Killifer orchestrates Sanchez's cunning escape; he gun butts the driver of the van and forces the vehicle to plunge into the ocean, where the drug lord is assisted by frogmen and transported safely away. Sanchez then orders swift, sadistic reprisal: while Della is raped and murdered off screen, Felix is lowered into a shark tank in a warehouse (lifted from the *Live and Let Die* novel), where he is viciously attacked but not killed (losing his right arm and half of his left leg). Sanchez watches with twisted satisfaction.

When Bond discovers Della dead and Felix maimed at their home, he loses it and goes after Sanchez. He checks out the warehouse and runs into Milton Krest (Anthony Zerbe, the vampire-like baddie from *The Omega Man*). He's a drug-runner for Sanchez using his marine biology lab as a front. On his way out, though, Bond notices one of Felix's discarded buttonholes, and returns later that night with Sharkey. He eludes the shark that attacked Felix and makes his way into the lab, overcoming one security guard with a handful of maggots and another with the help of an electric eel. Bond finds Columbian cocaine, and Killifer captures him. But Sharkey shows up and Bond gets even with Killifer by throwing his briefcase with the $2 million at him, which makes him fall into the shark tank, where he's gobbled up.

The following day, Sharkey tips off Bond that Krest's ship is called the Wavekrest and that it's anchored nearby. But before he can leave, Bond is confronted by a local DEA agent about his rogue efforts. Bond protests that their unwillingness to pursue Sanchez leaves him no choice. The agent then hands Bond over to a couple of MI6 operatives, who escort him to the lush-looking Hemingway House, where he encounters an angry M. It's the *Goldfinger* reprimand all over again: "You have an assignment! I expect you to carry it out objectively and professionally!" M commands. Only Bond refuses to hold back his emotions and suggests they owe Felix a debt, echoing his plea to help Tracy in *OHMSS*. But M counters that Felix knew the risks and has no use for such "sentimental rubbish."

This leads to an open confrontation with Bond resigning and M revoking his license to kill. As we've seen, Brown's M has been more tolerant of Bond's failings than his predecessor. Thus, when Bond refuses to hand over his Walther and escapes, we can see how much this pains the head of MI6. He naturally instructs the agents not to shoot. "God help you, Commander," he ruefully whispers. It's the first of many defiant exchanges that will carry over to Dalton's two successors, burdening Dench's more complicated M.

Disguised as a manta ray underneath a cowl, Bond swims to the Wavekrest and sneaks onboard undetected. He discovers a container of drugs and finds Lupe asleep in her cabin. The sight of the scars on her back only hardens his resolve. Then his anger intensifies when he spots Sharkey's corpse brought aboard the ship. He shoots the killer with a harpoon gun (a la *Thunderball*), grabs his scuba equipment, and jumps overboard. Krest's men give chase in a surface mini-sub and other vessels.

Coincidentally, Sanchez's men arrive by seaplane to conclude another drug deal with Krest, allowing Bond to intercede. First, he breaks into the vessel's cargo compartment and starts destroying the drugs until he's spotted and flees again. He harpoons the pontoon of the departing seaplane, holding on tight to the water skis with Krest's men still in hot pursuit, and deftly climbs aboard. It's reminiscent of his predecessor's wild acrobatics, only this isn't played for laughs. Bond then throws the pilot out and furiously fights with the co-pilot, who loses control and nearly crashes. But Bond tosses him out and regains control, smiling as he hurls some of the drug money into the sea to the dismay of Krest. Bond steals the remainder of bounty — $5 million.

Bond later sneaks into Felix's house at night, goes into his computer, and looks over the Sanchez file. He also notices Felix's list of contacts, all of whom are dead except former CIA pilot Bouvier, the woman he saw with Felix at the wedding reception. Bond intercepts her at a local bar, where she's waiting for a meeting with Felix. He tries to warn her about Sanchez, when they're interrupted by his henchman, Dario (Benicio Del Toro), who took part in the rape and murder of Della. Dario recognizes Pam and wants to hire her to charter a plane. But Bond and Pam start a fight, which breaks out into a barroom brawl. They make their way of the bar and escape by speedboat, and Pam's shot by one of Sanchez's men. Not to worry: she came prepared with a Kevlar jacket and her wounds are only superficial. So they argue about who saved whom back at the bar, and whether she's tough enough to join Bond as a former army pilot. Meanwhile, they realize that the boat's fuel line has been severed by gunfire and they run out of gas: so much for the film being devoid of humor.

Pam wears down Bond's resistance enough to fly them to Isthmus City. He tries to send her packing once they reach the hotel, but she refuses to leave. Clearly, Bond's worried about her well-being, given what has already happened to Della and the trail of dead women he's left behind. But Pam convinces Bond that she's actually safer with him. Fine, but he gives her money to dress more appropriately, which pisses her off.

Bond deposits the $5 million in the local bank run by the drug lord at the very same time that Sanchez shows a group of Chinese businessmen around the bank. Looking very sexy, Pam catches up to Bond and the bank manager and introduces herself as his executive secretary. Bond merely smiles in amusement.

Later that night, Dalton's Bond goes gambling for the first time. He intentionally loses $250,000 at blackjack before easily winning it back, further

impressing Pam. But the point is to impress casino owner Sanchez, who sends Lupe as the new dealer to win back his money. But she warns Bond that his luck has run out and that he should leave Isthmus immediately. But when she informs Bond that Sanchez is planning a party for the Chinese the following night, he insists that she take him immediately to the drug lord. Left alone at the bar, Pam burns with jealously at the sight of Bond leaving with Lupe.

Sanchez actually enjoys meeting the man who stole his $5 million and then rubbed it in his face at the blackjack table. Bond explains that it's his business to "prepare for the unexpected," and then offers his considerable services as a "problem eliminator." Sanchez says he'll think it over and instructs his men to have Bond checked out.

*Licence to Kill* is definitely more *Miami Vice* than *FRWL*. "One of the things you learn as an actor is that you have to give them levels to play," Dalton explained in stressing Bond's lack of nuance here. "He drives the story along, but you find that every other character in a James Bond movie is a new character. So they've often been written quite interestingly because they've often been written afresh. "

However, there's a pleasant surprise waiting for Bond when they return to the hotel: Q. A worried Moneypenny's been trying to help Bond on the sly until M puts a stop to it, so she's arranged for Q to assist him. His sudden appearance is quite touching, and *Licence to Kill* offers the most screen time for the curmudgeon: it's a sentimental turn that stands apart from the rest of the franchise. Except Bond immediately tells Q to go home. This really is Bond's personal vendetta. But Q fights back: "Remember, if it hadn't been for Q Branch, you'd have been dead long ago," and so Bond relents. Then Q trots out a suitcase full of goodies, which includes an explosive alarm clock, exploding toothpaste, and a signature gun disguised as a camera with an optical palm reader.

This marks the second consecutive film in which Dalton's Bond turns sniper, but he tries again to get

rid of his accomplices. Q insists on staying, though, yet Bond counters that he works better alone. First, he lines Sanchez's apartment window in the casino with the toothpaste explosive and plants a timer inside a pack of cigarettes. Then he spies on Sanchez in his office, where he entertains the Chinese in an attempt to expand his drug operation in the Pacific. Sanchez even offers to show them his local processing plant the following day.

After that Sanchez meets in his apartment with the president of Isthmus (Pedro Armendariz Jr., whose father played *FRWL's* Ali Kerim Bey), whom he's bought off and threatens to kill when he balks at his amount being cut in half. Bond sets up across the street from the casino, poised to detonate the explosive and shoot Sanchez with the rifle. However, he spots Pam giving an envelope to Sanchez's head of security, Heller (Don Stroud, best-known for his hippie roles such as *Coogan's Bluff*). Bond detonates the explosive, but before he can kill Sanchez, he's suddenly attacked by Hong Kong Narcotics agents with orders to capture the drug lord. Curiously, Dalton's Bond is not as adept at martial arts as his predecessors and is easily taken captive.

They take Bond to their safe house where they're joined by a British operative with orders from M to return Bond to London. Just then, they are attacked by Sanchez's local militia and the room explodes, killing everyone except Bond. He is carried out and taken to Sanchez's luxurious lair.

When Bond awakens, he's graciously greeted by Sanchez and then privately warned by Lupe that the Wavekrest is on its way. Bond takes advantage of Sanchez's most apparent weakness: fear of betrayal. Bond tells the drug lord that the Chinese were a freelance hit team and that they took him prisoner because they were afraid he'd warn him. To bolster his claim, Bond admits that he used to work for British Intelligence. Bond then plants the seed of paranoia by suggesting that it was an inside job planned by Krest. Sanchez appreciates Bond's cooperation, but insists that he stay at his mansion. Sanchez then prepares to deal with Krest.

But Bond has no intention of being held prisoner,

so he convinces Lupe to let him hide underneath the powerboat she drives into town. When Bond returns to the hotel, he instructs Q to leave for the third time, which has become a running joke. Then he angrily throws Pam onto the bed and confronts her about the meeting with Heller. She screams that Heller had agreed to help them retrieve four Stinger missiles from Sanchez in exchange for a letter of immunity from Felix. But Bond's unsuccessful assassination attempt has made a mess of everything, and now her life is in danger as well.

Bond now realizes that he's underestimated Sanchez and that he can't work alone any longer, so he instructs a heartened Q to bring the Rolls Royce to the front. Bond withdraws the money from the bank, and, later that night, after Pam boards the Wavekrest pretending to be a harbor pilot and rams it into the dock, Bond sneaks aboard and plants the money to incriminate Krest. Then he instructs Pam to fly Q to Miami, where he'll meet up with them after it's over. This time, Bond merely wants to ensure her safety.

Of course, Krest denies his betrayal when confronted by Sanchez, who seals him in a pressurized chamber and pops him after turning up the pressure. It recalls what happened to Kananga in *Live and Let Die*, only much more gruesome.

Bond returns to Sanchez's place, where he's financially rewarded for tipping him off about Krest. But Bond further fuels his paranoia by implicating Heller in the plot to overthrow him. Before finally luring Bond into bed, Lupe divulges that he will get to see where the drugs are processed the following day.

But while Bond accompanies Sanchez and the others to the plant, Lupe visits Q and Pam to warn them that Bond's in danger. She's fallen for Bond after spending the night with him, which only fans the flames of Pam's jealousy. "Look, don't judge him too harshly, my dear," Q appeases later when they're alone. "Field operatives often use every means at their disposal to achieve their objectives." "Bullshit!" Pam barks.

But Pam isn't about to sit still and concocts a plan

to help Bond. Sanchez and his contingent arrive at a meditation institute run by scamming televangelist Joe Butcher (famed Vegas fixture Wayne Newton). But it's really a front for the drug operation, where they dissolve the cocaine in gasoline so that it's undetected. While Sanchez's accountant, Truman-Lodge (Anthony Starke), leads them on a tour of the plant, Pam charms her way into Joe's private meditation chamber with a basket full of money, and then pulls a gun on him and locks him in the room. Butcher is so taken by her, though, that he just sits and smiles.

However, Dario recognizes Bond from the bar in Florida, and all hell breaks loose when Bond lights a fire to the place. While the Chinese flee and Truman-Lodge panics, Sanchez instructs his men to evacuate four gas tankers full of drugs. He then deals with Bond by forcing him onto the conveyor belt that leads to the machinery. While hanging precariously from the handrail, Bond divulges that he knows all about the Stingers and that Sanchez can't trust anyone. But, unlike the close call with the laser in *Goldfinger*, Bond can't bluff his way out of this jam. Sanchez leaves Dario to finish off Bond, but Pam arrives and nicks Dario with her lone shot, allowing Bond to recover and pull him into the machinery ("Switch the bloody machine off!").

Sure enough, as the whole place explodes around them, they find Heller dead and Sanchez now in possession of the Stingers. Sanchez murders his accountant as well. So Pam pilots a crop dusting plane and lowers Bond onto one of the tankers. He deftly maneuvers his way into the tanker's cab while Sanchez fires at him. Then Bond takes control, driving a second tanker off the road, and spectacularly tipping his tanker on its side (a la the *DAF* Vegas chase) to elude a Stinger missile that blows up the other tanker behind him. However, Sanchez's men shoot out his tires and Bond's tanker winds up on the edge of a cliff. Pam then swoops in to dust them off, allowing Bond to topple his tanker over the edge and smash into a third one below.

Next, Bond gets into one of the tanker cabs and eludes another group of baddies by popping a wheelie (in a throwback to Moore's Bond), leaving behind a flaming wreck. Bond then goes after Sanchez, who's in the fourth tanker. While climbing aboard, Bond smartly empties the gas, causing the vehicle behind him to burst into flames and hurl into the air, but nearly hitting Pam's oncoming aircraft. Then Sanchez fires a missile at Pam, but merely hits the tailpipe, allowing her to safely land.

Bond and Sanchez then fight it out on the tanker, which hurls down an incline and overturns. Both combatants are bloodied and drenched in gas, but Sanchez overtakes Bond and prepares to finish him off with a machete. "Don't you want to know why?" Bond craftily mutters. He then pulls out the lighter from Della and Felix and ignites Sanchez, who bursts into flames. Never has a personal gadget come in handier.

After phoning Felix to find out how he's recovering, Bond attends a party with Q and the two latest women in his life. But when Pam sees Bond kissing Lupe, she storms off, leaving Q to shake his head in disappointment. But Lupe's now smitten with the president of Isthmus, and when Bond finally realizes that Pam's fallen for him, he gallantly pursues her and drags her into the swimming pool with him (a Connery throwback). They smile, they kiss, and a happy glow returns to Bond.

But it's the last image we have of Dalton's Bond. Between the fallout from *Licence to Kill's* unpopularity and MGM/UA being sold to Pathe, Bond didn't return for six years: the longest inactive period in franchise history. So, despite a third film still remaining on Dalton's contract, there was a mutual parting of the ways when the studio's new regime finally bankrolled *GoldenEye* in 1994, and Michael Wilson and Barbara Broccoli took control of Eon. That's when Pierce Brosnan ironically entered the picture again.

# PIERCE BROSNAN: BACK TO BASICS

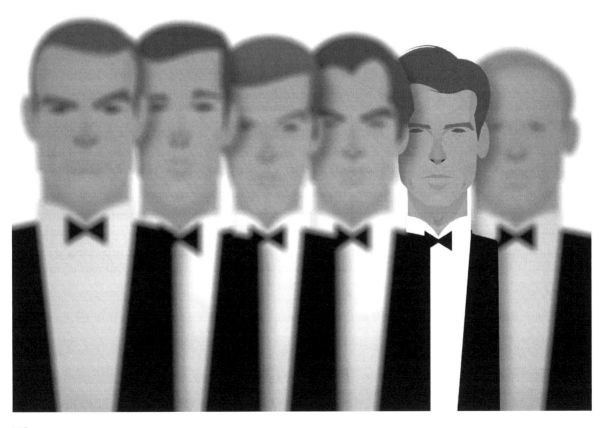

When Brosnan and Bond finally came together in 1995, it couldn't have occurred at a more crucial time. The actor floundered after his wife, Cassandra, passed away from ovarian cancer in 1991, and Bond entered his fourth decade with a mid-life crisis. The world had changed during his absence: the Soviet Union collapsed, the Berlin Wall came down, the Cold War was over, and the spy game was in transition. Plus Bond's notorious image was now politically incorrect.

Still, considering how far they strayed with Dalton, the time seemed right for a return to a more classic Bond. This definitely suited the darkly handsome Irish native (born May 16, 1953). Brosnan first showed promise as the cold-blooded assassin in *The Long Good Friday* (1980), and was positively charming as the thief-turned PI in *Remington Steele*. But the seminal moment occurred much earlier:" I was brought up on James Bond and wanted to be James Bond ever since I saw *Goldfinger* when I came from Ireland to London as a boy," he recalled.

Thus, with a familiar mixture of sex, violence, and humor, Brosnan rejuvenated the franchise, and even managed to evoke some of the spirit of Connery, since his Bond enjoyed fighting as much as shagging. It was just what audiences wanted, too, and Brosnan's four-film stint broke box office records for 007 (topping $100 million domestically for the first time and each one out grossing the last). He was also the first to admit that the delay made him a better Bond. Brosnan was older and more experienced and the pain he suffered gave him a tougher edge.

"I wouldn't have been Bond if *Remington* hadn't happened, so everything has its purpose," Brosnan reflected. "[Bond] had been in my life before and had gone out of my life. I saw it as a glorious opportunity to go out there and do it. And I tried to keep it as simple and as honest as possible because there was a lot at stake for myself and for [director] Martin Campbell. It was intense being up on the wire — do or die — and we did it and it worked."

*GoldenEye* also affected Brosnan's personal life as well. He was falling in love with Keely Shaye Smith (whom he would marry in 2001) and adjusting to a new life together: "being a family man, dealing with all the kids. I was very proud but anxious — anxious to do well."

But it wasn't easy for Bond, who clung to the tried and true even when it appeared anachronistic to the rest of the world. As always, though, Bond proved resilient. He survived by relying on his legendary charm, panache, and resourcefulness, not to mention the cutting edge gadgets supplied by the grandfatherly Q — the only holdover from the Connery era. But M was now a strict maternal figure whose tough love grounded Bond in reality.

"I think Pierce's Bond is much nearer the book than any of the other guys, no matter how dazzling Sean was or amusing Roger was," insisted Michael Apted, who directed *The World Is Not Enough*. "That wonderful tightrope Pierce walks between having a licence to kill and being vulnerable and complex, interested in people and respectful of women."

Although Brosnan says he had his own style, he has no idea what it was. "I just hope that it [was] truthful and believable, having the time of his life killing people, drinking martinis, and shagging his way through the high society of every country he goes to."

But Brosnan was never satisfied with playing it safe. Like Dalton, he tried to stretch the limits of the character, even when he encountered resistance

> **I just hope that it was truthful and believable, having the time of his life killing people, drinking martinis, and shagging his way through the high society of every country he goes to.**
>
> *Pierce Brosnan*

from the producers and the studio. "Bond has its restrictions; it has its own discipline and its own style, which has been built up over the years," he acknowledged. "And it has a rich tradition that you have to give up to and deliver. And it is a formula. So to go off and do *The Tailor of Panama* [2001] was highly enjoyable. It wasn't probably as much fun as Bond, but it was playing another aspect of the world of the spy game."

Even so, Brosnan got to flirt with Bond's vulnerability and dark side in his desire to return to the source. "He was born from the pen of Fleming with a perverseness," he relished. "There's always a shadow in those stories. If it was up to me, you would have scenes that have [kinky] sex. That's what this man is about. There would be lovemaking scenes that are palpable, like in *Thomas Crown Affair*, which were easy on the eye and exciting and erotic and tasteful. And I think you can work that into Bond as well.

"And violence, too; this man has a license to kill. But how does he kill? And you [would] see that violence. But I would love to take the censorship off it without being gratuitous, without being distasteful. Just sort of, ha! So you could be more believable. So you could have both: the intensity of the killing, which is very clinical and matter of fact, and then go into the humor. You go back to the flip side of things."

In other words, Brosnan wanted to peel away the onion to get at the core of Bond. But as producer Michael Wilson countered, "What happens when you peel away the onion? There's nothing there."

"I said it once and probably said it once too many times," continued Brosnan, "there are situations where you can play with it so I can make it my own. How do I make it my own? Connery had such ownership over it. And there's only one. What Roger did was great and he did it well, but how do you do it so it's dangerous and sexy and free?

Although Brosnan had his heart set on making *Casino Royale* and returning to the source, his license was unceremoniously revoked in 2005 when the producers went younger for the origin story. Brosnan may have also priced himself out of existence during his negotiations. But as far back as November 2002, Wilson told me that he wasn't sure Brosnan was the right Bond for *Casino Royale*.

"For me, it's been the greatest joy," Brosnan said about his roller coaster ride. "There have been moments when it's like pulling teeth, maybe, when you're in week number 25 and you just got off of four weeks of night shooting. But, above all else, it's creating the role, getting away with creating the role, having a love affair with the piece as a fan, and the pride in the work and being part of this legacy."

How did Bond fit in a post-Cold War world? That was the question that vexed everyone, particularly Michael Wilson and Barbara Broccoli, who now oversaw the franchise. Although there was talk of modernizing Bond, they instead reverted to the glam traditions: tuxedo, martinis, Aston Martin DB5, gadgets, humor, *chemin de fer* — the entire Bond package. This made sense both commercially and in deference to Cubby.

"When I did *GoldenEye*, it was a turning point for the franchise," Brosnan recollected. "Cubby was dying; Barbara and Michael were carrying on the torch. And, for me, I was the new kid on the block. I had no say in it. I didn't even want to have a say. I didn't know what to say, even if I could say something. I just knew that it was an opportunity from an acting point of view. I had nothing to lose and everything to gain, and knowing that if I pulled it off, it would change the course of my life. And it has changed my life."

At the same time, there were some notable changes: They chose New Zealander Martin Campbell as the new director. He was best-known for the 1985 *Edge of Darkness* British miniseries, and was well equipped to usher Bond into the nineties with Brosnan. "*GoldenEye* was his first time out and we didn't get as fantastical as they did later on," Campbell told me. "And perhaps Pierce played it straighter, so it made it that much better."

While reintroducing a sense of style and fun, Campbell also ramped up the violence and intensity. Peter Lamont returned as production designer, adding considerably more sheen; cinematographer Phil Méheux joined the team for his hard edge; and a new editor, Terry Rawlings, moved Bond along at a swifter pace.

"The good thing about a Bond film is being on the curve or ahead of the curve of what is global amid all this fantasy," Brosnan emphasized. But for every new Bond there is an initiation process — a trial by fire — and this one had to reaffirm his relevance at the end of the 20th century.

Indeed, when political commentator/satirist Bruce Feirstein came aboard to polish the script by Michael France and Jeffrey Caine, his motto was: "The world has changed. James Bond has not."

And that became the template for *GoldenEye*, the 17th Bond film, inspired by Fleming's Jamaican retreat as well as the code name of a plan he developed as a naval commander during World War II to secure Gibraltar against Nazi attack.

The gun barrel with Brosnan underscores a no-nonsense attack: he stands upright and fires without hesitation (for the first time the barrel is computer-generated, making the rifling spiral sharper and shinier). We then see a mysterious figure dressed in black and scurrying across the top of a dam at the Arkangel chemical weapons facility in the Soviet Union. He adeptly bungee jumps down below, enters through an air duct, and makes his way through the bathroom. "Beg your pardon, forgot to knock," Bond quips to the surprised soldier sitting on the toilet before knocking him out.

At first, this seems like a *Goldfinger* riff, but it suddenly gets more complicated. A mysterious figure gets the jump on Bond, who turns out to be Alec Trevelyan, 006 (Sean Bean). They proceed to plant explosives and it's evident they're closer than colleagues: "James, for England," he cheers. "For England, Alec," answers Bond.

Yet right after Bond complains that it's all too easy, Alec is captured by Colonel Ourumov (Gottfried John) and they're surrounded by soldiers. Bond refuses to surrender and secretly resets the timers from six minutes to three. Ourumov then shoots Alec and Bond stealthily makes his way across the room, shielded by a trolley of gas barrels. When a trigger-happy guard tries to shoot Bond, endangering everyone, Ourumov kills the guard. Bond leaps onto a conveyor belt and hurls the barrels at the soldiers below.

Outside, Bond boards an aircraft along the cliff-top runway, but is thrown out along with the pilot during a scuffle. Bond hops onto a motorcycle, hurls over the cliff, and free-falls after the aircraft. He miraculously catches up and climbs aboard in an absurd bit of Moore-like acrobatics. Bond then regains control of the plane just in time and steers a steady course as the Arkangel explodes below.

After Daniel Kleinman's inspired main title sequence (going beyond Binder with a woman destroying the hammer and sickle: commemorating the dawn of a new era), we rejoin Bond speedily driving the Aston Martin DB5 in the hills above Monte Carlo. Yet it's nine years later, which means that Arkangel took place in 1986 during the end of the Cold War. Now everything's changed; Bond's even subjected to a mental evaluation by a female psychologist in the car with him. It appears that MI6 wants to tame him, but Bond won't have it, so he recklessly swerves down the winding lanes in a test of wills with the lady. Then he spots a beautiful brunette in a red Ferrari and a familiar race ensues with Bond running her off the road. Just for kicks, Bond pulls out a bottle of champagne and seduces his petrified passenger, proving he hasn't lost his touch.

Then, in a further echo of *OHMSS*, Bond notices the Ferrari parked outside the casino and pursues her at the gambling table. Played by Famke Janssen, she's more like Trench than Tracy, smoking a cigar and salivating at the opportunity to get even. But when Bond slyly beats her at baccarat, she sneers, "Enjoy it while it lasts." "The very words I live by," he counters.

It's a snarky reminder of the short life span of a Double-0. He orders his signature martini and proudly proclaims, "The name's Bond. James Bond." She's Xenia Onatopp, and he's delighted at the sexual innuendo. But before he can bed her, Onatopp leaves with an admiral ("I like a woman who enjoys pulling rank").

With the aid of some digital snaps of Onatopp and her escort boarding a boat, Bond gets a transmission from Moneypenny that she's a former Soviet fighter pilot now working with a Russian crime syndicate

called Janus in St. Petersburg. Onatopp, we observe, gets her S&M kicks in bed by squeezing the admiral to death between her thighs (better than Bambi and Thumper).

Bond sneaks aboard the boat the next day and discovers the admiral's corpse. He deduces that Onatopp and an accomplice posing as the admiral are planning to steal the local Tiger helicopter prototype that's impervious to electronic interference. Unfortunately, security guards prevent Bond from thwarting the theft during a public exercise.

Onatopp flies the Tiger to the Space Weapons Control Center in Severnaya, Siberia, where they are joined by Ourumov, now a general and in charge of the space division. He grabs the activation keys and control disk for their secret satellite weapon system, and Onatopp machine-guns the technicians in the room a la Zorin with orgasmic satisfaction (they would've made a great pair). However, two computer programmers manage to flee Severnaya: the obnoxious Boris (Alan Cumming) and the beautiful Natalya (Izabella Scorupco). Ourumov then programs the satellite to obliterate the facility before leaving with Onatopp.

Back at MI6 headquarters, Bond finds a friskier Moneypenny (Samantha Bond), who's "dressed to kill" for a date and in no mood for what she now describes as his sexual harassment ("Someday you'll have to make good on your innuendos"). He then encounters friction from the new female M (British theater staple Judi Dench) during a briefing by Tanner (Michael Kitchen). Tanner's now friendlier toward Bond and enlightens them about the possibility of a Russian space-based weapon system called GoldenEye that's armed with a destructive electromagnetic pulse. It makes perfect sense to Bond, but M remains skeptical until a blinding flash of light knocks out one of their satellites when the Siberian outpost is destroyed. Feeling vindicated, Bond proposes that the massacre was a cover for the theft of GoldenEye and that the Tiger was the perfect getaway vehicle.

M then has it out with Bond privately in her

office over bourbon. While she appreciates his intelligence expertise, she berates him for being "a sexist, misogynist dinosaur; a relic of the Cold War." Bond has no respect for her either, so M declares that she's no bean counter and that she's got the balls to send him to his death. But she won't do it on a whim, even with his "cavalier attitude towards life."

With that, M sends Bond to find out how Ourumov is connected to Janus and to destroy GoldenEye. But, in an allusion to *Licence to Kill*, she cautions against a vendetta to avenge the death of 006. Bond admits the guilt he still harbors but promises not to make it personal. But everything will be personal to this Bond in one way or another. It's also an interesting foreshadowing of a similar warning at the outset of *Quantum of Solace*. She then briefly lets her guard down: "Bond... Come back alive." It's the beginning of a relationship in which they bring out the humanity in one another.

Meanwhile, in St. Petersburg, Ourumov deceives the Russian Security Council, including Defense Minister Mishkin (Tchéky Karyo), into believing that the Severnaya massacre was the work of Siberian separatists and that GoldenEye has been destroyed. But Ourumov is surprised to learn from Mishkin that Boris' colleague, Natalya, also survived the massacre. Given the new geopolitical landscape and Russia's tenuous transition, it's no wonder that Ourumov has aligned himself with Janus. He's merely a more extreme version of Orlov from *Octopussy*.

Fortunately, nothing's changed between Bond and Q, though the wily gadget wizard fools the new 007 into thinking that he's broken his leg because he's wearing a cast, when he's actually "hunting" with his latest experiment. He introduces Bond to his new BMW containing Stinger missiles behind the headlights and hands him a couple of new personal gadgets: a repelling cord that fires a piton hidden in a belt buckle and a nifty pen grenade.

In St. Petersburg, Bond meets his new CIA contact, Jack Wade. He's played by Joe Don Baker, who was arms dealer Brad Whitaker in *The Living Daylights* and co-starred in Campbell's *Edge of Darkness*. With his bedraggled appearance and

broken down car, Wade is more of a relic than Bond.

Bond asks Wade where he can find the mysterious head of Janus, and he suggests contacting rival Russian crime lord Zukovsky (Robbie Coltrane). Not surprisingly, he's a former KGB official that Bond has tangled with many times, stealing his car, his girlfriend, and giving him a permanent limp. While Bond meets with Zukofsky at his nightclub, Natalya steals her way into a computer salesman's office and emails Boris, who arranges to meet her at the Church of Our Lady of Smolensk. But it's a trap because the nerdy hacker works for Ourumov.

Zukofsky, who's reinvented himself in the new Russian market economy, relishes the chance to get even with Bond; however, 007 bargains for his life by offering to help Zukofsky defeat Janus if he sets up a meeting. Zukofsky can't resist and tells Bond that the head of Janus is a traitorous Lienz Cossack, the group that collaborated with the Nazis during World War II.

After taking a relaxing swim in the hotel pool, Bond is interrupted by Onatopp, who has come to kill him. He can't resist her seduction, which quickly turns into sadistic foreplay. Onatopp gets Bond between her thighs, but she underestimates his strength and his own propensity for violent sex, so they do the dance and Bond eventually overtakes Onatopp and forces her to take him to Janus. This is just the kind of palpable sex Brosnan wanted to see more of in the Bond films.

They wind up in a macabre setting: a graveyard full of discarded statues, busts, and other broken mementos from the glory days of the Soviet Union. But it's appropriate when Alec emerges from the relics to shock Bond: back from the dead and scarred from the explosion at the chemical weapons factory. "What's the matter, James? No glib remark? No pithy comeback?" "Why?" asks Bond, who is totally unprepared for the first betrayal within the ranks of MI6.

Alec then proceeds to throw everything Bond stands for back in his face. "Everything you risk your life for has changed," he charges. "It was the job we were chosen for," barks Bond. But Alec condescendingly scoffs back: "Her Majesty's loyal terrier, defender of the so-called faith."

As Bond tries to hold onto his trust and faith in a world turned upside down, Alec reveals his dark tale of disillusionment: His parents were Lienz Cossacks betrayed by the British and hunted by Stalin's executioners after the war. But, in an ironic twist of fate, Alec "went to work for the government whose betrayal caused the father to kill himself and his wife." Thus, while Bond and Alec are both orphans, Bond's parents died in a tragic climbing accident and Alec's were caught in the post-war political crossfire. That is why Alec created Janus, the two-faced Roman god, to avenge the death and dishonor of his parents.

Yet Alec also blames Bond for blowing up Arkangel and for disfiguring him. While he gets no sympathy from Bond, it's still a lot to digest. Earlier Q told Bond to grow up (which becomes a running gag between them), but that's exactly what he must do to survive this ordeal with Alec. At the same time, the confrontation gives Bond the motivation to prove that he's not a relic; that he continues to be "the one stabilizer within the whole genre."

But before Bond can shoot Alec, he's hit with a tranquilizer dart in the neck. When he awakens, Bond finds himself tied to Natalya in the Tiger, programmed to self-destruct. He alertly head-butts the emergency escape button and they are fired out just ahead of the incoming missiles that are doubling back again to hit the Tiger.

Now Bond has to contend not only with a wary Natalya but also with the Russians. They are arrested by the police and taken prisoner in a holding cell. Bond tries to gain her trust while finding out what happened. But she only tells him of Boris' betrayal. Then they are interrogated by Mishkin, who immediately asks Bond how they should execute him. Bond sarcastically yearns for the old days when sinister interrogation was an art.

Bond alerts Mishkin of a traitor in his midst and Natalya confesses that it's Ourumov. When Mishkin asks why, she says it's because he's got a second GoldenEye with a nuclear weapon. But then Ourumov bursts in and takes command of the interrogation, seizing Bond's Walther and shooting a guard and Mishkin. But before he can frame Bond, the two prisoners flee into the military archives where a gun battle ensues and Natalya is captured. However, Bond escapes with the aid of the repelling line from his belt.

Bond steals a tank and explodes his way through the streets of St. Petersburg to slay Ourumov and rescue Natalya. It's Brosnan's Bond at his most heroically iconic. He destroys everything in sight, including a truck filled with Perrier (a shattering display of product placement as well as a nod to Russia's stab at commercialism), only stopping to adjust his tie to uphold his suave image. But when he realizes that the general has taken Natalya aboard Alec's ICBM train, Bond stakes out a spot, straddles the track, and lies in wait. Then when the train approaches, he blasts it, abandons the tank, and causes the train to derail inside the tunnel.

Bond boards the train and manages to hold Alec and Onatopp at gunpoint, but finds himself in a standoff because Ourumov still holds Natalya captive. As Alec attempts to use Bond's fatal weakness for women to his advantage, Bond tries to pit Ourumov against Alec by divulging that he's a Lienz Cossack. It doesn't work because the general has been offered a fortune: "Mr. Bond here will have a small memorial service with only Moneypenny and a few tearful restaurateurs in attendance," Alec teases.

Bond has no choice but to bluff his way out: He tells Ourumov to kill Natalya because she means nothing to him. His hesitation gives Bond the split-second timing he needs to shoot him and save Natalya. But Alec escapes with Onatopp and deviously sets the train to self-destruct in three minutes to get even with Bond. Then while Natalya outwits Boris in a computer showdown and discovers that Janus is based in Cuba, Bond cuts through the floor with his new Omega laser watch and they escape before the train explodes.

Bond and Natalya rendezvous with Wade in the Caribbean. He continues to look like a tourist with floppy hat and ugly floral shirts, calls Bond "Jimbo," and disavows any official involvement in the mission. However, he delivers a care package from Q and Bond exchanges his BMW for Wade's plane to search for the secret satellite dish.

But Bond takes a quiet moment on the beach to contemplate what it's like having a friend turn foe that he now must kill. Natalya tries to comfort Bond, but then challenges his cold-blooded nature.

"It's what keeps me alive," he rationalizes. "No, it's what keeps you alone," she retorts. Natalya then asks if he meant what he said on the train about her meaning nothing to him when he told the general to kill her. "Yes. Basic rule: always call their bluff." But in lonely desperation, Bond and Natalya take solace in one another on the beach.

The following day, while searching for the satellite dish, their plane is shot down by an underwater missile and they crash land in the jungle. But as they emerge from the wreckage, Onatopp rappels down from a helicopter and attacks Bond with sadistic delight. They struggle and he shoots down the chopper, killing Onatopp when she crashes into a tree. When the lake drains, though, Bond and Natalya spy the satellite dish.

They infiltrate the installation and Bond uses the care package from Q to plant bombs next to the fuel tanks while Natalya excitedly hacks into the computer system and changes the access codes. She relishes getting the best of rival Boris. After a brief gunfight, though, in which the fuel tanks are pierced, causing a pool of flammable liquid to form, Bond and Natalya are captured and the bombs are disarmed.

Of course, Alec can't resist regaling Bond with his ingenious plan for revenge. He's going to steal a fortune from the Bank of England and then use the new GoldenEye to destroy all the financial records, thus sending the UK back to the Stone Age and plunging the world into economic chaos. He's like Goldfinger and Blofeld rolled into one. When it comes to megalomania, some things never change. But when Bond persists in psychoanalyzing Alec, his former mentor throws it right back: "I might as well ask you if all the vodka martinis ever silence the screams of all the men you've killed? Or if you find forgiveness in the arms of all those willing women for the dead ones you failed to protect?"

But when Boris realizes that Natalya has reprogrammed GoldenEye to blow up in space, Alec threatens to kill Bond if she doesn't change it back. However, Bond gets the break he needs when Boris picks up his grenade pen and nervously clicks it. Bond anxiously waits for him to activate it, and then knocks the grenade into the pool of leaking fuel and the room erupts in flames. In the confusion, Bond and Natalya escape and Boris furiously tries to save GoldenEye.

Bond attempts to destroy the transmitter, but is attacked by Alec and chased onto the antenna platform. They finally do the dance while Natalya, who's become quite heroic after overcoming Boris' betrayal, takes command of a chopper and its pilot. During their hand-to-hand, though, Alec discovers that Bond has attained greater strength and determination when he's able to jam the antenna and thwart Boris' repositioning of GoldenEye.

Eventually, their fight takes them to the bottom of the antenna but still high above the dish. Yet Bond prevails and kicks Alec off the side of the platform. Holding onto Bond's boot for dear life, Alec realizes that it's all over: "For England, James?" "No, for me," Bond admits before giving Alec the boot. The baddie falls and lands at the bottom of the dish yet still survives. GoldenEye burns out in the upper atmosphere and the place explodes, but Natalya comes to Bond's rescue with the chopper and they escape just as the antenna collapses and crushes Alec below. Boris, who thought himself invincible, freezes to death from a shower of liquid nitrogen.

Bond and Natalya ditch the chopper and flee into the jungle for privacy until Wade comes to the rescue with the Marines and they're airlifted to safety: Just like old times. Except, after metaphorically confronting his evil twin, Brosnan's Bond is now better prepared to serve Her Majesty's Secret Service.

# TOMORROW NEVER DIES

After the smash success of *GoldenEye* (which achieved a new box office milestone for the franchise with $106.4 million domestically and $352.1 million globally), the new producers continued down a retro path of Kiss Kiss Bang Bang with Brosnan. Fittingly, as the first Bond film produced after the passing of Cubby, *Tomorrow Never Dies* (1997) served as the perfect bridge between the past and the present.

"*GoldenEye* was a lovely success," Brosnan recalled. "And there was a new generation that wanted to bring the romance back and the familiarity of something they had grown up on. And then, of course, the second time around they pulled out all the stops with wall-to-wall action."

But when Martin Campbell declined to return, they recruited British ex-patriot Roger Spottiswoode (*Under Fire*) to direct the 18th Bond adventure about a maniacal power grab by an old media baron during the dawning of the internet.

Although Brosnan was ready to start walking "that wonderful tightrope between having a license to kill and being vulnerable and complex," the opportunities were few and far between in Feirstein's fast and furious script.

Indeed, like *GoldenEye*, *Tomorrow Never Dies* begins with another exciting pre-credit obstacle course for Bond. Only this time, the setting is an arms bazaar on the Kyhber Pass separating Pakistan from Afghanistan. We don't even see Bond, only his POV surveillance with a small video camera. This is uplinked to MI6 headquarters, where M observes on a large screen and guides Bond with the help of her chief analyst, Charles Robinson (the dashing Colin Salmon). He astutely identifies the terrorists and the weapons of mass destruction, while also communicating directly with Bond using his code name, White Knight. American techno-terrorist Henry Gupta (Ricky Jay) becomes the center of attention when he purchases a GPS encoder stolen from the CIA.

However, M and Robinson are not alone. As a result of a post-Cold War power struggle with the military, they're joined by Russian General Bukharin and British Admiral Roebuck (Geoffrey Palmer, who co-starred as Dench's husband in the popular sitcom, *As Time Goes By*). In fact, the admiral despises both M and Bond and takes command of the mission by ordering a missile strike, to M's chagrin, who now has to get her top spy out of harm's way. But when Bond quickly discovers two nuclear torpedoes mounted on an L-39 jet fighter, he refuses to pull out and the admiral unsuccessfully tries to recall the strike.

Bond obviously lives for such high-octane moments, and steps into action, hijacking the L-39, and taking off just ahead of another fighter as the incoming missile blows up the base. New composer David Arnold (who remained with the franchise through *Quantum of Solace*) wastes no time utilizing the "Bond Theme" at every action-filled opportunity.

But the unconscious co-pilot suddenly awakens and grabs Bond from behind, adding yet another obstacle. Bond skillfully steers with his knees to prevent crashing into the mountains and getting shot down by the fighter's missiles. He then craftily positions himself beneath the other aircraft and ejects the co-pilot, who crashes into the other fighter, which explodes. Bond safely flies off, saving the mission and rubbing it in the admiral's face.

Not surprisingly, the GPS encoder turns out to be the MacGuffin. It's used by Gupta to throw the H.M.S. Devonshire off-course in the South China Sea, resulting in a threat by two patrolling Chinese Air Force MIGS. Then the Devonshire is attacked by a sea drill launched from a stealth ship undetected by its radar. As the Devonshire begins sinking, the captain wrongly presumes they've been attacked by a Chinese torpedo and signals the Admiralty. The stealth ship then shoots down one of the two Chinese MIGS with a missile. The blond-haired commander, Stamper (Gotz Otto), later guns down the remaining survivors of the Devonshire, and steals one of its missiles. This sparks an international crisis between the British and Chinese.

It recalls the old SPECTRE deception of pitting one superpower against another. Indeed, the mastermind, media mogul-turned terrorist, Elliot Carver, even invokes Blofeld by wearing a black Nehru suit. He's played with theatrical flair by Jonathan Pryce (Tony winner for *Miss Saigon*). The white-haired Carver sits in his high-tech office like a sinister Rupert Murdoch, crafting the story's lurid headline on a wall screen for his tabloid, *Tomorrow*, and then salivates at the rest of the gloom and doom during a video conference with his staff of "golden retrievers." There's nothing stealth about Carver's megalomania: he wants to create the mayhem and profit by it as the most powerful global leader with a new 24-hour satellite news network.

Carver isn't the only one on a high: We find Bond in bed with his Danish language tutor at Oxford (with the Aston Martin DB5 parked outside). It's about time this Bond enjoy some recreational sex to ease the tension. But of course he's interrupted by Moneypenny to return to London, and she even delivers the film's best double-entendre, upping the sexual tension between them: "You always were a cunning linguist, James."

M continues her turf war with Admiral Roebuck, who persuades the Defense Minister (Julian Fellowes) to send the British fleet to the China Sea in retaliation. But M wants to avoid direct confrontation until they can at least check out a mysterious GPS signal they intercepted when the Devonshire was attacked. It's an interesting reversal of what General Gogol used to go through on the other side in fighting his hawkish opposition.

Bond enters with a copy of Carver's *Tomorrow*, touting a banner story about the slaughter of the Devonshire crew survivors by the Chinese, which is all the ammunition the Minister needs to side with Roebuck. But M buys Bond 48 hours to investigate Carver's connection to the Devonshire disaster and to prevent a naval attack.

When M briefs Bond in a speeding car, there is no hint of friction between them. In fact, she not only confides that the GPS signal actually came from one of Carver's satellites, but that she's also aware of Bond's past involvement with Carver's wife. She even insists that Bond use her to get to Carver. For once, Bond hesitates: "I doubt she'll remember me," he lies. "Remind her," M demands. "Then pump her for information." Moneypenny can't resist throwing in her two cents: "You just have to decide how much pumping is needed, James."

Bond's off to Hamburg to confront Carver. He's met by Q at the airport's rental car desk, where the wily old gadget master officiously goes over the insurance damage-waver form (with a nice exchange of double-entendres). He then presents Bond with a tricked out BMW 750i containing stinger missiles, machine guns, and female voice-activated control system (whose voice sounds suspiciously familiar to Bond). Best of all, Q also provides Bond with a remarkable Ericsson mobile phone, which features a fingerprint scanner, a lock pick, the ability to produce an electric shock, and a remote control device for driving the BMW. But when Q advises Bond that the remote control is tricky, he nimbly presses the keypad and the BMW obediently responds like most women in Bond's hands.

Later that night, Bond attends Carver's lavish reception for the launch of his satellite news network posing as a banker. But he has competition: A pretty Chinese journalist, Wai Lin, sneaks in and charms Carver. She's played by martial arts expert Michelle Yeoh. Carver even tips his hand by offering her a position in his Chinese bureau. But she cleverly points out that he doesn't have a Chinese bureau.

Bond then approaches Carter's wife, Paris (Teri Hatcher, *Lois & Clark: The New Adventures of Superman*). The dark-haired beauty greets Bond by slapping him in the face."Was it something I said?" "How about the words, 'I'll be right back?'"

It's the old occupational hazard of getting too close for comfort, and Bond assures Paris that he won't pressure her into helping him, though Paris insists that she has no intention of betraying her husband. Their conversation, meanwhile, is monitored by Gupta, and Carver jealously observes them from afar. He interrupts them to introduce Paris to Wai Lin, and Bond wastes no time tweaking Carver about his future plans and the destruction of the Devonshire. It's very similar to the way Bond openly provokes Largo about his SPECTRE

association when beating him at baccarat.

Carver abruptly leaves and confronts Paris about her relationship with Bond. She lies about being roommates with his ex-girlfriend, but Carver doesn't believe her and orders his goons to beat up Bond, which they do in a sound proof room while Carver gives a thinly veiled broadcast speech about his plan for world domination. However, Bond recovers after taking quite a beating and gives as good as he gets, and then humiliates Carver by turning off the building's power supply and cutting off his speech.

Later, Bond sits in his hotel room, drinking and brooding. Paris walks in to seduce Bond, which he was expecting and dreading. Carver has sent her as a test of her loyalty. We're reminded of Tracy, of course, in Bond's effort to shield Paris from harm. He tells her to go home; he doesn't need her to get to Carver. But Paris knows she's trapped and still cares

for Bond."I used to look in the papers every day for your obituary," she laments. "Sorry to disappoint you," Bond replies. But he can't resist one screw for old time's sake.

At the same time, Gupta confers with Carver about Bond's record being suspiciously clean ("If it sounds too good to be true, it always is"), as well as the recorded conversation between Bond and Paris, which proves she misled Carver. So he orders her killed by bringing in "the doctor."

Bond implores Paris to leave the country and promises to protect her. But she explains there's no hiding from Carver. Still, her loyalty shifts after sleeping with Bond, and so she tells him where to find Carver's secret lab.

Bond sneaks into Carver's building and uses the mobile phone to steal the GPS encoder from Gupta's safe. But first he must overcome an attacker on a

**Michelle Yeoh and Pierce Brosnan discuss a scene with director Roger Spottiswoode on the set of _Tomorrow Never Dies_.**

catwalk above a rotary press line. It's a brutal hand-to-hand, ending with Bond hurling him into the newsprint, causing a bloody mess (recalling the snow machine in *OHMSS*). But, as film historian David Bordwell astutely points out in his blog post, "Bond vs. Chan: Jackie shows how it's done" (*Observations on film art*, Sept. 15, 2010), there's a frustrating lack of clarity to the cutting in comparison to the more coherent and dynamic Hong Kong fighting style of the period. It was part of a larger trend, which eventually culminated with the dizzying *Bourne* franchise. It makes you long for Peter Hunt.

Bond trips the alarm and runs into Wai Lin, who's apparently there for the same reason. However, Bond must strenuously fight his way out while she escapes with ease using a wrist piton that allows her walk vertically down the walls.

After fleeing, Bond gets a call from Carver requesting that he return his two possessions — the encoder and his wife. Bond rushes back to his hotel room, locks the encoder in the glove compartment, and activates the BMW's security system. But his worst fear is realized when he finds Paris strangled to death in his bed. As he absorbs the shock and guilt, we're reminded of Alec's stinging analysis about Bond finding forgiveness for all the dead women he's failed to protect, recalling Tracy once again.

Bond also finds Paris' killer, Dr. Kaufman (Vincent Schiavelli, *One Flew Over the Cuckoo's Nest*), waiting for him. He's got a tape that will be broadcast by Carver implicating Bond in the murder of Paris and pointing to suicide. Kaufman is a trick shot like Scaramanga and a sadistic bastard that likes to torture people, but with a twisted sense of humor: "My art is in great demand, Mr. Bond. I go all over the world. I am especially good at the celebrity overdose."

But Bond makes them all look like fools when they're unable to break into the impregnable BMW. Stamper even phones Kaufman to let him know that they can't get the red box without Bond's help. After such an arrogant display, the assassin embarrassingly asks for the security code and Bond hands him his mobile phone. But, as in *FRWL*, the booby trap allows Bond to strike first when Kaufman gets an electric jolt. Bond throttles Kaufman ruthlessly and

gets even for Paris by shooting him in the head with his own gun.

Bond escapes just ahead of the police and intercepts his car in the garage, releasing a gas charge and leaping into the back window. Bond deftly drives the BMW with the remote control while being pursued by Stamper and his cronies, allowing him to unleash the entire arsenal of gadgets as he ascends to the top level. But Bond is forced to sacrifice the BMW when trapped on the roof. He snatches the encoder, jumps out, and hides; then remotely hurls the car off the roof. Funnily, the car crashes into the rental car office across the street where it belongs.

Bond then hooks up with Wade, the surrogate Felix, at the U.S. Air Force base in the South China Sea. Once again, Wade's assistance is unofficial, but he confirms that the Devonshire was indeed thrown off-course because the encoder was tampered with. Bond asks Wade a favor: to arrange a perilous HALO (High Altitude Low Opening) free-fall parachute jump in Vietnam where the ship sank. It's another acrobatic tour-de-force exploit for Bond, who explores the wreckage and discovers a missile is missing before running into Wai Lin again. A rock slide occurs and Bond signals that their only way out is through a narrow passage back to the deck. But they must abandon their oxygen tanks. However, when they resurface they find Stamper and his crew waiting for them.

They're captured and flown to Carver's headquarters in Saigon, where he's begun writing their obits. Bond learns that Wai Lin is a Chinese spy; she learns that he's with MI6; and they both learn that Carver is in cahoots with General Chan of the Chinese Army.

Although Bond and Wai Lin pretend they've been onto Carver for months, he doesn't buy it. He introduces them to his private collection of small metal Chakra torture tools. They were a favorite of Dr. Kaufman, the idea being to probe the heart or the genitals and inflict torture for as long as possible while keeping the victim alive. Dr. Kaufman's record was 52 hours. Ironically, Stamper was Kaufman's protégé, and he's instructed by Carver to torture Bond and Wai Lin. But even handcuffed together, Bond manages to throw one of the sharp tools into

Stamper's leg.

Bond and Mai Lin fight their way out and make it to the roof. Once trapped, though, they smartly use the large banner of Carver's face to descend the skyscraper, tearing right down the middle in a symbolic victory. When they run out of room, they crash through a window to enter the lower floor, and wind up stealing a motorcycle in the wildest and most daring action sequence.

Racing through the streets of Saigon on the motorcycle, Bond and Wai Lin replay the competitive rivalry from *Spy*, arguing about control while being pursued by Carver's cronies in cars and chopper. But they make a good team with Bond expertly driving and Wai Lin precariously navigating. He leaps above the hovering chopper at one point and, even more impressively, slides underneath it when cornered and facing near death from the rotors. Wai Lin then throws a washing line into the rotors and causes the chopper to crash.

Afterward, Bond suggests they work together, but Wai Lin says she only works alone. She soon reconsiders after being ambushed at her place by a gang of thugs. Even though she holds her own, Bond enters the scene and prevents her from being shot. But Wai Lin will only team up if Bond acts professionally. And so the remainder of the film becomes an obstacle course in which Bond must earn her trust and take better care of her than Paris.

Wai Lin gets Bond up to speed on what she knows: The general has been stealing stealth material, and Bond deduces that Carver has stolen the nuclear missile from the Devonshire, which he plans to launch from his stealth ship, in the hopes of starting World War III.

Then she escorts Bond to her secret gadget room that would make Q envious. Bond even remarks that it reminds him of home. Among her toys are a Chinese fan that shoots sharp webs of rope and an ejector seat that she demonstrates when slamming an intruder sent by Carver. Bond, though, acts very flirty as he trades up to the Walther P99 and a new Omega Seamaster watch with detachable remote detonator for grenade launching. They begin trying to figure out where Carver's stealth ship could be stationed. There's one secluded bay that makes the

most sense, so they signal their respective bosses and set off to locate it, which they do rather quickly. But while setting mines, Wai Lin is captured by Stamper; and Bond fakes his own demise by hiding behind the dead body of one of Stamper's gang.

Carver tells Wai Lin that he's planning on firing his missile at Beijing during a meeting of its top military and political leaders, throwing the country into chaos and blaming the British, whose fleet will be obliterated by the Chinese. Carver will then set up Chan as the new leader of China and gain exclusive broadcast rights for the next century.

Bond captures Gupta and tries to make a trade for Wai Lin. But when Carver suddenly shoots his scientist, Bond detonates the grenade he's planted, which rips through the hull of the ship. The explosion is picked up by radar and the British fleet is on its way. Bond and Wai Lin reunite and fight it out with Carver's men. Wai Lin even disables the engines while Bond creates mayhem with a rocket launcher. He then engages in a running gunfight with Stamper, but the British fleet fires at the ship and Bond is nearly burned alive by a fire ignited by Stamper.

But Bond cagily survives, though captured by Carver, who crows about his escape plan and how the British fleet will even destroy the evidence. However, Bond manages to activate the sea drill and make a bloody mess of Carver ("You forgot the first rule of mass media, Elliot — give the people what they want!").

Bond deals with Stamper, who's captured Wai Lin in chains and lowers her into the water. But Bond's booby trapped the missile with explosive charges, and even though the henchman pummels Bond, he stabs him in the leg and traps him so he blows up when the missile self-destructs.

Bond then rescues Mai Lin in the sea as Carver's stealth ship is destroyed, prompting M to craft Carver's obit: suicide. Bond and Mai Lin remain undercover and consummate their relationship.

If only Bond's next mission were as simple as this one.

# THE WORLD IS NOT ENOUGH

Like Moore, the third time was also the charm for Brosnan, but obviously for different reasons. With the hiring of director Michael Apted, who specialized in intimate dramas (the acclaimed *Up* TV documentary series, and *Gorillas in the Mist*), Brosnan finally got the chance to tinker with Bond's emotions. In fact, the presence of Apted signaled a precedent for prestige that would continue during the Craig era with the additions of Marc Forster (*Quantum of Solace*) and Sam Mendes (*Skyfall*).

"With *The World Is Not Enough*, I saw an opportunity of articulating the human side and the mystique as well with Michael Apted, who's got a body of work that covers documentaries and character-driven dramas, and so much of his fingertips dealing with relationships." Brosnan recalled.

For his part, Apted was thrilled to "redress the balance a bit between action and the other stuff… I went back to Ian Fleming because I found it very empowering and reassuring."

Just one look at Brosnan and you can instantly tell they've aged and matured him. His hair is more stylishly coiffed with a touch of gray on his right temple, and he carries Bond off more smoothly, if pensively, during trying moments.

"There's a certain confidence that you gain after years of making Bond," Brosnan revealed, "a high degree of assuredness and relaxation that wasn't there in *GoldenEye*, which had its own fears and trepidations."

*The World Is Not Enough* is all about overcoming fear and dealing with pain. The title refers, of course, to the Bond family motto, previously mentioned in *OHMSS* (which Brosnan told me he wanted to remake). But we finally grasp its meaning in the 19th Bond adventure when the pursuit of world domination proves a soulless exercise. Delivered by Bond in a throwaway line, the motto is what ultimately separates him from his opponents.

The pre-credit sequence starts out deceptively enough, with an impeccably dressed Bond meeting with a Swiss banker in Bilboa, Spain. He's ostensibly come to retrieve £3 million taken from a Double-0 agent that was murdered. But as he eyes the banker's sexy assistant, who hands out cigars, Bond admits that what he really wants is the name of the assassin. The banker refuses but Bond persists, even after being reminded that he's outnumbered. "Perhaps you failed to take into account my… hidden assets," Bond asserts.

Then Bond smiles, looks down, and presses a button on the side of his sunglasses that activates a stun flash from his Walther P99 on the table. This gives Bond the opportunity to overpower the three henchmen and give the banker one last chance at the point of his gun. But before he can comply, he's killed by a knife in the neck hurled by the cigar girl, who leaps out the window and escapes on a wire. Bond grabs the case with the money, but is held at gunpoint by one of the henchmen. Just then a red dot appears on Bond's chest and the henchman is shot through the window by a guardian angel. Bond escapes with the money out the window using one of the henchmen as a counterweight.

Back at MI6 headquarters, Bond greets Moneypenny with a souvenir from his trip, a phallic cigar tube, which she angrily tosses in the trash ("Oh, Moneypenny, the story of our relationship: close, but no cigar").

Bond then joins his colleagues and is introduced to Sir Robert King, M's friend from Oxford law school, whose money he retrieved. But Bond is leery of the Russian report King purchased with the money: it's intended to identify the terrorists that have been attacking his pipeline. King has been building his pipeline along the southern end of the Caspian Sea in direct competition with the Russian lines to the north.

King thanks Bond, even teases M about luring Bond away from her, and leaves to collect his money. But Bond literally smells a trap when he notices a strange scent and bubbling from his drink. He shouts and rushes through the corridors and reaches the steel doorway, but he's too late. The bomb explodes as King's about to grab the money; the blast instantly kills King and rocks the building. A wall and section of the roof are gone, and Bond enters to investigate. Outside, the cigar girl lines up Bond with the infra red telescopic sight on her rifle from a high-tech speedboat. Bond sees the red light on his chest and dives for cover. She fires and makes her escape along the Thames.

But Bond leaps into Q's unfinished hydro boat (sans weaponry), and chases after her, passing London's new Millennium Dome, and trailed by police speedboats. Despite the great maneuverability and unique propulsion system of the Q boat, Bond still struggles to keep up with her. In fact, the discomfort of the water constantly splashing him is palpable. It makes Moore's boat chases jaunty by comparison. Then when she blocks his route and unloads machine gun fire at him, Bond launches off her boat and into the air before landing back onto the Thames. But in a desperate attempt to catch up to her, he jumps onto the docks and through a fish market.

She finally reaches her destination and hops into a hot air balloon. As she prepares to take off, however, Bond arrives and races toward her. He grabs hold of one of the tethers and hangs on for dear life. He implores her to give up, but she kills herself by shooting the helium tanks, causing the balloon to explode. Bond lets go and falls hard onto the Millennium Dome. Thus ends the longest and most ambitious pre-credit sequence in franchise history, clocking in at nearly 15 minutes.

At King's funeral procession in Scotland, Bond wears a black sling on his left shoulder as a result of the fall, and observes M warmly embracing King's alluring daughter, Elektra (Sophie Marceau, *Braveheart*). He's definitely drawn to her.

However, during a briefing at MI6's Scottish headquarters — a castle —Tanner reveals that Bond unwittingly set off the chain reaction that led to King's assassination. Bond delivered the bomb and King's lapel pin detonated the liquid explosive coating the money. M looks distraught and Bond tries to hide his head in shame. Robinson adds that obviously someone close to King switched lapel pins.

M then declares war on the perpetrators in an uncharacteristically impassioned speech, except Tanner informs Bond that he's been relieved of active duty because of his injury. So Bond promptly "skirts the issue" by seducing his attractive physician into giving him a clean bill of health, despite a dislocated collar bone.

On his way back, Bond encounters Q, who complains that the boat he destroyed was intended for his retirement. This becomes no ordinary exchange: it's the last, poignant, goodbye to the beloved gadget master, allowing Llewelyn a memorable exit. Q introduces Bond to his bumbling, fumbling assistant (John Cleese of Monty Python fame), whom he's groomed as his replacement. Bond jokingly refers to him as R. He's well-aware of Bond's sarcasm and misuse of equipment. But for once, Q joins in the fun at his assistant's expense. While showing off the latest enhancements to the BMW Z8, Q needles his nerdiness; then pulls the chord while the hapless assistant demonstrates an inflatable ski jacket, which totally envelops him like a balloon and rolls away. All the while, Bond looks on with reverence.

Screenwriter Feirstein (who shared credit with newcomers Neal Purvis and Robert Wade) describes the moment in his script as Merlin saying goodbye to Arthur, in which "Bond fights the sentimentality." "Pay attention, 007. There are two things I've always tried to teach you. First: Never let them see you bleed." "And second?" "Always have an escape plan."

And just like that, Q disappears in a puff of smoke behind a secret door like the Wizard of Oz, and Bond nods in a final gesture of affection.

Then, while quietly researching the case, Bond discovers that King's daughter, Elektra, was kidnapped. He's visibly shaken as he watches the footage of Elektra looking frightened and helpless in captivity. He tenderly reaches out and touches her crying face on the computer monitor. This is exactly what Apted meant about Brosnan's Bond being "interested in people and respectful of women." On a hunch, Bond then calculates that the $5 million he retrieved for King is the same amount as the ransom demand for Elektra. But he's denied further access to Elektra's file by M.

Bond immediately confronts M about shutting him out and being too personally involved. She was obviously closer to King than she let on and there's more to the kidnapping than meets the eye. M clears the room and reprimands Bond for his insubordination. But he needs to know what happened. M explains that King came to her for help in dealing with the kidnapper. Against all her instincts, though, M persuaded King not to pay the ransom while she went after the kidnapper using Elektra as bait. Fortunately, Elektra escaped. But Bond tells M about the money and that the kidnapper killed King.

Bond learns in a subsequent briefing that their target is the notorious terrorist, Renard (Robert Carlyle, *The Full Monty*). After Elektra escaped, M assigned 009 to kill Renard. But Renard miraculously survived a bullet to the head, which remains lodged in his brain. While viewing a large holographic image of Renard's skull, Bond discovers that the terrorist is impervious to pain and can push himself longer and harder than any normal person. Eventually, the bullet will kill him, but for now, it's like a living death.

M assigns Bond to guard Elektra. Since they both have a personal stake in her safety, this provides

**Denise Richards, Maria Grazia Cucinotta, Pierce Brosnan & Sophie Marceau at the Royal Premiere of *The World Is Not Enough* at the Odeon Leicester Square, Nov. 22, 1999.**

an added dimension not normally associated with a Bond film. First, it makes M an active participant for the first time (which will be even more demonstrative in *Skyfall*), and also puts Bond in an emotionally vulnerable position because of his guilt. So this becomes a redemptive mission that will ultimately bring Bond and M closer together.

Bond travels to Azerbaijan, where he encounters Elektra overseeing the construction of her pipeline. But there's a vocal protest among the villagers and Elektra defuses the situation by ordering the route changed in defiance of her father and at a cost of millions. The oil once belonged to her mother's family until the Russians seized it; now she's reclaiming it, but not by destroying the environment. Bond's impressed with her diplomatic skill and sense of humanity. But when she asks if he's ever lost a loved one, he quickly changes the topic to avoid mentioning Tracy.

However, when Elektra then tests Bond by skiing down the slopes to see if he can keep up with her, it rekindles memories of Bond and Tracy. She's impressed and he needs to catch his breath. But then they're fired on by parahawks (a combination paraglider and snowmobile), so Bond instructs Elektra to ski on while he lures them into the forest, where he cunningly forces them to crash into each other. But this results in an avalanche, and Bond comes to Elektra's rescue when she's frightened. He inflates his jacket into a protective bubble. However, the sudden claustrophobia causes her to have an anxiety attack and Bond holds her tenderly, telling her that he will protect her.

Back at her villa in Baku, Elektra tries to seduce Bond but he resists. Elektra confides that after the kidnapping she was afraid of everything until she discovered an inner strength to overcome her fear. Now she likes living on the edge. She teases him for being afraid, as he anxiously leaves.

Bond visits his old pal, Zukovsky, at his nearby casino in an effort to find Renard. Sporting X-ray sunglasses, Bond surveys the room to see what he's up against and finds that even the girls are packing firearms. He orders a martini and strong-arms his way into Zukovsky's office. Thanks to Bond's help in *GoldenEye*, the gangster's more prosperous than

ever. He even has his own caviar label. Bond gives him a scarf to identify that he confiscated from a parahawk. Zukofsky says it belongs to the Russian Atomic Energy Anti-Terrorist Unit. But what's the connection to Renard? Zukovsky divulges that Renard was too hot to handle even for the KGB and has gone freelance. He could be working for any of the four pipelines in competition with King's.

Elektra then unexpectedly walks into the casino and casually drops a million on a single game of High-Low. Bond can't protect her from herself, but she's no Tracy. "There's no point in living if you can't feel alive," she declares. He can't resist her any longer, and Elektra finally lures him into her bed. She massages his sore shoulder and they suck ice together. He asks Elektra how she survived and she says she seduced a guard and grabbed control. She asks Bond how he survives, and he thinks for a moment before somberly replying: "I take pleasure in great beauty."

Meanwhile, Elektra's security chief, Davidov, secretly meets with Renard at the Devil's Breath, a place of holy pilgrimage where the flames never extinguish. Renard obviously feels at home here, touching a hot rock and feeling nothing. They're joined by Dr. Arkov, a nuclear scientist, who arranged the unsuccessful ambush of Bond with the parahawks. Renard blames Davidov for the blunder, and presses one of the rocks into his hand to punish him. But instead of killing Davidov, he pulls the old Blofeld trick and shoots Arkov. He then instructs Davidov to impersonate Arkov when they leave the following morning.

But Bond sneaks out of Elektra's mansion in the middle of the night and stumbles onto Davidov's plan and kills him. He gets on the flight to Kazakhstan, posing as Arkov. They arrive at a former Soviet nuclear test facility, where Bond is introduced to the sexy scientist in charge of clean-up, Dr. Christmas Jones (Denise Richards, *Starship Troopers*). But, like Pussy, Christmas discourages Bond from trying to seduce her. She wants to be taken seriously as a scientist. So Bond is happy to oblige, which only drives her nuts for not trying.

Bond finally encounters Renard inside the mine where he's extracting a nuclear missile for some world domination plot. Bond takes Renard by surprise and holds him at gunpoint, but the terrorist taunts him. He can't kill him, he's already dead ("Not dead enough for me"). Renard then divulges that he spared Bond's life at the banker's office and threatens to kill Elektra. Bond thinks he's bluffing, so Renard makes him jealous by suggesting that he broke her in for him. Bond pistol whips him: "I usually hate killing an unarmed man," Bond confesses. "Cold-blooded murder is a filthy business… But in your case, I feel nothing, just like you."

Then Renard drops a bombshell: "But then again, there's no point in living if you can't feel alive." Bond is shaken to his core. Just then Christmas arrives with some guards and exposes Bond as an imposter. He tries to explain that Renard is the imposter, but the terrorist resumes command and orders Bond taken away. Renard laughs at Bond's inability to kill him and then presses hard on his collar bone ("I knew you couldn't shoulder the responsibility"). What a contrast: Bond's hyper sensitivity to pain and Renard's desensitized condition.

But Bond's presence forces Renard to machine gun everyone and confiscate the nuke. He seals up Bond and Christmas in the mine, but Bond orchestrates their escape just before it explodes. Bond now has a new companion in going after Renard.

Elektra calls M and tells her that Bond is missing and that her security chief is dead. She requests that M come at once to Baku. M, of course, rushes to her side, despite Tanner's objection. Bond then returns to Elektra's mansion and accuses her of falling in with Renard. He describes "Stockholm Syndrome," in which hostages fall in love with their captors. But Elektra vociferously denies it and accuses Bond of betraying her.

M arrives and Bond gives her a locator card that he retrieved from the nuke, and they quickly realize that Renard has planted it inside the King pipeline. Bond and Christmas attempt to defuse the bomb, but discover that half the plutonium is missing. Bond convinces her that the only solution is to let the bomb explode, which will rid them of Elektra's domination.

Believing Bond is now dead, Elektra gives M her father's lapel pin, and admits she's glad he's dead for failing to rescue her. She then executes M's associates and takes her hostage in Istanbul, where she reunites with Renard at Maiden's Tower, an ancient, ornately decorated lair. The lovers embrace and he shows her the plutonium ("Touch your destiny"). She leads him to M, who sits in a jail cell. Before leaving them alone, Elektra vows to reclaim her mother's kingdom. The imprisonment of M pleases Renard, who chides her for clumsily sacrificing Elektra just to get to him. "She's worth 50 of me," he bellows. "For once, we agree," M whispers. As a reminder of what she's done to him, Renard leaves a clock in the room. Time will run out for M at noon the next day.

In bed, Elektra cruelly makes fun of Renard's impotence and how she misses Bond's sexual prowess. Renard smashes his hand in a desperate attempt to feel pain. She tries soothing him with an ice cube and then runs it seductively along her body to remind him of what pleasure is like.

Thus, Elektra represents the franchise's first female super baddie, surpassing even Rosa Klebb, who technically worked for Blofeld. She's turned weakness into strength, preying on both Renard's living death and Bond's guilt.

Bond and Christmas visit Zukovsky at his caviar factory off the Caspian Sea. But the gangster's gold-toothed assistant, Goldie (Clifford Price), works for Elektra, and sets a trap for Bond when a helicopter armed with buzzsaws attacks the warehouse. Bond alertly uses his remote control to launch the BMW's missile launchers to destroy the chopper. Then another buzzsaw chopper arrives, and Bond takes it out with a flare gun and the warehouse gas pipe, causing it to explode.

Zukovsky winds up in a large vat of caviar and Bond agrees to fetch him out only if he confesses his involvement with Elektra. The gangster admits that he delivered a nuclear sub, commandeered by his nephew, in exchange for the million dollars she lost in his casino.

Once apprised of the situation, Zukovsky escorts Bond and Christmas to the Soviet security bureau office in Istanbul, where they deduce that Renard plans to turn the sub into a large nuclear bomb by putting the plutonium into the reactor. This will appear as an accident, destroying millions, eradicating the region, and creating an oil monopoly for Elektra (shades of *Goldfinger*).

Elektra informs M that her time is nearly up yet foolishly leaves the clock close enough for her to grab. M attaches the locator card, which signals her whereabouts to Bond. He recognizes the signal but before he can react, the office blows up. Bond and Christmas are captured by Goldie and Elektra's men while Zukovsky lies unconscious. Renard takes command of the sub, poisons the crew, and prepares the plutonium, then says goodbye to Elekra. He laments that he won't live long enough to rule the world with her. Bond and Christmas are taken to Maiden's Tower, where they're greeted by Elektra, who drops the façade and is more maniacal than ever. She orders Christmas taken to Renard on the sub and then deals with Bond, who's forcefully restrained by two guards.

"I could have given you the world," she brags. "The world is not enough," he defies. "Foolish sentiment," she scoffs. "Family motto," he boasts.

Bond is then strapped to an ancient torture chair in which his neck is placed in a metal collar. Elektra warns that five turns of the screw will break his neck, and takes great pleasure in torturing Bond both physically and mentally. "There's this ménage à trois that is rather perverse when you think about it," Brosnan explained. "I mean, this secret agent who just goes through women, but for the first time he's kind of lent himself to this woman out of guilt. And not only that, she's a great seductress, too, and she knows it. And just when he's near the edge of the abyss, the worm turns."

With each turn of the screw, Elektra reveals another aspect of her megalomania: her power over men, her obsession with oil as a birthright, her desire to rule the world, and her indestructibility. Bond realizes that she turned Renard and that the kidnapping scheme was her idea all along to gain control of her father's empire and recapture her maternal legacy. Bond tries to appeal to her better nature, but it's too late. She kisses him before saying goodbye. As a harbinger of *Casino Royale's* famous torture scene, however, Bond only has his wit to fall back on: "One…last…screw?"

But Zukovsky rushes in, kills Goldie, and sacrifices himself to save Bond. After Elektra turns and shoots him, Zukofsky realizes he only has the strength to get off one last shot. So he looks Bond in the eye, smiles, and craftily shoots one of the restraints. Bond escapes and races up the staircase after Elektra, with a short detour to free M.

Bond demands that Elektra call off Renard, but she still doesn't believe he'll kill her, so she calls his bluff and he unhesitatingly blows her away ("I never miss"). M enters the room and observes Bond tenderly caressing Elektra's corpse. She feels sad about Elektra, of course, but also has compassion for Bond and nearly bursts into tears. It's a transcendent moment and Brosnan's highlight as Bond.

Bond now has the strength to go after Renard and complete the mission. He dives into the water and enters the sub: First, he rescues Christmas and then fights and shoots his way into control of the sub. But instead of resurfacing, the sub hits the bottom of the Bosphorus, which ruptures the hull. Renard grabs the plutonium rod and heads to the reactor room. Bond figures the only way to stop Renard is to swim out of the sub and re-enter through the reactor room escape hatch, so he instructs Christmas how to open the hatch to let him back in. He fearlessly swims his way to the reactor room and soon has Renard in a choke hold. But he notices Christmas drowning nearby, so he knocks Renard down and rescues Christmas before resuming their struggle. While Renard momentarily overpowers Bond, he outsmarts the baddie by ejecting the plutonium rod into his chest. Bond and Christmas then torpedo out of the sub before it harmlessly explodes.

After everything Bond's endured, he enjoys having "Christmas in Turkey." But in a throwback to the Moore era, Bond and Christmas are surreptitiously caught having sex by MI6, thanks to satellite thermal imaging, causing M to shout: "007?!" Fortunately, Q's replacement alertly shuts off the computer transmission to save further embarrassment.

"I thought Christmas only comes once a year," Bond quips before continuing with his latest conquest.

But Bond's next assignment will be torture.

# DIE ANOTHER DAY

Obviously a lot had changed in the three years since *The World Is Not Enough* opened at the end of 1999. Brosnan, who fulfilled his three-film obligation and happily exercised the option for a fourth, said it was surreal returning as Bond after the terrorist attacks on Sept. 11, 2001.

"We didn't adjust," Brosnan admitted. "The script came in at the end of summer; then 9/11 happened and it took me a while to come out of the paralysis of that and realize that, after a few days, we had a movie with Bond to make that deals with this planet, and blowing things up, and world domination. This film is a celebration of Bond at a time when we need to embrace heroes."

Still, the franchise strived to be as topical as ever with the 20th Bond film, *Die Another Day*. Purvis & Wade were back with their second script (they've been the go-to scribes ever since), and tapped escalating territorial tensions between North and South Korea as the political backdrop.

But since *Die Another Day* also marked the 40th anniversary of the Bond franchise in 2002, the screenwriters were additionally tasked with paying homage to the previous 19 films. So they cleverly came up with an array of references, from Halle Berry's introduction as Jinx coming out the water in an orange bikini a la Honey Ryder from *Dr. No*, to the central plot device of a diamond-powered laser satellite lifted directly from *DAF*, to Q's secret stash of memorabilia (including *FRWL's* shoe blade and attaché case, the jet pack and re-breather from *Thunderball*, and the mini-jet and crocodile sub from *Octopussy*). Then there were more obscure references, such as the title of the book Bond picks up called *Birds of the West Indies*. In reality, this was written by a certain James Bond, the author whose name Fleming borrowed for his superspy.

The trick was not allowing the sentimental journey to take over the movie. But new director Lee Tamahori, best-known for creepy thrillers and hard-hitting action (*Once Were Warriors*), made sure he kept 007 grounded in the present while still showing "great reverence for the old Bond movies."

"To see Lee and Michael and Barbara pull Bond into the 21st century, to get them to use CGI, and get them to put Bond in tougher situations is so satisfying," Brosnan remarked.

Indeed, the first and probably best instance of CGI occurs when Bond fires the bullet straight at us during the gun barrel opening. From there, we glimpse three surfers slipping into North Korea in the pre-credit sequence, which is muted and gray. It's Bond and two South Korean allies infiltrating the base of Colonel Tan-Sun Moon (Will Yun Lee). Bond impersonates a dealer who's come to trade African conflict diamonds for weaponry. Moon wants to annex South Korea by force and obliterate the West. But the Oxford-educated soldier comes off as a spoiled brat. He furiously kicks a canvas bag and then pulls out his anger management trainer, who's been beaten to a pulp. All along, he defies his father, General Moon (Kenneth Tsang), by secretly plotting war.

Bond's cover is easily blown by Moon's accomplice, Zao (Rick Yune), with the help of a mole at MI6. Moon then blows up Bond's helicopter with a depleted uranium gun. But Bond detonates the C4 in his diamond-filled briefcase with his Omega watch and flees in a hovercraft. The blast even scars Zao's face with diamond shards. Bond destroys the base and shoots up the heavily mined demilitarized zone (DMZ) while being pursued by Moon's men. Moon runs away in his own hovercraft when he fears his father's reprisal. Bond eventually tangles with Moon and sends him plunging over a waterfall to his apparent death, grabbing onto a bell at the last instant ("Saved by the bell").

But the angry general takes Bond prisoner and the pre-credit action spills over into the main titles for the first time, in which Bond is brutally tortured. He's beaten, water tortured, and he's attacked by scorpions.

When Bond emerges from imprisonment 14 months later (looking like Robinson Crusoe with

long hair and a beard), the general interrogates him one last time, trying to make sense of his son's destructive behavior. But Bond remains defiant: he tells the general that his son got what was coming to him. Bond's prepared to face a firing squad, but instead is swapped at the border for Zao. Bond's picked up by Robinson, who's accompanied by snarky NSA chief Falco (Michael Madsen). He snarls at Bond's release and tries browbeating M at every turn.

Aboard an MI6 ship that serves as a floating hospital, Bond's examined and sedated and then harshly interrogated by M (separated by a pane of glass). She tells Bond that he's suspected of leaking information under duress and that she considered the price too high for his release. Bond agrees it was a bad trade, but insists he's not the source of the leak. It's too late: M has already cut him loose from Her Majesty's Secret Service. Bond has no choice but to escape and prove his innocence, which he ingeniously accomplishes by stopping his heartbeat (recalling James Coburn's Bond imitator from *Our Man Flint*). He then eludes security and swims to Hong Kong harbor.

"Here's a man who has killed so many people," Brosnan recounted, "who lives with blood on his hands, sometimes messy killings, dealing with death on a constant basis, [grappling] with the idea of his own death. And that's hard to do with something, which is geared now toward kids. But you find the guy captured, you find him on the run between friend and foe — a renegade — you find him outside the circle of his own people. The writing isn't as deep as you'd like, but there are beats that are a good throwback to the Cold War."

Still, Tamahori wanted to take it a step further with a wild idea for explaining the 40-year continuity of the franchise. "What if Bond gets a mysterious phone call from a stranger summoning him to Scotland?" he told me. "And what if that stranger turns out to be Sean Connery, who explains that he was the original 007 and that after his retirement he was replaced by a series of successors?" He then proceeds to instruct the latest 007 on how to conduct himself as a renegade spy since he once found himself in similar circumstances. Of course,

Wilson and Broccoli didn't go for the idea.

In any event, Bond casually wanders into the Rubyeon Royale Hotel drenched in hospital clothes and asks for his usual room and tailor at the front desk. The manager comes to his aid, and, after looking more like himself in his hotel room, Bond is greeted by a girl who wants to give him a massage. But Bond spots a trap and uncovers an attempt by the manager to videotape him having sex (a nod to *FRWL*). The manager's with Chinese intelligence and Bond elicits his help to capture Zao.

Bond then travels to Cuba and traces Zao with the help of a sleeper agent to an island called Isa Los Organos, where he first encounters the beautiful but lethal Jinx Johnson, who turns out to be an assassin. In fact, she's as kick-ass as Bond, who poses as an ornithologist when they first meet. But she seduces him into bed, gets on top, holds a knife during their wild sex, and leaves him in the morning.

"She has a maturity, sexuality, and sensuality that make men and women feel so at ease," said Brosnan in describing his co-star — the only Bond girl to ever win an Oscar, which she nabbed for her performance in *Monster's Ball*. No wonder they considered spinning Jinx off into another film franchise.

The following day, Bond and Jinx separately infiltrate a gene therapy clinic where Zao seeks a complete makeover (a throwback to *DAF*). We eventually learn that Jinx works for Falco at the NSA, who still doesn't trust Bond and has assigned her to kill Zao. But Bond gets to Zao first and tortures him during the aborted treatment. However, the albino-looking terrorist with permanent facial scarring eventually overpowers Bond and escapes by helicopter. Jinx vanishes too before Bond can catch up to her. But Zao leaves behind a pendant containing conflict diamonds, which Bond traces to flamboyant British billionaire Gustav Graves (Toby Stephens).

Bond returns to London and witnesses the daredevil parachuting from a plane to accept his knighthood (a Union Jack, of course). He then follows Graves to the Blades Club (culled from the *Moonraker* novel) and challenges him to a fencing duel, but not before flirting with Graves' instructor

Verity (Madonna, who wrote and performed the theme song).

The match starts off in Bond's favor, but then goes way over the top when the petulant Graves refuses to give up. He insists on grabbing larger swords, but he's met his match in Bond. They thrash the club and spill blood before Graves' fencing partner and assistant, Miranda Frost (Rosamund Pike), puts a stop to their "cockfight," as Verity calls it.

Graves pays up but is so impressed that he invites Bond to a soiree he's hosting in Iceland for a scientific demonstration. Bond immediately tries flirting with Frost, but gets a chilly reception after asking if he'll enjoy her in Iceland: "I'm afraid you'll never have that pleasure, Mr. Bond."

Bond then meets M in an abandoned underground tube station, which serves as a refuge of last resort for MI6. She divulges that Frost works for them but can't get the goods on Graves and Zao. "You burned me and now you want my help?" Bond sneers. "Did you expect an apology?" M retorts. But as she explains, "Knowing who to trust is everything in this business." It's a refrain that will vitally carry over into the Craig films.

Cut to MI6 headquarters being invaded and M accosted. Bond enters and shoots the place up and saves M. But it turns out to be one of Q's latest gadgets: a virtual reality training system. They argue about Bond passing the test, but this Q seems to have gained confidence. At one point, Q even gets the better quip: "You know, you're cleverer than you look," Bond chides, "Still, better than looking cleverer than you are," Q responds.

On the way to Q's underground lab, Bond enjoys looking at a few of the aforementioned mementos from past assignments. He picks up the poison spiked shoe with particular fondness. Q demonstrates a sonic agitator ring, which shatters a sheet of unbreakable glass when twisted. Then he unveils the latest Aston Martin, the Vanquish, which offers an invisible cloaking device along with two machine guns under the hood, front firing rockets, air canons under the chassis, and spring-loaded ejector seat. Yes, they replay the *Goldfinger* Aston Martin intro. Bond even remarks, "You must be joking," to which Q replies, "As I learned from my predecessor, Bond, I never joke about my work."

While Bond's reinstated with renewed confidence and sent packing to Iceland with Q's latest and greatest gadgets, M meets with Frost to inform her that she'll be working with Bond. She only has disdain for 007: "He'll light the fuse on any explosive situation, and be a danger to himself and others." But M suggests that Bond's recklessness is precisely what they need. It's the best ringing endorsement of this Bond she's ever provided.

Bond reunites with Jinx at Graves' ice palace in the Arctic (one of production designer Peter Lamont's most lavish sets). She even pulls up in a sparkling red Ford Thunderbird. Ever the thrill-seeker, Graves tries breaking the land speed record with his ice-dragster. And when Jinx and Frost first meet, they seem destined for a cat fight. Frost immediately thumbs her nose at Jinx, who cuts her down to size by saying how much she's enjoyed "the thrust" of Bond's "Big Bang theory."

Later that night, Graves puts on a dazzling demonstration of his latest project: Icarus, an orbital mirror satellite, which harnesses solar energy (thanks to the conflict diamonds) for year-round crop development. Bond's not impressed: he's been in this situation before and realizes there's some world domination plot behind Icarus. But Frost saves Bond from capture while he's snooping around, and she finally decides to try him on for size in bed ("I know all about you — sex for dinner, death for breakfast").

Jinx infiltrates the command center in the palace. But she's captured by Zao, who arranges for her to be laser sliced a la *Goldfinger* while she trash-talks him ("Yo' mama"). Of course, Bond comes to her rescue, using the re-breather underwater to reach the command center, and tangling with a thug. However, Jinx winds up saving Bond by zapping the baddie with the laser. Jinx tells Bond that she spotted another gene therapy machine in the compound. That's when Bond realizes that Graves is actually Moon in disguise. Indeed, it's a variation on the Drax doppelganger ploy from the *Moonraker* novel, only here Moon has assumed the identity of what he most despises: Western decadence.

Bond sneaks up on Graves, who's become every

megalomaniac he's ever encountered rolled into one. Then Frost intervenes and reveals that she's the double-agent (she attended Oxford with Moon). Once more, Bond's weakness for women gets the best of him. But he escapes by using the sonic ring to shatter the glass floor beneath them.

Bond then flees in Graves' ice dragster while Graves tries to zap him with the Icaraus beam. It's a mad dash that ends with Bond parasailing over a cliff and surfing his way out of a jam (with really bad-looking compositing).

Jinx is recaptured by Frost and taken prisoner in the ice palace. Bond then hops into the Aston Martin, but his vanishing act doesn't fool Zao, who pursues him in his tricked out Jaguar XKR (door panel rockets, front grill machine guns, rear-mounted Gatling gun, and trunk-mounted mortars). It's a car cockfight between Bond and Zao on the pack ice, and Bond can't shake him (even though he gets to use the ejector seat to flip right side up). However, when Graves turns the Icarus beam on the ice palace, Bond switches gears and drives inside the rapidly-melting structure in search of Jinx. Zao is right behind him, but Bond strategically uses the Vanquish and the elements to his advantage, and finally lures Zao to his death under a collapsing chandelier. Bond then rescues Jinx from drowning just in time. He whisks her away in the Aston Martin and uses the sonic ring to break the windshield.

Bond and Jinx then HALO jump into North Korea, but Bond is unable to kill Graves with a sniper rifle. So they stow away in his Antonov plane in a nod to *The Living Daylights*. Graves now dons an armored suit that communicates electronically with Icarus and also allows him to deliver a deadly 100,000-volt surge.

Graves meets with General Moon and divulges his true identity to his father along with his plan to take back South Korea using the Icarus to burn up the DMZ, and then render the West defenseless. But he has shamed his father and dishonored his family. In an attempt to restore peace, the general holds his son at gunpoint. But Graves stuns him with an electrical charge and then shoots him.

Jinx takes control of the plane and Bond confronts Graves, who delights in explaining that his new identity has been modeled after him. "I paid attention to details: that unjustifiable swagger, the crass quips, the self-defense mechanism concealing such inadequacy."

"My self-defense mechanism's right here," Bond responds, holding his Walther P99. He tries to shoot Graves, but his aim is deflected and he pierces one of the windows, causing the plane to depressurize (in another nod to *Goldfinger*). Jinx stabilizes the plane, but is attacked by Frost. However, she manages to alter the plane's course toward the Icarus beam. They subsequently engage in a brutal sword fight, which ends with Jinx surprising the henchwoman with a hidden knife from *The Art of War* ("Read this… bitch!").

Bond battles Grave and, like the fencing duel, scores an early hit. But Graves activates the suit and stuns Bond long enough to retrieve a parachute from a locker (he teasingly hurls the spare out of the plane). Yet, like his villainous predecessors, Graves is undone by hubris. He can't resist gloating about his apparent triumph. Bond cunningly grabs the ripcord and forces open the chute ("Time to face gravity"). As Graves desperately clings to the side of the plane, Bond then presses the button on his suit and the electrical charge hurls Graves into one of the engines. Fortunately, the Icarus beam is shut off with his demise.

Bond and Jinx then escape the disintegrating plane using a helicopter in the cargo hold. Cut to Bond finally having his way with Moneypenny at her desk. But wait: it's only Moneypenny using the virtual reality device. "It's rather hard, isn't it?" Q interrupts. "Yes…very," she sighs.

We then hear Bond and Jinx having some sly off-screen fun in bed. "Wait. Don't pull it out. I'm not finished with it yet," Jinx pleads. "See? It's a perfect fit," Bond offers. But this is deceptive, too. They're playing with a stash of diamonds and Jinx has one in her belly button. If only they didn't have to return them, she wishes. They're still the good guys, but Bond's not sure how good Jinx really is. "I am so good," she insists. "Especially when you're bad," he adds. It's a fitting end to the successful Brosnan era.

But after toying with 40 years of Bond, it's time to start all over again and get real.

# DANIEL CRAIG: BOND REBORN

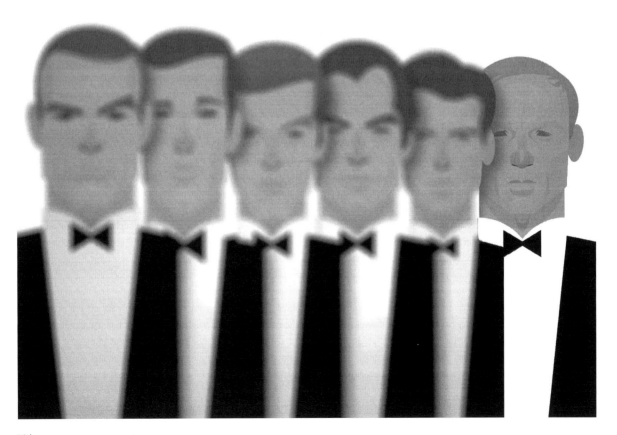

Daniel Craig has certainly broken the Bond mold with his blond hair and rugged features (not to mention the fact that he's the shortest 007 at 5' 11'). Sure, the fanboys jumped all over him for looking more like a Bond baddie than Bond. But that didn't matter: Craig returned to Fleming's description of Bond in *Casino Royale* as "ironical, brutal, and cold."

In the end, it turned out for the best: *Casino Royale* became the highest grossing Bond film to date (earning $594.2 million worldwide), redeeming Craig's rough-and-tumble portrayal. *Quantum of Solace*, the sequel, even topped it domestically ($168.3 million), solidifying Craig as Bond, despite the mixed critical response.

"For me, I couldn't have seen doing it any other way than with *Casino Royale*," Craig admitted. "I had to feel like we could begin again here, not in any broad way, but to try and find some of the subtlety of who this person is. And, therefore, hopefully, give us a springboard."

The Cheshire, England native (born March 2, 1968) had plenty to work with: After re-reading all of the Fleming novels, he discovered that Bond's always in trouble, always struggling with his personal demons, which is why he's such a "blunt instrument."

And to think it was all made possible because Eon's old nemesis, Kevin McClory, failed to launch his own Bond franchise with Sony Pictures, which lost a court battle with MGM in 1999. Sony owns Columbia Pictures, which made the *Casino Royale* spoof, and was forced to give up its rights to the property. Ironically, though, Sony wound up financing and distributing *Casino Royale* when it led

> I couldn't have seen doing it any other way than with *Casino Royale*. I had to feel like we could begin again here, not in any broad way, but to try and find some of the subtlety of who this person is.
>
> *Daniel Craig*

a consortium to take over MGM in 2005. And Eon has enjoyed working with Sony's new regime ever since.

Still, Craig's ascension as Bond took everyone by surprise when it was presumed that Clive Owen would assume the mantle after his suave turn in *Croupier* in 1998. But Eon shrewdly went outside the box again for the origin story. Although Craig made a career out of playing tortured souls (*Road to Perdition*, *Sylvia*), he turned up the heat as the charming yet deadly drug dealer in *Layer Cake*. Craig looked like he could "light the fuse on any explosive situation." Even though director Martin Campbell was skeptical at first, Barbara Broccoli knew she had her Bond.

"Nowadays it would be inappropriate for him to revert to some of the older conventions," Broccoli asserted. "9/11 changed everything. We need a Bond that fits the times. The world is a very different place. Human intelligence is so vital in the world we live in today. It comes down to individuals doing pretty heroic acts, putting themselves at personal risk. We realize that more than ever."

They also realized that the spy genre had changed dramatically after the surprising success of the rival *Bourne* franchise (starring Matt Damon as dour amnesiac Jason Bourne), which launched just ahead of *Die Another Day* in 2002. But *Casino Royale* proved that audiences were ready for a more serious and grittier Bond as well.

"When I picked up *Casino Royale* again, I was reminded what a lean and mean book it is," Craig noted. "Funnily enough, I re-read it when I got the call [about becoming Bond]. It was on a Wednesday and I started it on Tuesday, and I only had two more chapters to go as I went to bed that night. The following morning I finished them in the cab on the way to my meeting. It's a really good read — it's a really good story. And I had forgotten how much it sets up and how complicated he makes Bond. That was one of the impetuses for me to actually think it was possible to do."

The other impetus, of course, was having a solid script by Purvis & Wade and Oscar winner Paul Haggis (*Crash, Million Dollar Baby*). This provided the foundation for Bond's riveting rite of passage and coming full circle back to Fleming. And it certainly helped having the return of director Martin Campbell to break in his second Bond actor. But this was different: "He's thinking more with his heart than with his head, and things go wrong," Campbell noted.

That's because Bond doesn't have all the answers. Craig, who's been more directly involved than any other actor in the development of Bond's character, made sure of that. "There are a couple of simple equations that you can apply and that I have always applied to the work anyway," Craig explained. "And that has to do with fallibility, which is much more dramatically interesting. But his argument to M was, 'You gave me the job — you gave me a Double-0.' He doesn't have to phone up before he kills somebody. If he's got the shot, and he feels it's the right thing to do, then he'll do it. I want the audience to go, 'Is that the right decision at this particular moment?' Hopefully, at the end, we ultimately see that he was right: that there was a grander plan, there was something that he was thinking about. Then we're going to be covered. But during the movie it should go either way."

There's also the grueling physicality of the role, which demanded three weeks of rigorous training: all that running and jumping and fighting, getting cut, bloodied, and bruised. Craig would wake up, roll out of bed and go, "I can't move."

But the greatest opportunity has been showing Bond's vulnerable side. In *Casino Royale*, he meets and falls in love with Vesper Lynd (Eva Green): the enigmatic accomplice that finances his high-stakes poker match against terrorist banker, Le Chiffre (Mads Mikkelsen). She melts Bond's cold heart and vice versa before shockingly betraying him and committing suicide. This crucially defines his character.

"I wouldn't have touched this movie if I didn't see an element of where we saw him change," Craig suggested, "where we saw him go through something — a revelation — and that revelation was Vesper."

The counterbalance is Bond's relationship with M, the strong maternal figure and the most stabilizing force in his life. "They have this relationship that is genuinely almost one of love," Craig revealed. "That wherever he is, in spite of everything, no matter how alone in the world he is, she's there for him."

Then, in *Quantum of Solace*, there's unfinished business, as Bond is torn between vengeance and duty, searching for answers about Vesper and the powerful, SPECTRE-like organization behind her betrayal. "I think he's just beginning to get his head around the fact of what he might have to achieve and what he might have to do," Craig asserted. "That doesn't bother me. I think everybody was saying he's now the person we know. He's not. He's somebody who's just been badly hurt and so his reactions after this are going to be extreme."

The theme of trust continues in the upcoming *Skyfall*, Craig's third outing as Bond, whose loyalty to M is tested when her past comes back to haunt her. "What I'm interested in is a refining of the character," Craig offered. "He can't go in guns blazing all the time, or whenever he'd like to. He's gonna have to start thinking. But still there's that possibility, when it comes down to it — and Sean was very good at it — he can pick up a table and smash it in somebody's face."

*Skyfall*, the 23rd Bond film, opens Oct. 26 in the UK and Nov. 9 in North America. What a nice 50th anniversary present in 2012.

When Eon finally made *Casino Royale*, the franchise Holy Grail, it was a new start for Bond — a hard reboot. At long last, he was the center of the story, with "real scenes and real dramas going on," and the establishment of a character arc, as the origin story unmasked the enigma.

We were now privy to the genesis of the gun barrel opening, how Bond attains his Double-0 status, why he prefers his martinis "shaken, not stirred," and the derivation of the famous tagline: "The name's Bond. James Bond."

But more important, we learned about the events that shaped Bond's attitudes toward killing and women — and how he's been hardened by them. "It's that whole process and change that I thought was gonna make it an interesting movie and also give us something to work with now," Craig suggested.

However, *Casino Royale* is obviously unique: it's not a prequel because it starts all over again contemporaneously, so it's like looking forward and backward at the same time. It actually belongs to a special category common to comic books called "retroactive continuity" or "retcon," in which historical events are revised to fit new circumstances. That helps explain why *Casino Royale* reintroduces Judi Dench as the first M, and alters Bond's first encounters with Felix Leiter and the Aston Martin DB5. The results are disconcerting at first but ultimately reassuring in maintaining franchise continuity.

"It's a testament to the writing that we've managed to get most of the Bondisms into the movie without belaboring the point about them," noted Craig. "And making them, hopefully, for a new audience to go, 'OK, I've heard that that's the movie where it came from.' But also for hardened Bond fans to say, 'We accept it — we have to have them in there but take it this way.' I don't see any reason why we don't get them into later movies. But we've set it up so that we don't have to hammer them home."

The reinvention begins immediately with the absence of the traditional gun barrel opening. But we commence the pre-credit sequence in black and white to denote its importance. We are in Prague and a car pulls up outside an ultra-modern building in the middle of the night. A man gets out and enters the building and rides the elevator (note that he gets off at the sixth floor and not the seventh). He enters his office (whose look by production designer Peter Lamont was modeled after *The Ipcress File*). He moves to open a hidden safe, but it's ajar. Bond sits in the shadows waiting for him. His name is Dryden (Malcolm Sinclair), the MI6 section chief, and he's been caught selling secrets by M. Dryden surreptitiously pulls out a semiautomatic from a secret panel. "Your file shows no kills," Dryden confidently suggests. "But to become a Double-0, it takes…" "Two," Bond interrupts.

Cut to a violent flashback that looks grainier and washed out by cinematographer Phil Méheux: Bond struggles to get his first kill in a brutal hand-to-hand. He throws the baddie against the wall of a bathroom stall and kicks him and slugs him, and the two men tumble chaotically in the confined space, easily breaking the partitions.

Dryden pulls his gun on Bond, who remains emotionless: "Shame, we barely got to know each other," he slyly offers. Dryden pulls the trigger. Click. Bond holds up the magazine. "I know where you keep your gun, I suppose that's something," Bond wryly suggests. Dryden realizes that he's underestimated Bond at his own peril. "True. How did he die?" he asks. "Your contact? Not well," Bond dryly responds.

Cut back to the fight: Bond drags the man and forces his head into the basin, overflowing with water, knocks the gun out of his hand, and holds it under for what seems like an eternity until he stops writhing and kicking. He lets the body slide to the floor and steps back. The unclean kill unnerves him.

"Made you feel it, did he?" Dryden sneers. "Well, you needn't worry, the second is…" Bond coldly shoots him dead with his silenced Walther P99 (a hand-off from the Brosnan era along with the Omega Seamaster watch): "Yes. Considerably," Bond drolly concludes. This forms the basis of the ideal cat-and-mouse/chess match: Bond assesses his opponent's weakness, lulls him into a false sense of security, and strikes by surprise. If only it were so easy from here on out.

Cut back to the bathroom: Bond picks up his gun, and sees a reflection of the man aiming a pistol at his back. Bond whirls and fires one shot that explodes out of his Walther. We view it from inside the victim's gun barrel. Red blood flows down the screen as Bond stands frozen against the white wall. From now on, whenever we watch any of the previous Bond films— or future ones, for that matter — we'll have a frame of reference for what the gun barrel opening means. It will no longer be as abstract.

"The bathroom sequence I made brutal, tougher, and grittier," Campbell explained. "The idea being that Bond's past is important because he has difficulty dealing with the violence when he pushes the guy's face into the basin and he stands back and it's kind of rough on him. And that's very much about what the navel-gazing part of the film is."

Craig said it bothers Bond so much that it leaves the slight undercurrent of a death wish: "The shot where he has to take a breath, it's pretty nasty," he added. "We have to feel that it's his first one and he's been ordered to go out and do it."

Meanwhile, there are no silhouetted naked ladies in the animated main title sequence. Daniel Kleinman instead morphs playing cards with red hearts into a series of violent graphics inspired by the cover design of Fleming's *Casino Royale*, while Bond fights with baddies in silhouette to convey the spirit of the danger and love story.

In Uganda, rebel leader Obanno (Isaach de Bankole) meets with international banker and money launderer Le Chiffre ("The Cipher") and mysterious liaison Mr. White (Jesper Christensen) to safely stash his war chest. Le Chiffre, who must constantly use an inhaler, also introduces the physical deformity trope with a scar running down his left eyelid (recalling Blofeld in *YOLT*). However, Le Chiffre is not to be underestimated: He's a mathematical genius but also shrewdly profits in the stock market by enlisting terrorists to bomb companies he's bet against.

We next encounter Bond pursing a bomb maker (free runner Sébastien Foucan) in Madagascar, which results in the film's longest and most thrilling action sequence. The elaborate foot chase through a construction site tells us a lot about Bond: unlike the bomber, who's a very graceful athlete and adept escape artist, Bond has no finesse whatsoever. He's like a raging bull. But he's relentless, using every shortcut available to keep up. In fact, he literally bulldozes his way to the bomber, who begins climbing the framework of the building. Bond follows in hot pursuit, running across narrow girders, impervious to danger. He doesn't even flinch when a crashing welding rig causes an explosion.

The bomber eventually leaps onto a crane and rushes to the top while Bond hits the quick release lever on the side mechanism to catch up. The bomber hurls his gun at Bond in frustration after he runs out of bullets. Bond snatches the gun and throws it back at the bomber's face; he nearly falls off the crane but quickly regains his balance. They furiously fight 200 feet up and Bond holds his own until the bomber smashes his face against the ironwork. The bomber leaps off the crane onto the arm of a second crane below. He then spectacularly jumps onto the roof of a building and free runs away. Bond freezes but then takes the plunge. He hurts himself when hitting the second crane and nearly falls off the roof. It's painful. He then pursues the bomber as relentlessly as ever down an empty elevator shaft and crashes through the wall to keep up with him outside. This is definitely the antithesis of Connery's effortless Bond.

The bomber heads for the Nambutu Embassy for sanctuary, and Bond follows and hops the fence. Bond then forces his way into the ambassador's office, grabs the bomber, and drags him through the embassy, shooting the place up in the process. But with nowhere to run outside, security catches up, and Bond pretends to give up. Then he shoots the bomber dead and fires at a gas cylinder, which starts an explosive chain reaction with the other cylinders. Bond vanishes. The military attaché is flabbergasted. Outside the embassy, Bond looks through the bomber's backpack and finds a cell phone along with a bomb. He notices that the last call was to "Ellipsis." This is exactly what Craig meant about Bond using questionable tactics but somehow still getting the job done. After recklessly blowing up the embassy, he stumbles upon the lead that will eventually take him to Le Chiffre.

Speaking of whom, Le Chiffre handily wins a poker match aboard his yacht (one of the guests includes Tsai Chin, Bond's Hong Kong fling at the beginning of *YOLT*). But in another physical display of vulnerability, he weeps blood ("a derangement of the tear duct — nothing sinister"). Then news of the bomber's demise wipes the smirk off his face.

M storms out of the House of Commons with her assistant, Villiers (Tobias Menzies), cursing the politicians as well as Bond: "Is the man deranged?! And where the hell is he?! In the old days, if an agent did something so embarrassing he'd have the good sense to defect! Christ, I miss the Cold War!"

Inside a dark apartment, Bond pulls a SIM card from the bomber's cell phone and plugs it into a laptop and traces the signal for Ellipsis to the Ocean Club in Nassau (*Thunderball* country), and then quickly copies the zone map and relevant info onto a memory stick when he hears someone getting out of the elevator. M enters and shockingly finds that Bond has broken into her home. He sits quietly on the other side of the room and she has it out with him, questioning his judgment as well as her own for prematurely promoting him. But Bond gives as good as he gets, and nearly blurts out what M stands for before she threatens to have him killed. Then he unexpectedly strikes a somber note when reminding her that "Double-0s have a very short life expectancy."

"Bond, this may be too much for a blunt instrument to understand, but arrogance and self-awareness seldom go hand-in-hand," she lectures. "So you want me to be half-monk, half-hit man," he quips. "Any thug can kill," she continues. "I need you take your ego out of the equation and judge the situation dispassionately. I have to know I can trust you, and that you know who to trust. And since I don't know that, I need you out of my sight. Go and stick your head in the sand somewhere and think

about your future."

M sends Bond on his way and warns him never to break into her house again. But once more, a questionable tactic has gotten him closer to Le Chiffre, thanks to the Nassau lead that he snatched from her laptop. After he's gone, she realizes that Bond's smarter than he looks when she glances at her laptop.

But beneath the tension there's fondness between them. Indeed, it's a very different dynamic from the male-centric dick-swinging of the early Bond films. "But he gets in her apartment, and even though he's, 'Fuck you, mum,' he respects her totally," Craig emphasized. "He knows he's pissing her off and he likes that. And we have her struggle a bit, which is interesting. And I like that feeling because that gives a balance to his other relationships in the movie."

At the Ocean Club, Bond quickly discovers that the bomber was hired by Alex Dimitrios (Simon Abkarian), a terrorist middle-man. Again, Bond uses crude tactics, smashing a car in the parking lot when the owner confuses him with a valet, and then using the distraction to break into the security office, where he looks over the footage to identify his target pulling up to the entrance in a '64 silver Aston Martin, of all things.

Bond then flirts his way into booking a suite with the cute receptionist and finding out where Dimitrios lives. This is more like the old Bond we know and love. He checks out the baddie's beach home and spies his beautiful wife, Solange (Caterina Murino), riding through the surf on a horse. But in a clever *Dr. No* reversal, Bond is seen as the sexual object of desire coming out of the water wearing swimming trunks. Back in his suite, Bond connects Dimitrios to Le Chiffre by hacking into M's computer account. All the while, Villiers monitors Bond's activities. M doesn't like his methods but is impressed with the results.

We then get a sense of that adrenaline rush Bond receives from gambling, especially when mixed with danger and sex. He easily beats Dimitrios at poker, even winning his Aston Martin. After sizing up the unhappy Solange, though, Bond picks her up in his latest prize outside the hotel, and seduces her into a drink back at his place. Bond even displays that sly

sense of humor by gunning the engine and driving in a circle. Of course, having sex with Solange is a familiar position for Bond, who likes to keep his relationships simple with married women, but who easily learns that Dimitrios is on his way to Miami.

Bond follows Dimitrios to the Science Center, where he's arranged to rendezvous with another bomber, and leaves a coat check tag at the bizarre Body Worlds Exhibit of cadavers. Fittingly, it's at a poker table. Bond saunters over but Dimitrios pulls a stiletto on him. They struggle and just when it looks like the baddie's going to get the best of Bond, he glances away, diverts his attention, turns him with an arm lock, and thrusts the blade into his back. Bond sits him down in a chair, grabs his cell phone, and checks for sent messages. He locks in on "Ellipsis." Realizing the tag is gone, Bond looks around and spots the bomber and follows him to the airport.

The bomber passes undetected through security, disguises himself as a maintenance worker, and prepares to blow up a target with a key ring detonator. But when Bond loses the bomber through security, he phones MI6 for help just as the fire alarm is triggered as a distraction. After some quick intel by Villiers, M informs Bond that the target is the new Skyfleet prototype — the largest plane in the world. Apparently Le Chiffre has invested all of the rebel leader's money in shorting Skyfleet stock, and would make a fortune off the destruction of the prototype.

On a whim, Bond types "Ellipsis" on the security keypad, and pursues the bomber outside on the tarmac. The bomber intends to ram the jetliner with a fuel tanker with the key ring detonator attached. So Bond charges up a mobile stairway and leaps onto the top of the tanker. The bomber swerves back and forth but can't shake Bond until he's forced to leap off to avoid getting crushed by an oncoming vehicle. Bond races to catch up with the tanker and jumps back on (this is a far cry from *Licence to Kill's* tanker climax).

Then after the tanker unavoidably slices a bus in two, causing an explosion, Bond seizes his chance and enters the cab through the shattered windshield, and the two men start pummeling each other. Police shoot out the back tires and the tanker nearly

collides with an oncoming plane. Bond gets him in a choke hold, but he smashes Bond with his elbow and throws him through the side door. But Bond holds on and notices the key ring detonator. He gets back in and grabs hold of the bomber, but he manages to escape. Bond then barely prevents the swerving tanker from hitting the Skyfleet.

Bond rolls out of the tanker and collapses on the ground, as security guards catch up and hold him down. Safely away, the baddie detonates the bomb; however, during the fight, Bond deftly attached the key ring to the bomber's belt loop. The bomber realizes he's been fooled and blows up off-screen while Bond watches and smiles ever so slightly. It's a twisted look of satisfaction that takes us all the way back to the sadistic killing of Dent in *Dr. No*.

Bond returns to Nassau, where he notices the corpse of Solange before being briefed by M and having a probe implanted in his arm: Le Chiffre has set up a high-stakes poker tournament at Casino Royale in Montenegro in an attempt to win back the more than $100 million he lost in the Skyfleet fiasco. Since Bond is their best poker player, his mission is to beat Le Chiffre, forcing him to seek refuge at MI6 in exchange for information about his superiors.

On the train to Montenegro, Bond meets Vesper in the dining car. She's the Treasury official assigned to supervise his budget: a dark-haired beauty who tries to hide it. "I'm the money," she says matter-of-factly. "Every penny of it," Bond replies. It's a nice pun on Moneypenny.

Bond's immediately put on the defensive, though, when Vesper makes it clear that she's against the mission — she doesn't trust Bond with such a vast sum of money. However, he explains that poker is all about bluffing and reading people, which merely incites further sarcasm. So Bond tries to cut her down to size with a blunt psychological assessment: Vesper worries that she won't be taken seriously because of her beauty, and "overcompensates by wearing slightly masculine clothing and being more aggressive than her female colleagues, which gives her a somewhat prickly demeanor and, ironically, makes her less likely to be promoted by her male superiors, who mistake her insecurity for arrogance."

He then deduces that she's an orphan because she didn't flinch at an earlier quip about her funny name.

Vesper rises to the challenge and sizes Bond up: "By the cut of your suit you went to Oxford or wherever and actually think human beings dress like that. But you wear it with such disdain, that my guess is that you didn't come from money and all your school chums rubbed that in your face every day, which means you were at that school by the grace of someone else's charity, hence the chip on your shoulder. And since your first thought about me ran to orphan, that's what I'd say you are."

Bond's impressed and Vesper continues the psychoanalytical foreplay:"You think of women as disposable pleasures rather than meaningful pursuits. So as charming as you are, I will be keeping my eye on our government's money and off your perfectly formed ass."

Vesper leaves Bond feeling skewered, like his lamb, but he's hooked. He realizes they're kindred spirits. "Because she has this sense of mystery about her and that's what he falls in love with," Craig said.

When they arrive in Montenegro, Bond finds a new Aston Martin DBS waiting for him ("I love you too, M"). They also meet their local MI6 contact, the charming and caustic René Mathis (Giancarlo Giannini). After Le Chiffre buys off the local police chief to increase his odds, Mathis arranges to have him removed from office with the help of Photoshop, and buys off his successor at a more affordable price for MI6.

Meanwhile, Bond and Vesper surprise one another with last-minute gifts and a hidden display of affection before the tournament: He gives her a stunning purple dress so she'll look fabulous in distracting the other players, and she gives him a stylish tux so he looks like he belongs at the table. When Bond notices that it's tailored, she replies, "Oh, I sized you up the moment we met." We now have her to thank for introducing more glam to this Bond.

Instead of baccarat, they play the more modern and familiar Texas Hold 'em in the otherwise retro-looking casino. But while there are 10 opponents (including Wright's Felix), it's all about the showdown between Bond and Le Chiffre. It's their cat-and-mouse and dance rolled into one since they never actually have a physical fight. Bond even dispenses with his cover and uses his real name, figuring that Le Chiffre is smart enough to already know his identity.

"With the poker stuff, it was trying not to confuse the audience," Craig explained. "Of course, there'll be people in the audience that play poker and know what's going on, but we need to appeal to everybody. We need to have a sort of sparring and that was the key to making it work."

The poker match is divided into three sequences: the first obviously involves Bond and Le Chiffre sizing each other up. In fact, early on when Bond closes in on a flush, he notices a slight twitch of Le Chiffre's eye. He nonchalantly pulls his finger up to hide it, and so Bond goes all out to learn the meaning of the routine. But, suddenly, Vesper enters from behind Bond and kisses him on the cheek. Only it's the opposite direction from what they discussed. Still, the effect is the same in distracting the other players. When Le Chiffre stops twitching and doubles the bet, Bond calls, and Le Chiffre lays down a full house. Bond shakes his head and throws his cards away. Bond calls the barman over and orders his signature dry martini:"Three measures of Gordon's, one of vodka, half a measure of Kina Lillet, shake it over ice then add a thin slice of lemon peel."

Several other players order the same and Bond scores a minor triumph in turning attention back to him. He then walks over to the bar and kisses Vesper to further infuriate Le Chiffre. Bond explains to Vesper and Mathis that he's discovered Le Chiffre's "tell" of twitching when he's bluffing. No matter that he won on the last card: that was blind luck. Bond also likes the martini he's just concocted and starts thinking of a name. Mathis, who's displayed a romantic side and taken a liking to Vesper, inquires if she's melted his cold heart yet.

During a break, Le Chiffre is accosted by Obanno, the rebel leader, in his hotel suite demanding his money. He threatens to chop off the arm of Le Chiffre's girlfriend with his machete and Le Chiffre doesn't even flinch. But Le Chriffre promises to return his money in the morning, putting more pressure on the poker match. Bond and Vesper hear the girl screaming while in the elevator and Bond rushes to her aid, taking on the rebel leader and his henchman in the stairwell. Bond shoots the henchman and goes hand-to-hand with Obanno, who tries to slash him with his machete. It's a brutal, bloody, claustrophobic fight, reminiscent of Bond's first kill. Vesper's scared to death and tries to hide. Bond has him in a choke hold as he tries to grab his Walther on the floor. Vesper tries to move the gun and Bond finally strangles him to death. Vesper's in shock but he sends her to find Mathis to clean up. Bond then stumbles into his suite and tries to compose himself and wipe the blood off. He stares at himself in the mirror, once again having difficulty with the killings.

Bond briefly returns to the game to let Le Chiffre know that he's in the for the poker fight of his life. But later that night, he finds Vesper cowering in the shower in their suite. Wearing bra and panties, with the water cascading on her, Bond rushes over and holds Vesper in his arms. It's a tender, emotionally naked moment, enhanced by the introduction of David Arnold's somber "Vesper" theme. There are definite echoes of *OHMSS*, including the water motif, which, of course, will have a horrifying payoff. "You're all wet," she remarks when noticing his presence. She tells him she couldn't even get the blood out from under her fingernails. He looks at her fingers and there's no trace of blood. He puts each finger in his mouth in a non-sexual act of kindness. "Better?" Then he turns on the hot water and they silently enjoy a strangely romantic interlude.

"Well, the shower sequence is key," Craig acknowledged. "That vulnerability she shows — she opens herself up and it's a shock to him. I don't think many people do that to him."

Bond gets an even bigger shock when he returns to the game. Convinced that Le Chiffre's bluffing, Bond bets everything on his full house, only to be fooled by the poker master, who draws four of a kind. Bond's devastated. Then he's infuriated when Vesper refuses to authorize the remainder of the money to buy back in. "I made a mistake," he admits. "I was impatient, maybe arrogant, but I can *beat* him." But Vesper's unconvinced. She thinks

he's all-ego and that beating Le Chiffre won't stop terrorism. He fumes and rushes into the bar. When the bartender asks if he wants his martini shaken or stirred, Bond replies, "Do I look like I give a damn?" It's a perfect example of turning a Bond convention on its head to reveal a character twist.

Out of desperation, Bond rushes to try and kill Le Chiffre with a knife, but is stopped by none other than Felix Leiter, who introduces himself and suggests it would be to their mutual benefit if he staked him the money to buy back in the game. Bond agrees to hand over Le Chiffre to the CIA in exchange for the winnings.

Just one more obstacle: Le Chiffre's girlfriend poisons Bond's martini. He staggers out of the casino and into the bathroom, where he induces vomiting, and then staggers out of the hotel and into his Aston Martin. He grabs the medipac from the glove compartment, jams the surgical needle into his arm, and attaches the lead from the box to his handheld. He contacts MI6 and a doctor attempts to walk him through using the portable defibrillator. M is alerted that Bond has gone into cardiac arrest. Bond follows the instructions, but when it comes time to press the red button for the charge, he notices that one of the leads has fallen off. Bond starts blacking out. But Vesper comes to his rescue by reattaching the lead and pressing the red button to revive him. When Bond comes to, he asks if *she's* all right. He composes himself and returns to the casino.

"Sorry, that last hand almost killed me," Bond mutters to Le Chiffre when resuming the game. Of course, back from the dead, Bond now has the confidence to beat Le Chiffre. Only this time, he does it with panache, letting Le Chiffre think his full house is better than Bond's flush. Except Bond has pulled a straight flush! A small red globule appears in the corner of Le Chiffre's eye, which he wipes away.

Bond's suddenly famished and celebrates with Vesper in the restaurant. "You know, I think I'll call this the Vesper," he says about his martini. "Because of the bitter aftertaste?" she replies. "Because after you've tasted it…it's all you want to drink." They both loosen up but she fidgets with her necklace. Bond tells her that he's figured out what it is: an Algerian love-knot. She pretends it isn't important.

He pretends that the killing doesn't affect him. Like Natalya in *GoldenEye*, she tries to convince him to leave his dangerous profession. But he turns the discussion back to her by suggesting there's something's driving her and that he hasn't a chance of ever finding out what it is.

Le Chiffre has no choice but to snatch Vesper and Bond gives chase in his Aston Martin, which he rolls to avoid hitting her in the middle of the road. When Bond awakens, he's in a warehouse; Vesper's taken to another room. Le Chiffre stands with a carpet beater in his hand; and Bond's dragged to a cane-bottomed chair. His hands and feet are bound. He then strikes Bond's genitals with the carpet beater and he screams in agony. Le Chiffre even plays the Vesper card: they will torture the account number out of her, but he needs the password from Bond. But Bond will not give in. His only recourse is humor: "I've got a little itch down there, would you mind?"

"I like black humor — always have," Craig revealed. "I know it's a British thing and a Scandinavian thing. I love the fact that it's under pressure making the joke — gallows humor — and

that's really what Bond was always to me. It's there even in this rather brutal torture scene. Bond may think he's going to die, but he doesn't want to lose. He likes making a joke when it's inappropriate and it gives him a kick, and, hopefully, that gives us a thrill."

Indeed, the humor not only makes the torture easier to watch, but also helps explain its importance as a defense mechanism. It's all part of Bond's test of wills with Le Chiffre, taking everything he sadistically dishes out: "Now you can tell all your friends that you died scratching my balls," he laughs. But Le Chiffre makes a crucial mistake in telling Bond that he's willing to divulge what he knows to MI6. That's enough to save Bond when Mr. White enters and shoots Le Chiffre ("Money isn't as valuable as knowing who to trust").

Bond convalesces at a clinic on the beautiful Lake Como in Italy accompanied by Vesper and Mathis. But he doesn't trust Mathis because Le Chiffre indicated that he was a double-agent. In fact, while conversing on a porch, Bond arranges for Mathis to be drugged and taken away for questioning by MI6.

**Producer Michael Wilson introduces Queen Elizabeth to Daniel Craig at the Royal Premiere of *Casino Royale* at the Odeon Leicester Square, Nov. 14, 2006.**

Bond and Vesper continue falling in love during his convalescence. "The truth is, you can have me anywhere," she declares in the garden. It turns out that his password for the Swiss bank account is "Vesper." He reveals a bigger surprise when baring his soul: "I have no armor left," he confesses. "You've stripped it from me. Whatever is left, whatever I am, I am yours." A few weeks later, they test how much he's recovered when attempting to have sex in his room, knocking over hospital equipment.

They escape to Venice with the money, and during their romantic sojourn aboard a yacht, Bond admits that he's ready to resign from MI6 and find an honest job: "Like you said, you do what I do for too long and there won't be any soul left to salvage." She even stops wearing her Algerian love-knot necklace, believing she can hide from the past. But when Vesper spots one of Mr. White's goons, everything falls apart. She takes the money and runs, and Bond gets a panic call from M about returning the money.

"At the beginning of the movie, I don't think he cares if he lives or dies," Craig revealed. "It's his job, it's what he does, and this woman blows his mind — absolutely exposes him and breaks his heart."

Bond races after Vesper (easy to spot in a striking red dress and an image inspired by *Don't Look Now*), and chases her down in a courtyard. He finds her handing over the money to some henchmen. He's torn between saving and killing her. He fires at them and they scatter into a renovated building along the Grand Canal. Bond follows them inside on a rampage. He shoots one through the eye with a construction nail gun. The gunfire splits the air bag at the bottom and the building starts creaking and sinking. Bond efficiently dispatches the others and the money floats away, but he finds Vesper trapped in a sinking elevator. Bond attempts to rescue her but she conveys how sorry she is and forces the gate closed. Then she drowns herself and Bond is powerless to stop her. Yet he refuses to give up. He pries open the door and drags her body to the surface. He tries to revive her outside but it's too late. Bond's both enraged and grief-stricken and cradles the lifeless Vesper in his arms over the plaintive love theme. Mr. White, who's retrieved the money, observes from above.

Again, the influence of *OHMSS* is unmistakable. You just know that in devising Vesper's demise the writers were influenced by Tracy's attempted drowning, and were fully aware of the parallels they were drawing with Bond's two tragic love stories. In fact, just like the book, the film version of *Casino Royale* now casts a shadow over *OHMSS*. As a result, there's more of a haunting quality to Bond's rescue of Tracy and a sense of doom about their fleeting romance — and her shocking death carries an even greater ironic sting. Likewise, the loss of Vesper shapes Bond's ambiguous attitude toward women: his attraction/repulsion, his need to rescue and abuse, his inevitable misogyny to protect himself.

In the meantime, Bond learns a painful lesson about getting too emotionally attached. He was unable to read the enigmatic Vesper and paid the price. Now he doesn't trust anyone and puts the mask back on, proclaiming, "The bitch is dead." While this pleases M, she also points out over the phone that Vesper was coerced into cooperating after they kidnapped her Algerian boyfriend, yet still sacrificed her life for Bond's.

"Vesper's soul is un-savable, or so it would appear, and so is his," Craig said. "I love that. I haven't thought about it too much. But maybe she feels she can't save her own but she can save his."

Besides, Vesper knows Bond well enough that he won't stop until he uncovers the truth. Therefore, she leaves a valuable number in her cell phone, which he discovers along with the necklace while going through her purse.

A car pulls up to the courtyard of a villa on Lake Como; the wily Mr. White gets out and answers his cell phone: "Who is it?" A shot explodes and hits his knee. He falls in agony but crawls to the front door leaving a trail of blood. A man steps in his path: It's Bond, dressed to kill, wearing a blue pinstripe suit (inspired by the classic suit worn in *Goldfinger*), and holding a submachine gun. He flip closes Vesper's cell phone: "The name's Bond. James Bond," he coldly utters. He then cracks a malevolent smile as "The James Bond Theme" unfolds for the first time over the end titles.

But Bond's rite of passage is far from over.

# QUANTUM OF SOLACE

After the great commercial and critical success of *Casino Royale*, the Bond team had no problem picking up the thread in a direct sequel, the first in franchise history. Besides, the 22nd Bond film cried out for a continuation with such a dramatic cliff-hanger: Bond's been betrayed by the love of his life, who's dead, and he's angry and confused. He believes their love was a lie after the way Vesper tricked him, and he needs to find out why. How could the great poker player have been fooled so easily? And what is the story behind this enigmatic femme fatale? Therefore, Bond needs to solve the mystery of Vesper as well as the mystery behind the secret organization that blackmailed her. At the same time, he needs closure so he can move on with his life and perform his job properly.

Of course, Fleming framed it perfectly at the end of the *Casino Royale* novel: "But now he would attack the arm that held the whip and the gun. The business of espionage could be left to the white collar boys. They could spy and catch the spies. He would go after the threat behind the spies, the threat that made them spy." Thus, Craig's Bond now has a similar mandate and sense of urgency. The title of Fleming's second novel even provided a fitting motto: "*Live and Let Die.*"

"We started off something with *Casino Royale*," Craig told me. "We had a great storyline; we had a novel by Ian Fleming that was solid; and had a really strong love story. And when it came time to shooting this movie, it was like, we can't just push that aside, we have to develop that — we have to tie up the loose ends. And that's what *Quantum of Solace* is about. He's not on a vendetta, he's not after revenge. He's after finding his place in the world and who his allies are."

However, Martin Campbell was not conducive to such navel-gazing, and so they went with a director totally outside the mainstream, Marc Forster, to turn Bond inside out. Like Michael Apted, Forster was not accustomed to big-budget franchise movies, but could provide emotional resonance, and a striking visual look. He not only directed *Monster's Ball*, the searing drama starring Halle Berry as the wife of a convicted murderer on death row, but also *Finding Neverland*, the gentle J.M. Barrie biopic starring Johnny Depp. Born in Germany but raised in Switzerland, Forster was the youngest director to helm a Bond film as well as the first not from the British Commonwealth. In fact, Forster was born in 1969, the same year that *OHMSS* was released, which, not surprisingly, happens to be his favorite Bond film.

Yet it was the humanistic appeal of *Casino Royale* that attracted Forster to Bond, who approached it as an art film. "It's interesting that you have someone who is an assassin and has lost someone and how this changes his perspective on killing," he told me. "What does that really mean? And Daniel Craig adds so much more humanity and vulnerability. He is someone we can finally relate to."

*Quantum of Solace* also evokes something loftier than the usual Bond title, even though it's culled from Fleming's off-beat short story in the *For Your Eyes Only* anthology. It's about a dinner conversation concerning "the amount of comfort" that's required for human relationships to survive, convincing Bond that people aren't as easy to read as he thought: "When they go wrong, when there's nothing left, when the spark has gone, when the fire's gone out, there's no quantum of solace," Craig explained. And afterward, a "bestial cruelty" is unleashed in the person hurt most by the relationship.

This provocative theme was applied to the Bond/Vesper story and serves as the subtext of the sequel. Bond turns inward and becomes a killing machine in search of the people responsible for turning Vesper against him. Yet because it's never formally addressed, the title left many viewers confused about its meaning.

But in functioning as a revenge story, there's no confusion about Bond confronting his dark side. Unlike *Licence to Kill*, though, *Quantum* avoids dragging Bond away completely because of its character arc. It also evokes the spirit of classic Ken Adam in Oscar-winning Dennis Gassner's (*Bugsy*) post-modern production design, using a pattern language based on Craig's striking blue eyes and "angular, chiseled, textured face." But since the conspiratorial plot hinges on the control of natural resources, Forster also symbolically focuses on air, water, fire, and earth. Indeed, each action set piece is built around one of these elements.

"One of the locations I chose is the desert," Forster explained. "He is lonely out there in this desolate place and doesn't know who he is. He's as much a mystery to himself as he is to the audience. Trust is the root of the story and what I tried to do is use the other characters to provide him with a different perspective, and, ultimately, at the end, give him a little self-awareness."

Here's a director specializing in emotionally repressed protagonists trying to make Bond implode. But despite the fact that Purvis and Wade were back laying the foundation and Haggis returned for a polish, the writing did not go as smoothly as *Casino Royale*. That's because the Writers Guild of America strike hit in 2007/2008, and Forster and Craig were pressed into substantial rewriting duties on set. Both have since voiced disappointment at *Quantum's* lack of narrative clarity and depth, but Craig has gone even further in suggesting that it was never intended to be such a direct sequel and failed to deliver what was expected of a Bond film.

Even so, *Quantum* effectively carries us through the completion of Bond's origin story. As such, it's really the second part of *Casino Royale* and works best when viewed together. Of course, *Quantum* has a completely different vibe: it moves like the speeding bullet fired from Bond's Walther in the main title sequence by MK12 (which reintroduces the erotically silhouetted girls frolicking in sand). No wonder it's the shortest Bond film at 106 minutes.

Speaking of guns, the first thing we notice is that there's no gun barrel opening (Bond's journey is not complete). Instead, we immediately jump to the pre-credit, in which Bond races in his Aston Martin from Lake Como to Siena, Italy. He's chased by some baddies and winds his way perilously through a quarry. They knock his door off, but Bond disposes of the last car with his submachine gun, running them off the cliff. Then arrives at a safe house and pops the trunk. Mr. White cringes from all the excitement. "It's time to get out."

Bond looks totally drained when gulping down a scotch. He gets a stern lecture from M about the messy way he's handled the situation. She also informs him that Vesper's boyfriend, Yusef Kabira, was allegedly murdered, but that a DNA check of his wallet and ID didn't match a lock of his hair found in Vesper's apartment. "I wouldn't have thought Vesper the sentimental type," Bond gripes. "Well, we never really know anyone, do we?" M cautions. Ironically, this applies to her as well since she no longer trusts Bond again. She tells him he'd be a "pretty cold bastard" if he didn't seek revenge. On the one hand, Bond tries to reassure M that he has no interest in finding the boyfriend, while on the other he snatches his photo and stuffs it in his pocket.

During Mr. White's interrogation, he teases Bond that they would've killed him if it weren't for Vesper and that his love for her betrayed him. M threatens the baddie with torture and he merely cackles at how clueless they are about his organization. "And the truth is, you don't even know we exist," he suggests. "Well, we do now, Mr. White, and we're quick learners," M counters. "Oh, really? Well, then, the first thing you should know about us is that we have people everywhere. Am I right?"

Mr. White turns to Mitchell (Glenn Foster), M's bodyguard, who open fires. M drops to the ground and Bond chases after Mitchell in the confusion through the cisterns. They emerge outside during the running of the Palio di Siena horse race, and now two frantic chases occur in parallel, with Mitchell shooting bystanders that are in his way. Then, after entering an apartment building, they knock over a bowl of cherries (symbolic of the bloodshed) when racing to the roof, where they continue the chase on the tiled rooftops throughout the city. Like the Madagascar chase in *Casino Royale*, Bond gets bumped around, particularly when leaping from a window onto a bus. When Bond finally catches Mitchell, they smash through the roof of an art gallery and get entangled in the construction scaffolding. While Bond precariously hangs from the ropes, reaching for his gun, Mitchell struggles to grab his weapon on the scaffolding above. Bond wins the race and blasts the traitor in a close-up revealing that malevolent look.

Bond meets up with M in Mitchell's London apartment. She's aghast at how ubiquitous this organization is and yet they've never heard of them. But even her sarcasm doesn't reach Bond: he remains emotionless. Back at MI6 headquarters, redesigned with a smart room containing a large electronic table with touch screens and graphical user interface, they trace Le Chiffre's money laundering activities to an operative named Slate in Haiti. M displays more hands-on involvement in MI6's high-tech surveillance activities.

Bond breaks into Slate's hotel room and the baddie takes him by surprise. But Bond quickly recovers and overtakes him in a brutal, *Bourne*-like fight, which ends on the balcony, where Bond coldly stabs Slate in the jugular and watches him die (talk about "bestial cruelty"). Many have criticized *Quantum* for appropriating too much of the jarring *Bourne* style. True enough, but there's no lack of clarity here and we can feel the pain of the blows.

On his way out, Bond luckily grabs a package intended for Slate at the front desk. Outside, he's picked up by a young and attractive Latin American woman, Camille (Olga Kurylenko), who mistakes him for Slate. They drive off in her car and are immediately followed by a man on a motorcycle, and Bond realizes that Slate was hired to kill her. Camille pulls a gun on Bond and he jumps out. He knocks the man off his motorcycle, and follows her to a harbor hideaway, observing from afar.

Camille storms past edgy-looking henchman, Elvis (Anatole Taubman), sporting a bowl cut, and confronts her lover, Dominic Greene, calmly checking receipts. Although you couldn't guess by his slight appearance, Greene's the super baddie, played by acclaimed Frenchman Mathieu Amalric (*The Diving Bell and the Butterfly*). And that's the point: Greene's very inconspicuous and so is his cover as a prominent businessman and environmentalist. But he represents a new kind of Bond villain whose evil ambiguously resides beneath the surface. Greene operates like a master politician, charming his way among the powerful elite, making corrupt deals behind the scenes, and staging military coups.

But Greene's also a pitiful weasel. He authorized the hit on Camille because he caught her arranging a secret meeting with one of his disloyal geologists, whose corpse floats in the water. They pretend to kiss and make up, but Greene still distrusts her. He tells her that disloyalty makes it feel like "ants under his skin," and describes how he took an iron to one of his mother's piano students as a youngster when he overheard her saying nasty things about him.

With the arrival of exiled Bolivian General Medrano (Joaquin Cosio), Greene suddenly realizes that Camille was only sleeping with him to get to Medrano. Greene and his organization have been overthrowing Third World governments in exchange for control of their natural resources, and they've arranged to do the same in Bolivia and put Medrano back in power as a sympathetic ally. What Greene desires in return is a seemingly barren piece of desert. Medrano claims there's no oil to be found there. Undeterred, Greene sweetens the deal by throwing in Camille if he will dispose of her. It turns out that Camille is also Bolivian and that Medrano knew her late parents.

But Bond immediately senses danger when Camille boards Medrano's vessel. What he doesn't realize is that she's plotting to kill him. She misses her opportunity, though, when Bond drives a trail bike over several fishing craft and steals a small power boat and rams Medrano's vessel. During the collision, he scrambles aboard and grabs Camille and takes off in another power boat. She puts up resistance before realizing that Bond's not associated with Greene. An elaborate battle ensues that's much tougher than the *Live and Let Die* boat chase. The sequence certainly lacks clarity but one can make the case that the disorientation evokes Bond's state of mind. Medrano's men attack from several inflatable dinghies, and Camille gets knocked unconscious after hitting her head, but Bond violently wipes out a boat by driving straight over it and then skillfully uses an anchor to take out the last one and make his escape.

In a throwback to Connery, Bond carries the

unconscious Camille off the boat and plops her into the arms of an unsuspecting dock worker ("She's seasick"). Bond then calls MI6 to get some intel on Greene. M's already peeved that he killed Slate, but is intrigued after her call to the CIA gets transferred to the South American section chief, Beam (David Harbour), who tells her they have no interest in Greene. Why would Beam take the call if Greene was so inconsequential? M immediately learns from Tanner that Greene is bound for Bregenz, Austria, and instructs Bond to follow him but to refrain from killing every potential lead.

By sheer coincidence, Beam and Felix escort Greene and his henchmen on the plane. Greene has arranged for the CIA to look the other way in Bolivia in exchange for the lease on any oil found. Felix sits silently with a sullen look of disapproval. Then Greene asks Beam to ID a photo of Bond on his cell phone. Beam draws a blank and passes the phone to Felix, who refuses to help them. However, it's a test of Felix's loyalty because Beam immediately informs Greene that it's Bond of British Intelligence. Greene asks Beam to dispose of Bond for him, which he agrees to do. After they land, Felix complains about working with the corrupt Greene. "Yeah, you're right. We should just deal with nice people," Beam scoffs. He warns Felix about being a team player for the sake of his career.

Bond hits the jackpot: Greene and his fellow associates hide in plain sight at a lavish staging of *Tosca* on the floating stage at Bregenz. The Puccini opera's the perfect metaphor for seeing and being seen, capped by the central image of the giant blue eye symbolic of Bond. *Tosca* also refers back to *Casino Royale* with its violent depiction of torture, murder, and suicide.

First, Bond kills one of the members in the men's room of the lobby and steals his goody bag with Q insignia and electronic earpiece. Bond carries himself more confidently in a tux, listening intently to the meeting about the Tierra Project in Bolivia and Quantum's desire to control the world's most precious resource. This is obviously a much more modern, realistic version of SPECTRE, comprised of terrorists, corporations, and governments: a shadow organization that hides behind the mask of respectability. However, when a Brit, later identified as Guy Haines, an advisor to the British Prime Minister, questions the importance of the Tierra Project, Bond sarcastically interrupts: "I really think you people should find a better place to meet."

The members quickly and quietly disperse, now that they've been compromised, as Bond photographs them one by one with his smart phone, sending the files back to MI6. But Mr. White calmly stays seated with his date ("Well, *Tosca* isn't for everyone"). Bond stares down Greene in the corridor before making his escape, shooting his way through the restaurant and kitchen, where a fire starts, intercut with violent scenes from the opera in another artful example of parallel action (beautifully photographed by longtime Forster cinematographer Roberto Schaefer). Then Bond holds a burly goon at gunpoint on the roof, who tells him to "piss off." Bond tries to interrogate him, but is forced to push him off the roof (recalling the Sandor rooftop death in *Spy*). He lands safely on Greene's car, who orders him killed so he can't ID him.

Tanner informs M while she's drawing her bath of the various Quantum members they've ID'd: a former minister of Siberia, a telecom giant and former Mossad member, and Haines. She asks to be connected to Bond, but Tanner then relates the bad news that it appears 007 killed Haines' body guard, a member of Special Branch. When M gets Bond on the phone, she orders him to come in for debriefing. "And I would, but right now I need to find the man who tried to kill you," he replies. "Go back to sleep." We find a companion, in fact, asleep in her bed.

M terminates Bond's status and he has nowhere else to turn but to Mathis, who reluctantly greets him at his new Italian villa. Apparently Bond misjudged his ally, who wasn't a double-agent after all, and MI6 reimbursed him for his troubles.

"Come to apologize?" he asks. In a scene inspired by "The Nature of Evil" chapter in *Casino Royale*, the melancholy Mathis finds it odd that he's the only one Bond can trust. "But I guess when one's young, it seems very easy to distinguish between right and wrong. But as one gets older, it becomes more difficult. The heroes and the villains get all mixed up." Mathis then mourns the passing of

Vesper, telling Bond that she loved him and died for him, echoing M. But the wound's still too fresh for Bond.

He pulls out the Quantum photos and Mathis is familiar with all the players, so Bond takes Mathis with him to Bolivia, where he knows the lay of the political land. During the plane ride, however, they grow closer together. The "Vesper" theme plays while Bond nurses a martini and glances at the photo of Vesper and her boyfriend and the necklace. Mathis wanders over and Bond hides the evidence of his sentimentality. Mathis asks what he's drinking and Bond turns to the bartender, who recites the ingredients of the Vesper martini. Bond is on his sixth. Mathis wants to know what's keeping him awake: "I was wondering why you came with me?"Bond asks. "It takes something to admit you were wrong," Mathis replies. It's an important emotional breakthrough for Bond.

At the airport, Bond and Mathis are met by Strawberry Fields (Gemma Arterton), a spunky, retro-looking redhead from the consulate, who's come to escort Bond back home. Bond drags her with them to one hotel. But after one look at its modest accommodations, he turns right around and takes a lavish suite at the finest hotel in town, pretending to be teachers on sabbatical that have just won the lottery.

Bond then quickly melts her resistance in bed, attentively kissing her on the back. Fields feels guilty enough as it is when Bond tells her they're going to a party and that he's buying her a new dress. It's the first time that Bond has slept with someone since Vesper, but he has no qualms about using Fields to take his mind off his troubles and get to Greene without further interference.

Although she refuses to tell Bond her first name, Fields proves useful at the fundraiser for Greene's Tierra Project. In a persuasive speech, Greene blames the government for a severe water drought. While

**Daniel Craig and Director Marc Forster discuss the desert scene while filming *Quantum of Solace*. Forster wanted action sequences involving earth, air, water, and fire.**

Mathis has a drink with an old friend that's head of Bolivian police, Carlos (Fernando Guillen Cuervo), Bond rescues Camille from Greene after she tries to sabotage his fundraising activities. However, when Elvis tries to intercede, Fields trips him down a flight of stairs, pretending to be a ditzy drunk. But Greene can't resist picking apart Bond's character: "As MI6 says, he's difficult to control. Nice way of saying that everything he touches seems to wither and die."

In the car, Bond finally enlists the feisty Camille's support in bringing down Greene when she admits "there's something horribly efficient" about 007. Unfortunately, tragedy strikes again when the police pull them over and Bond discovers Mathis in the trunk. He's been brutally beaten and Bond is forced to use him as a human shield when the two officers fire at him. After killing both of them, Bond cradles Mathis in his arms. "Do we forgive each other?" Mathis asks. "I shouldn't have left you alone," Bond admits. "Vesper," Mathis whispers. "She gave everything for you. Forgive her. Forgive yourself." Mathis dies in Bond's arms. He was sentimental about friendship, love, and trust. It's the only currency that matters. But right now, Bond's survival mode kicks in. He places the corpse of Mathis in a dumpster and takes his money. Camille doesn't understand his coldness. "He wouldn't care," Bond explains.

Bond charters an old Douglas DC-3 aircraft and they survey the region Greene has earmarked for the Tierra Project. Camille tells him the geologist found proof that Greene was hiding something. We notice a difference in Bond — he starts opening up. When Camille asks him about his interest in Greene, he tells her that he tried to kill a friend of his. She guesses that it's a woman. Bond tells her it's not what

**Director Marc Forster watches Mathieu Amalric, Olga Kurylenko, and Daniel Craig perform a read through of the party scene while filming *Quantum of Solace*.**

she thinks. "Your mother?" she teases. "She likes to think so," he admits.

After spotting some sinkholes, however, they're attacked by an enemy fighter plane and Bond finds himself in a dogfight that pays homage to *North by Northwest*. Bond tries flying through a canyon to lose him, and eventually the swelling smoke from the DC-3 forces the other plane to crash in the side of a hill. However, a helicopter pops up and cripples them during the attack. Bond goes into a steep climb and they escape from the rear with only one parachute between them. They crash land in one of the sinkholes.

Meanwhile, M meets with the angry British Secretary of State (Tim Pigott-Smith), who echoes the CIA's Beam. Secret organization or not, they're in bed with Greene out of necessity for oil and Bond must be pulled in or the CIA "will put him down."

During a brief respite in the sinkhole, Bond continues to probe Camille to get his mind off Vesper. She reveals that Medrano killed her father because he was part of the opposition. She watched him shoot her father and then rape her mother and older sister. Then he set fire to their house but she survived and has sworn vengeance ever since. Bond apologizes for interrupting her assassination attempt on the boat. "It seems we're both using Greene to get to somebody," Bond concludes. "You catch whoever did it?" she wonders. "No, not yet," he replies. "Tell me when you do. I'd like to know how it feels," she mournfully wonders. So much for losing himself in Camille — there's no hiding from Vesper. But the painful lesson of Camille is that vengeance is an emotional dead end.

Ironically, Bond gets a break when they stumble upon a hidden dam in a *Chinatown*-like conspiracy to monopolize the water supply. But there's hell to pay when they return to the hotel. Bond gets a note at the front desk from Fields telling him to run away, and he instructs Camille to wait for him. He cautiously enters the suite and discovers M and several agents. After making sure that Camille is left out of it, he has it out with M about selling him out to the Americans for oil.

But Bond doesn't realize the severity of the problem until he discovers Fields' corpse on the bed drenched in crude oil. In a strange homage to *Goldfinger*, Bond is forced to confront his reckless behavior. M lectures him about being blinded by "inconsolable rage." She says, "When you can't tell your friends from your enemies, it's time to go." When Bond protests, M blames him for the needless death of Fields and ties her to Vesper: "Look how well your charm works, James. They'll do anything for you, won't they?"

But notice how M addresses him as "James." He's as much a son to her as a subordinate. She suspends him again and takes away his Walther. But Bond dispatches his colleagues in the elevator and doubles back and startles M in the corridor. He demands that she cite Fields' bravery in her report, and declares that they need to both see this through together. M realizes that she misjudged him and helps him escape. But when Tanner warns M, she throws caution to the wind: "He's my agent and I trust him. Go on."

Camille picks up Bond outside the hotel and he calls Felix and arranges a quick rendezvous at a local bar. Bond has 30 seconds to prove he's trustworthy and they both realize they're fighting for the same side. Felix tells Bond where he can find Greene and Medrano in the desert. "Thank you, Felix." "James, move your ass." Bond barely escapes the CIA ambush.

However, the desolate image of Bond in the desert with Camille says it all: Despite the terrible toll that betrayal and revenge have taken, he's on a mission to recover his soul. Bond skillfully shows her how to reassemble a gun and tenderly explains what she needs to do to kill Medrano: "Your training will tell you that when the adrenaline kicks in you should compensate. But part of you is not going to believe the training because this kill is personal. Take a deep breath. You only need one shot. Make it count."

At the golden, ultra-modern Eco hotel powered by fuel cells, Greene oversees the payoff and exchange of power between Carlos and Medrano. Of course, the sleazy Medrano momentarily balks when Greene springs the surprise about Quantum owning 60% of the water supply and that he will now pay double for utilities. But Quantum owns him and he has no choice.

Bond infiltrates the hotel with a bang, shooting Carlos on his way out for betraying their mutual friend, Mathis, while Camille makes her way to Medrano's room, where he rapes a young worker. The building rapidly goes up in flames, killing Elvis and forcing Greene to flee. Camille struggles with Medrano before stabbing him in the crotch and getting her revenge.

Bond catches up to Greene, who lunges at him with an axe like a wild animal, as they're enveloped in flames. It's an ugly fight but Bond gets a break when Greene accidentally stabs himself in the foot. But instead of letting Greene die, Bond lifts him up by the head and puts him down. Then he rushes after Camille, who's trapped by the fire and haunted by childhood memories of Medrano's force of evil. Bond cradles her in his arms and prepares to take one shot. She thinks he's going to put her out of her misery, and reminds him to "take a deep breath" and "make it count." However, Bond fires and causes an explosion, which blows a hole in the wall so they can escape.

Then Bond goes after Greene in one of the vehicles. After interrogating the baddie off-screen, Bond lets him out. Greene told him what he wanted to know about Quantum, and Bond gives him a can of motor oil and leaves him to die in the desert.

Bond drives Camille back to town and says goodbye. She complains about feeling unsatisfied: "Now what?" Bond suggests she help destroy Greene's operation in Bolivia. "Do you think they'll be able to sleep now?" she asks. "I don't think the dead care about vengeance," Bond concludes. They warmly kiss and Camille tells Bond that she wishes she could set him free but that his prison is inside his head. She's the first primary Bond girl that he doesn't have sex with.

Bond travels to dark and snowy Kazan, Russia, where he sits and waits for Vesper's boyfriend, Yusef (Simon Kassianides), to return home with his latest victim, a Canadian agent named Corrine (Stana Katic). It's similar to the Dryden scene at the opening of *Casino Royale*, only we don't know what to expect. However, he gently explains the trap to Corrine, showing the necklace he has that's just like hers. He then instructs her to return home because

he has "unfinished business" with this man. Yusef looks pitiful alone with Bond. He begs him to make it quick.

Bond calmly walks outside and joins M. She's surprised to learn that he didn't kill Yusef and they have a lovely exchange about trust and self-awareness: "Did you find what you were looking for?" she asks. "Yes." "Good. I assume you have no regrets." "I don't. What about you?" "Of course not — that would be unprofessional."

Bond has finally learned to take his ego out of the equation. But M's curious if he knows anything about the death of Greene, who was found in the desert with two bullets in his head and motor oil in his stomach. Bond shrugs and says he can't be of any help. But Bond's pleased to hear that Felix has been promoted.

Then Bond makes an extraordinary admission: "Congratulations, you were right," he confesses. "About what?" "About Vesper," he replies. They say goodbye and he starts to walks away. "I need you back," M declares. He turns around. "I never left," he reveals. He turns and walks away and M watches compassionately. The necklace lies in the snow as the "Vesper" theme plays. We stay on his blank face. At last, Bond has been set free.

Appropriately, the gun barrel finally appears over the "Bond Theme." But Craig moves faster than his predecessors. The barrel rifling is entirely new with grooves set farther apart, and, for the first time, Bond walks out of frame, inside the red Q that forms the film's title. "That was the scariest bit," Craig admitted. "We did it twice. We did it once and it didn't work. And I thought it has to be right, it has to be aggressive, and it has to work."

With Bond's rite of passage complete, he's solidified his relationships, attained his quantum of solace, and knows what's expected of him. "I think what we've got to keep doing is inventing new questions," Craig suggested. "There are characteristic guidelines that you have to adhere to because it's a Bond movie. And we try and do that, but within the parameters of that, you mess it up, and that's the challenge and exciting thing about doing this."

James Bond Will Return in *Skyfall*…

# LOOKING AHEAD TO *SKYFALL*

It's been four years since *Quantum of Solace* — the longest break for an existing actor. But it appears that the delay has benefitted Craig's third outing as Bond (thanks to MGM's prolonged bankruptcy and new Spyglass ownership, and the extra attention paid to the script by Purvis & Wade and *Rango* and *Hugo* scribe John Logan). He appears older, shrewder, and more comfortable in his own skin — and the most grizzled Bond ever pointing his trusty Walther in a neon-lit Shanghai club. It's an exquisite fusion of ultra-modern and retro. As Craig says, he's "Bond with a capital B."

Indeed, *Skyfall* melds into a serious and classical hybrid, with a grim-faced Bond also sporting a shorter haircut and gray suit along with the return of the silver Aston Martin DB5 (bearing the same license plate as the original incarnation from *Goldfinger*: BMT 216A).

But make no mistake: Craig's Bond is not unshakable. That's the way he was set up in *Casino Royale*, with his unclean first kill and the Vesper betrayal, and that's the way Craig wants him to continue. Yet it's also clear that Connery and Craig represent the two pillars of Bond: one effortless; the other fallible. But now that Craig's Bond is fully formed, he's come full circle. How fitting for the 50th anniversary of *Dr. No*.

Craig even cites *From Russia with Love* and *Live and Let Die* as major influences. That's not surprising since the former's his favorite Bond film and the latter's the first Bond he ever saw in a theater. It just so happens, that *Live and Let Die* was also *Skyfall* director Sam Mendes' introduction to Bond as well.

"I vividly remember the first time I saw one of the Bond movies, which was *Live and Let Die*, and the impact it had on me," Mendes regaled at the London press conference in November 2011. "But there was something else, which was, frankly... I got very excited when I saw my friend, Daniel, play James Bond in *Casino Royale*, and I thought it opened up all sorts of wonderful possibilities for the character."

However, even though *From Russia with Love* and *Live and Let Die* seem worlds apart, the opening passage from the *Live and Let Die* novel certainly shares a post Vesper vibe with *Skyfall*: "There are... occasions when he takes refuge in good living to efface the memory of danger and the shadow of death...."

To be sure, Wilson and Broccoli have pushed the action-centric drama in making Bond their own, securing the prominent Mendes, who, like Marc Forster, specializes in repressed characters but on a more mythic scale. Mendes goes back and forth between the British stage and Hollywood screen, and won the Oscar his first time out for *American Beauty* (1999) before working with Craig on his follow-up, *Road to Perdition*. But while Craig was certainly instrumental in persuading Mendes to helm *Skyfall*, he was actually first approached to direct *Die Another Day*. Mendes admitted to me a decade ago that he was flattered but that it just wasn't the right fit. It's funny how things have turned out with Craig becoming Bond and Mendes engineering the film that will likely define his legacy.

Mendes has assembled a *Skyfall* cast to die for: Oscar winner Javier Bardem plays a much more nuanced and nimble baddie; French actress/model Bérénice Marlohe co-stars as the glamorous and enigmatic Séverine; Naomie Harris appears as the rough-and-tumble field agent Eve; Ralph Fiennes portrays a government official; Ben Whishaw (who previously teamed with Craig in *Layer Cake* and starred in the British espionage series, *The Hour*) reintroduces a youngish Q; Helen McCrory (*Potter's* Narcissa Malfoy) introduces Clair Dowar, a member of Parliament; Rory Kinnear returns as a more active Tanner; and Albert Finney appears as Kincade, who has a fondness for 19th century English firearms. Ironically, Finney got his break as the angry young man in *Saturday Night and Sunday Morning* (1960), executive produced by Harry Saltzman, and later rose to stardom as the affable rogue in the Oscar-winning *Tom Jones* (1963), thanks to an assist from the popularity of Bond.

Mendes has also surrounded himself with several of his regular below-the-line collaborators: the great cinematographer Roger Deakins, who shoots the first digital Bond; production designer Dennis Gassner, returning from *Quantum* to expand his Craig-inspired pattern language; and composer Thomas Newman, who has scored all but one of the director's previous films, providing a sense of melancholy. In *Skyfall*, we follow Bond from London's Whitehall district of supreme political power to such exotic locales as Shanghai, Istanbul (an obvious nod to *FRWL*), and the wilds of Scotland (the ancestral home of Bond and Connery country).

Indeed, Bond finally returns home for refuge in the 23rd film. But the focus shifts to M for the first time when MI6 is attacked and she's implicated. In a dramatic reversal, though, it's Bond who must now protect his boss while uncovering her dark past to destroy the threat. What a culmination that should make. "I don't think I'll get a grip on who M is, or who anyone is who works in my office, either," Dench teased at the press conference.

While Wilson suggests they are continuing down the same path as *Casino Royale*, with even more of an emphasis on the early Connery films, Mendes assures us that *Skyfall* is not a direct continuation of the Quantum thread. This means that Bond's mission to destroy the new SPECTRE will have to wait. On the other hand, there has been rampant speculation that Blofeld might be reintroduced once again to match wits with Bond.

"Well, maybe. I think, if we set it up right," Craig mused. "But the great thing about the Blofeld character is if he's done right, as in the early Bonds, it's not that he's mad for the sake of power: the madness is a psychosis for anybody who's got that much power — that craziness. If done properly, it could be fantastic. He's one of the great movie villains."

Of course, it's all well and good to get more serious, with baddies lurking both inside and outside of MI6, but Bond is not George Smiley or Jason Bourne. He obviously rises above the rest with his unique mixture of action and humor.

"We're in a fantasy world here and that must remain constant because people come to see a Bond movie for that very reason," Craig stressed. "And that's why we owe it to make sure that the world we create is something out of the ordinary. And as long as you're on that level of fantasy, you can have as much reality as you want. We can hit you with the hardcore and we can hit you with the toughness."

Does this mean that Craig's Bond can relax more and start enjoying his work? "Daniel really understands the character very well now and how he plays in the scenes," Wilson interjected. "His interpretation is pretty much from the Fleming books. He's very focused on keeping it consistent and coming up with surprises."

But Craig maintains that you have to resist the temptation to raise the jeopardy with gadgets. "And that's maybe why they went the way they did with a lot of the Bond movies," he added. "But we've gotta find a way to make that work each time as opposed to making it… I don't want to get lazy about this. I don't think of myself as a lazy actor. When I leave this one day, I want to leave something that's gonna last a bit because that's the way I look at the work I've done. And I'm not scared of gadgets; we just have to get them in there in the right way. And with reason: not a gadget for gadget's sake. They shouldn't rule the movie. If they're not more than window dressing, then we're doing something wrong."

Speaking of gadgets, the sight of a potentially armed Aston Martin in full chase mode in Glencoe, Scotland, should delight generations of Bond fans weaned on Connery. At the same time, with Whishaw's Q now younger than Bond, this should make for an interesting new dynamic: a kind of sibling rivalry. Then again, the prospect of Bond reporting to a male superior would certainly restore a sense of classicism.

Both Craig and Mendes are adamant that the Bonds remain event films, family experiences, passed down from generation to generation like a ritual: the ultimate in cinematic comfort food. "I think it is still possible to make a big, entertaining, fabulous, glamorous movie and yet at the same time to say something about the world that we're living in," Mendes declared in his *Skyfall* videoblog.

Therefore, the great challenge of *Skyfall* is adding

layers of social realism while still keeping it Bond. Perhaps screenwriter Logan has the right approach in thinking of Bond as a continuum. Why, the generational pairing of Finney and Dench alone should take us back to the Cold War and provide another link to the early Bond films.

"It has nothing to do with being a standalone film, as far as I'm concerned," Logan told Collider. com (Nov. 27, 2011), "because I don't think these films are standalone, I think they're part of a legacy. When I was working on it, I was deeply aware as much of *Quantum of Solace* and *Casino Royale* as I was of *Thunderball*, as I was of Ian Fleming in the fifties writing it, you know you're a float in a parade. What was particularly thrilling about this is the freedom, because I had the fear that you would going into a franchise movie that you have to put all the toys back in the sandbox, but I've never felt anything but completely free as a writer to explore different material, to explore different ideas with these characters and this world."

Craig views his contribution thus far as providing a vital emotional context for Bond's actions: "I want to make sure that we continue questioning," Craig observed. "And, of course, the story will take over, but hopefully that will become a different experience. It's a really good place to start. The books are good, Connery set the movies up and probably gave them what they needed to last a long time, and the Broccoli/Saltzman partnership put the money on the screen. They put Bond on location, they made him stylish, and it's given it this impetus that's lasted this long. And Michael and Barbara love this franchise and protect it fiercely. And it's an unusual situation, but it's a very exciting situation as far as filmmaking is concerned."

We'll know soon enough what happens in *Skyfall*. And as long as Bond continues, *James Bond Unmasked* Will Return.

# CONVERSATIONS WITH THE BONDS

My journalistic journey with Bond actually started with an assignment for the *Los Angeles Times* to interview Pierce Brosnan and Michael Apted about *The World Is Not Enough* in 1999. I was intrigued about the new serious direction implicit in Apted's presence. Little did I realize at the time how involved I would become in covering Bond and what a serious turn the franchise would take with the coming of Daniel Craig as the sixth 007.

As you might expect, my interviews with the actors were thrilling adventures: Connery was charming and gracious and full of pride in reminiscing about his legendary creation, with only a hint of bitterness when discussing the business side. He was also quite humble in giving most of the credit to director Terence Young. George Lazenby was accessible for coffee at Starbucks in LA and revealing about his one shot at Bond, which made him a shooting star that quickly burned out. Roger Moore was affable and cagey over the phone. Not surprisingly, he was more

comfortable being anecdotal about the off-camera fun than getting analytical about playing Bond. Timothy Dalton was engaging and thoughtful in his analysis of being Bond at the Chateau Marmont in LA, providing an overview that would serve me well with this book. Pierce Brosnan was candid and generous in a series of interviews that spanned his last two films. It was instructive discussing the end of his tenure and then segueing to Craig's start as Bond. Craig was especially game with my speculative line of questioning when we met at the New York press junket for *Casino Royale*. By contrast, he was more curt and guarded in our second meeting in LA for *Quantum of Solace*. But then that was a quick roundtable setting rather than a relaxed one on one. I look forward to finding out all about his continuing evolution in *Skyfall*. I've included the transcripts so you can enjoy the full extent of their insights and the flavor of our conversations.

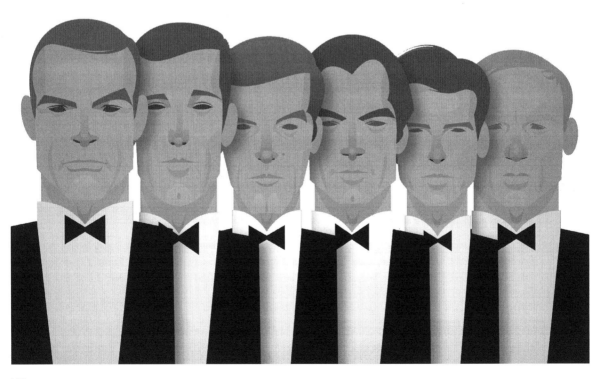

# Sean Connery

**Did you ever think Bond would last this long?**

No, I didn't. And anyone who says he did is a liar. Of course, it's gone through a lot of changes with the others actors.

**What accounts for the longevity?**

I think a great deal to do with the initial success was that it came somewhat after the "kitchen sink" dramas. It was refreshing and it had a certain kind of style, although it didn't cost anything because we only had a million to make the picture. And the idea that it was boosted by the popularity of *Dr. No*. And the fact that *From Russia with Love* was President Kennedy's favorite novel helped it as well. They were exciting and funny, and had good stories and pretty girls and intriguing locations. And it didn't take anything for granted.

**How responsible were you for the humor? You didn't seem to take it too seriously.**

Well, I took it seriously on one level, which was one had to be menacing, one had to be strong enough to do all this stuff. Or seem old enough to do it. And the humor was one element that was missing from the books of Fleming himself. And I knew Terence Young. I had done a dreadful film with him before called *Action of the Tiger*. And we did share a great deal of the same humor. When we went down to the islands to make *Dr. No*, and we got the script daily with all the scenes and what have you, Terence's contributions were enormous because he was always a great bon vivant. He was very much up on the latest shirts and blazers and was very elegant himself — whether he had money or not — and all the clubs and that kind of establishment. And also he understood what looked good — the right cut of suits and all that stuff, which I must say was not that particularly interesting for me. But he got me a rack of clothes and, as they say, could get me to look convincingly dangerous in the act of playing it. So it was a combination.

**How long was it fun playing Bond?**

Well, it was fun on *Dr. No* and *From Russia with Love*, which is a sad one in a way because we found out during the making of the picture that Pedro Armendariz was terminally ill [with cancer] and wanted to finish the film, so we changed everything around and it was a very strong, wonderful character. And it took a long time to shoot the film. And the next film was *Goldfinger*. That was quite fun too because I got to learn how to play golf. Then *Thunderball* started to become a problem, not because of the film per se, but because they committed from then on before they ever had the script ready. They were always looking for the next picture coming out, which is rather like the studios do now. And it's very expensive because you have to get a date for an opening and it's working ass-backwards. And I found that a demand on my time — the films got longer, like 18 weeks on a movie, or 20. This one [*The League of Extraordinary Gentlemen*] is like that because it's unavoidable because of what happened in Prague with the [flood]. But a great deal of this stuff like on *You Only Live Twice* where we were in Japan for months was ridiculous. We had the wrong time of the year when we got there; it was stormy. To get the script of a movie right, that's the first thing, and then you accommodate it by the time to go there. You don't have to shoot a lot of other stuff, or go at the wrong time and accommodate the weather. And that was the one thing. The other was we kept moving the goal posts because they couldn't commit to a definite date, and I was having to turn down work because I was contractually committed to doing the movies. And eventually I just wanted out. So I said *Diamonds Are Forever* would be the last one. But I was already getting disenchanted. Apart from the payment, which was puerile, they were bringing in a lot of science fiction stuff. You know, the stuff like the [shoe in *From Russia with Love*], or you follow somebody in a car because they had that gizmo under the bonnet, all these kinds of things, which today are commonplace and you can actually buy in a shop, they were a little bit ahead of their time. Well, that I didn't mind. It's when you get into nuclear stuff and launchings.

**What's your favorite Bond film?**

I think the one that worked for my money the best was *From Russia with Love*. And *Goldfinger*. Again, they were quite refreshing, I think, because of timing initially. And *Dr. No* cost [so little]. They are exorbitant now like everything. And they'll still be planned the same way.

**What were some of the differences between the three directors you worked with: Young, Guy Hamilton, and Lewis Gilbert?**

It's quite interesting, actually, because they're three directors with entirely different films. I think you have to give the credit to Terence because he was the first one. He molded it. The others went along after him. Guy Hamilton was very much in the mold of Carol Reed. He worked as an assistant to him and he was very conscious of certain thriller stuff.

**On the other hand, he had a lot of gadgets to deal with, right?**

Yeah, and so did Lewis Gilbert on *You Only Live Twice*. He had lots. He had the helicopter. There was another thing. The initial team had Ken Adam, who really was an exceptional talent.

**And what about Peter Hunt?**

Yes, the editor. Again, if the director hasn't shot it, the editor can't really edit it. They were just three different types.

**But there was a smooth transition with each one once you figured out their style?**

Well, once you had done the first two, you just moved forward because the rules were established. One wound up doing less and less as it were, because you did what you were expected to do and whatever else only up to a point. I think if anyone maybe Timothy made the mistake of thinking that it was going to be easier than it is. You have to work very hard to make something look easy. The movement, the fights, and whatever else are certain absurd situations.

**And it must've been hard moving back and forth for you?**

Well, I had done five films by then of the same character, and each one had become more and more successful; it's very difficult not to be influenced by that. So what was tried in the other films, as I say, the windows weren't that open because stop dates and start dates, and considerations because of the length of time.

**Even after you left Bond it was still a struggle to move on?**

And also not always successful. *The Man Who Would Be King* was not successful because of a bollixed job by Columbia and that happy to see bankrupt company called Allied Artists. They had the film in the U.S. and Columbia had it abroad, which is going in two different directions. And eventually it became recognized as a really marvelous film. It looks as good now on DVD as anything that's made.

**What do you think the Bond franchise needs to keep it fresh?**

Well, go back into the intrigue of the stories. You still always have to have some stunts and that links up the story, but make them more what people are living with today. And the other thing is villains. They are only as good as their villains. Well, there are enough women actresses now, you know. That would give it an edge.

**Would you ever consider returning as a villain?**

That wouldn't be a problem, but I don't think they could afford it. You know, they don't pay the money for the other parts. Now they pay the money for the Bond character. That wasn't the case when I was doing it.

**Have you watched any of the other Bonds?**

No, I haven't seen any of them. Actually, an odd one or two on the television. I have them on DVD in boxes and have a machine now, so I must catch up on all the other films.

# George Lazenby

**Why did you go after Bond?**

I was hooked on Bond. I think that in part gave me the drive to become James Bond. I was a James Bond fan. Connery was my hero. Every time a movie came out, I was there. And not only that, for the life of me, I didn't believe I could be as good as Connery — he created the character. I had to stay within the frame of Connery. I couldn't be me — the swaggering Australian. So here I was a non-actor: I changed my accent, I changed my walk, everything. I went to school, the same school as the British Prime Minister, Harold Wilson, who was from Yorkshire and half of England couldn't understand him. Nobody could understand him. I used a special voice coach and without her I never would've been able to get near an English accent. But the other thing was my walk. I swaggered. I walked like Prince Philip. I had to remember my accent, the lines, my walk.

**Did you ever meet Connery?**

We met briefly at Morton's. Connery came in right behind me and gave me a wink, as if to say, "There's no need for us to get up and shake hands." We shared the same dentist. I saw him another time and kidded him where I said I just read an article that said my Bond movie was the best, and he muttered something. Afterward he took my hand.

**You bluffed your way in but how'd you get the part?**

I think, first of all, I was very capable physically, I was a natural athlete. When I was in school, I never had any lessons or training. I just did it, and I would come in second or third. And Peter Hunt liked the idea of having someone outside of the acting world so he could not only get him to do what he wanted but to also have a lot of praise for being able to pull it off with an unknown. Because they were talking to people like Richard Burton and Roger, who I think was tied up at the time. I saw a lot of actors come and go and I knew their faces. When I was testing,

I tested for four months. I was there every day, and Peter would put me up with people who were trying out for other roles to give me experience because he had it in his mind right from the beginning that I was the guy. But Broccoli and Saltzman and the studio didn't want me. There was a lot riding on this and you had never had a male model becoming a movie star before. But what clinched it was when I decked a wrestler. I didn't mean to, but energy starts to flow and boom! I had the self-assuredness. When I came through a room, I practically broke the door down. They had me tone it down a bit because I was coming on too strong. And a lot of that was I was bluffing. I think that's what got me the part— being over the top. And also having nothing to lose.

**So you could handle the physical part. What about the rest?**

I was nervous. They put me in a love scene and had to yell cut 15 times. I thought I might as well enjoy it. Most other shots were no more than a take or two. I had a misunderstanding with Peter on the third day and we didn't speak the rest of the shoot.

**What was the misunderstanding about?**

There were some friends of his visiting the set and I didn't know who they were, but they were distracting me, and my line of vision, so I told them to leave when nobody else would. I tried several times to patch things up with Peter, I tried to at a party and invited him to dinner but he never spoke to me again but from then on he communicated to me through the assistant director.

**How did the whole opening come about with you breaking the fourth wall: "This never happened to the other fella"?**

Everything I did, whether it was doing a lot of press interviews or a fight scene, whatever, I kept saying, "I bet the other guy didn't have to do this." Finally, Peter said I could use the line in the opening scene, though they polished it slightly.

**Describe working with Diana Rigg and Telly Savalas.**

Everyone I worked with were seasoned pros and, of course, I didn't realize at the time that it would show my shallowness as an actor. The feelings weren't always there. I had never seen myself on screen as an actor before.

**But even though this was your only Bond, don't you get a lot of comfort in knowing it was the most emotional story?**

It's the only movie that closely follows the book, which is why the fans adore it so. Broccoli said I would've been the best Bond if I'd kept it up.

**What happened? Why'd you walk away?**

The late sixties was a rough time for Bond because of the hippies. When *On Her Majesty's* came out, *Easy Rider* was a hit movie. People were wearing bell bottoms and growing their hair and singing love songs against killing. And Bond wasn't about that at all. So it was a rough time for me in that sense as well. I thought the title song should be done by Blood, Sweat & Tears. That shows you where my head was at.

I gambled and walked away from a seven-picture Bond contract that was offered before the end of shooting the film. To be honest, it wasn't my thinking. I was convinced of that by other people. And they said you're a movie star now, go and do whatever you want. And I had never signed a contract. To this day, I've never signed a contract. I just said, "No, I've gotta walk." That's when they offered me money under the table. And United Artists offered me any movie I wanted to do in between Bonds trying to get me to sign the contract. And this guy, Ronan O'Rahilly, who owned a pirate radio station and was like the hip guy in London, was advising me. Bond is too conservative and it's Connery's gig anyway. He would get me movies. I couldn't because everyone was afraid to touch me. They either thought I was still tied up to Bond or was damaged goods. I went to Hong Kong for three years and hooked up with Bruce Lee, who died tragically. I did bit TV roles like *Hawaii Five-0* (Jack Lord changed my role from a suave guy to a bum). I had a chance role in *Saint Jack* as a gay American senator. I didn't want it, but

Ben Gazzara convinced me to do it. It was a very gratifying acting experience. I went sailing for a year. Months of drinking too much eventually led to a near-death experience that sobered me up quickly.

**What was it like shooting the death scene?**

It was the most gratifying emotional moment of my acting career. I was totally on my own. I'd come in and rehearse and I would say, "That was awful." And they'd say, "Don't worry — we'll get it from another angle." Peter knew what he was doing. It was the last scene we shot. One take I had tears, and the assistant director told me that Peter said James Bond doesn't cry. So I did it once more without the tears. Diana Rigg was lying on my lap and biting me on the leg. I don't know why— probably to get me to emote or something. What happened was I had the book with me and read it right before the scene and cried. I just read that scene again and I got the feeling. Where ever you can get it, you know?

At the time, I didn't understand that part of life — the dark side of what killing does. I can remember being in the Australian Army. I was 20, I was a sharpshooter, because I was brought up in the Bush, in the country, and I could shoot the eye out of a needle. And so when I was in the army, if somebody told me to shoot somebody, I would've done it without question. I think this is where Bond was coming from: "This guy's a bad egg for our country — take him out." And he would do it because he had this quality. And he then showed his emotions and lost it when they shot his wife. I don't think he ever chased a girl before. So it was confusing to me in a way, where I understood that he was falling in love and he had to decide what to do. Like many men, even if they're killers, they have that gene that compels them to mate with the opposite sex. And when you find that special one, you want to be with her. But I didn't know how to deal with the deeper aspects of acting: It's not just saying the words but how you feel. And so you're like an instrument. There are a few moments where he's more vulnerable that I'm quite proud of. I was never one to walk away from a risk and this was the biggest professional one I ever had.

# Roger Moore

**When were you first approached to play Bond?**

I wasn't aware of it at the time, but Cubby told me that I was on the short list for *Dr. No* with Sean and Patrick McGoohan. I had never heard of James Bond. I was tied up with *The Saint*. Had I known, I might've been more expensive.

**And then you were approached a second time before finally accepting?**

Yes, it was after Sean did *You Only Live Twice*. What happened was they had a script [for *The Man with the Golden Gun*] and it was supposed to be filmed in Cambodia, but it got pushed back because of all the problems. When they were ready to go, I was tied up and they went with George, and then Sean came back with *Diamonds*, and then they called me again and that was it.

**I suppose you had the easiest transition to Bond, given your work on *The Saint* and *The Persuaders*. But what was it like for you stepping in as Bond number three?**

Well, the way I play it, I make everybody look the same, I think. Rather like that wonderful character actor George Arliss many years ago, who played all those famous historical characters. He made them all look like George. As Spencer Tracy said, "Say the lines and hit the marks." As Lee Marvin said, "Say the marks and hit the lines." I carried somewhere in between.

**But there was obviously the consent to break away from the Connery mold.**

The only thing that Guy Hamilton had me not say [in *Live and Let Die*] was: "A martini shaken, not stirred." I played it for more humor. We changed directors on the third film, *The Spy Who Loved Me*, with Lewis Gilbert. He and I had more or less the same sense of humor, which is slightly off the wall. We had a marvelous rapport. "What are you going to say in this scene?" We would try something fun and Cubby would decide which one he liked best. So he played with the lines. John Glen came on the scene later and he was happy to go along with the way I was doing it, which was obviously successful.

**Since you knew Sean very well, did you have any conversations about Bond, even jokingly?**

No, no. It's a lot like discussing with Laurence Olivier how you're going to play *Hamlet*. I knew both Harry and Cubby, and we used to gamble during the bad days of the sixties and were seeing one another on a very regular basis. We had Michael Caine and Ken Adam and his wife and Harry and his wife…whoever would survive on Saturday nights would play gin rummy on Sundays, and Cubby and I played backgammon.

**What was stepping up into Bond stardom like for you?**

Well, it was already unique after seven Bond films, and it was an ongoing concern and it created tremendous press interest that was a distraction while shooting the films. I remember once we had 80 journalists waiting on set and I said: "You have a choice. We can sit here and do these interviews or I can do the movie. But we can't do both." In between, on a couple of occasions, I locked up the time doing other movies. But it was a big commitment, one Bond every two years and you have to be available for about six months. And then there's the promotion and publicity campaign and the worldwide tours. So it took up quite a lot of time.

**And dealing with Bond for the rest of your private life?**

Well, I had a number of years of dealing with Simon Templar and *The Saint*, and have dealt with stardom going back as far as *Ivanhoe* and then there was *Maverick*. So I was fairly well known. So it was always amusing to be recognized.

**How did Bond help or hinder you as far as being typecast?**

Fortunately or unfortunately, whichever you want to look at it, I was born with the looks of a leading man and I sort of fit the heroic roles. I personally would like to try all sorts of roles. I know my strengths and limitations as an actor and have been able to capitalize on this very successfully. All I had to do was *be* James Bond, but it was the villains who had all the fun and got to say, "You've really gone too far this time, Mr. Bond." I loved them all. Curt Jurgens, Michael Lonsdale, Christopher Walken. They have characters to come in, but Bond is just Bond.

**Did you attempt to find freshness over the course of the films?**

Well, you can't change the character. The one thing about filming, after the first day of shooting, you've set the tone and that's the way you're going to play it.

**Did you ever have any discussions beforehand about trying something new? For instance, with *For Your Eyes Only*, you have a darker revenge theme.**

I remember Lewis Gilbert reading a review once and he said that it's quite extraordinary the way people read into things. There are things we don't even think about. I don't self analyze.

**So for you it was all about maintaining the casual persona?**

Oh, yes. And also we had a wonderful atmosphere on the set. Cubby had this running backgammon game, which we never settled up until the last day of shooting. And if he was losing, they'd call me in from the set and he'd say, "You're gonna let the sonofabitch stay here so I can get my money back." And we just had a lot of laughs doing them. Maybe sometimes it got a bit hairy. But I find it much easier to work this way. I remember the last day of shooting [*The Man with the Golden Gun*], and I saw Cubby's head peering out from one of the sets, and a bucket of paste came flying down at me on one of those wonderful silk suits I was looking forward to stealing.

**What's your favorite Bond film?**

*The Spy Who Loved Me*. Great looking location shoots. The one in Egypt to start out with. We had a government censor on the set. After the scene where I fight Jaws [Richard Kiel] on the Temple of Karnak, which comes down, I had this great line, "Egyptian builders." But we were worried about the censor so I just mouthed the line. But the sound man wasn't in on the gag, so he yelled, "I didn't hear him — we'll have to do it again!" But they dubbed it in later in London. Friends in Egypt said it was the biggest laugh in Cairo.

**Did some of those famous throwaway lines come about spontaneously?**

Some of them. Some were scripted. Tom Mankiewicz wrote some great one-liners. I love *The Man with the Golden Gun* line he gave me. It was when I dropped the sight of the rifle to the nether regions and I say, "Speak now or forever hold your piece." Another one was when I told the tiger, "Sit!" I think that was in *Octopussy*. My god, at the end of the day, they all start to run together.

**What's the downside of playing Bond?**

The downside is the one day you're too old and too tired and they run out of villains who look old enough to be logically knocked down by you. And the leading ladies have become far too young. You have too many chins for them to look at.

**Have you watched the subsequent Bonds?**

I saw two reels of Pierce Brosan's first Bond [*GoldenEye*] because my son Christian was working on the production and I went down to the set and it was very sad because Cubby had died. Michael, Barbara, and Dana and I have remained good friends. Dana and I had known one another a great deal. They wanted me to see the two reels and I thought it was terrific — it was very good stuff.

**Were you surprised that you lasted seven films?**

When I first started, I was surprised that I lasted seven days.

# Timothy Dalton

**What's it been like as a former Bond?**

I did a humanitarian movie about wolves some time ago. And I lived with Eskimos in the north of the Brooks Range in Alaska, which is a very long way north and it's very cold. And when I got off a plane on the runway that skidded on ice, these very nice people came out and said, "James Bond."

**It's obvious you take a lot of pride in being part of the Bond family — a very select group. And despite his public distancing, I found that Connery still has a lot of pride himself.**

Why shouldn't he? He was damn good. For good or bad, Sean is the one that started it all. Those first three movies he did were the best James Bond movies there are. They captured the essence of the series. And they were responsible for establishing what has become the most powerful and probably the most enduring film image. There's nothing to compare with the notion of Bond in people's consciousness. He was great. He was one of the founders of some kind of dynasty anyway.

**What do you think is the best Bond film?**

Probably *Goldfinger*, though I love *From Russia with Love*. The interesting thing, you know — and I haven't paid attention to Bond in about 15 years — is that it's memorable for the train sequence, with the audience knowing that Robert Shaw was a double-agent who was going to kill him and knowing that Sean Connery didn't know that. I can't remember if it's 25 minutes or 30 minutes, but essentially the bulk of the movie was simply this one proposition: How or if Connery is going to find out that he's going to be murdered. When? How? All on a train! Now we couldn't do a sequence like that in a modern movie. Nowadays a sequence is five minutes! Bam! Bam! Bam! And this was all about the look in the people's eyes, what was going on — it was a real piece of drama!

**What was it like being considered for Bond when Connery first gave it up?**

Well, very silly, really… I was far too young. I would've been around 23, having done some big movies like *Lion in Winter*. I was a young up and coming actor. So it was a ridiculous notion, really, but I was very flattered.

**Did you actually test?**

No, no it was all a big secret, so I went along to see what it was all about. And then later I realized what it was all about. And then the second time was when Roger and the company always had these renegotiations after every one — it was probably in the seventies. But, of course, Roger did come around again. And then the last time was when I did do it.

**After Pierce said yes and couldn't get out of his *Remington Steele* contract?**

It was actually more complicated than that. There was somebody else — a big star.

**You mean Mel Gibson?**

I can't say. I don't mean to be coy. I had been asked to do it, but I couldn't…I think I was doing *Antony and Cleopatra*. So I was out of the picture. Then they asked Pierce and then somebody else, and it got delayed and delayed and delayed until finally [they wore down my resistance].

**So what did you think about being Bond?**

Well, you can't help thinking about it. It's one of the biggest roles in the movies and also there are some very good British movies, but it's about the only movie franchise that Britain has ever made that makes you an international star immediately. So you've got to take it seriously when they ask you.

**So once you said yes, how did you prepare?**

I read the novels and saw the first three movies. You realize immediately that the films aren't really like the books. Or they had become completely unlike the books. By the time I came in to do the first one, Bond was sort of jokey, flippant. But people liked that. And Roger was very, very experienced and skilled in carrying off that sort of flippant onion ball — lovely, lighthearted, but it had nothing to do with spy movies or *From Russia with Love*.

**Did you talk to Sean or Roger about it?**

No, they sent their best wishes. You know they can't tell you anything because whatever they can tell you only applies to them. But they were nice. The books were tough (the torture scene in *Casino Royale* is very brutal). In [*The Living Daylights*] short story, he's popping pills — he's doing uppers —so he has to stay awake for like three days on the job. And, of course, he drinks and he does all the kinds of things that they did try to capture in the beginning. You know people wouldn't let their kids go see James Bond when they first came out. He was a bit of a sensation. He killed people. Good guys didn't do that. And he didn't kill them fair and square.

**In *Dr. No*, he shoots a man in cold blood.**

You know, by the time I was doing them, people were saying that they wanted to take their seven-year-olds to see them. When they first opened, they were restricted if you were under 16.

**What do you think of *On Her Majesty's Secret Service*?**

It's a wonderful movie, a good movie.

**Pierce told me that he'd like to remake it.**

Does he? Well, it's a great story. Not that it matters that much but you see in that one event of marrying somebody and having her killed, a wonderful psychological basis for, if you like, his attitude

towards women. You can't fall in love; otherwise they're a target. You don't want to get too serious for these movies, but this one comes closest.

**Peter Hunt was very smart in keeping true to the book.**

Yeah, it was one of the best.

**And in a weird sort of way, George Lazenby's inexperience translates into an effective vulnerability.**

Well, I'm not so sure about that. I don't think he pulled it off, but it's a very hard one to pull off.

**Of course, we can only ponder what Sean would've been like. He complained that with each one there was less and less to do, but this would've been his greatest challenge as Bond.**

Well, he's gotten over that hurdle. It's like Harrison Ford and Indiana Jones. He goes on and does other stuff, and you always say, "That's Harrison Ford." You go through a period — and Pierce knows this now better than anyone — where everyone who has played James Bond has suddenly realized that the role overtakes the individual. There is a time when you are Roger Moore who has played this, or Timothy Dalton who has played that, Pierce Brosnan who has played this, that, and the other; Sean Connery. But you do a Bond and it's bigger than anything. People still ask me today to do an interview on TV [after all these years], and I say no. And there's this anniversary — and it still goes on. You incorporate it as part of your history. It rises out of proportion. Even for Connery. And then Roger was their James Bond. The consciousness of Bond was embodied by Roger — and rightly so. Whatever one says or whatever one would like to do, you have to deal with the concrete. And so you work off that.

**How did you handle *The Living Daylights*?**

There was little preparation for the first film. I was just flung into it. I remember the press conference was the biggest I'd ever done. It was hell with 600 people all shouting at me and masses of cameras from all over the world. I just started doing it. You can't think of it as being different from any other job. You do it scene by scene.

**But you have a distinct personality.**

Yeah, but that's for others to approach and like or dislike. It's hard. Twenty weeks, 15-hour days. It was very tiring. You've got to mediate, you've got to concentrate. It's interesting, these long shoots. You see wonderful freshness for about six weeks, then there's an ease and then you go on automatic pilot.

**How would you have changed *Living Daylights*?**

My version of going back to Sean Connery. Dry, tough humor. But you can't.

**Going into the second film, *Licence to Kill*, was it more tailored for you?**

No, I don't think so. I simply said don't write for me. Write a wonderful Bond story where there's danger, where there's humor. And my job is to play it, to fill it out. For some reason, the second one is a lot of people's favorite of my Bonds. I much prefer the first one. I thought it had a good story but it was too dour. Give me jokes. Of course, it was first called *Licence Revoked*, but MGM didn't think anyone would understand it. One of the things you learn as an actor is that you have to give them levels to play. It had that one theme of revenge. And it had a go at establishing a different kind of Bond. But it dragged it away completely. It came out at the time of *Lethal Weapon* and *Indiana Jones and the Last Crusade*. Why can't you have both —seriousness and droll, cynical wit?

**Like Connery?**

Yes. One of the difficulties, with the exception of Sean, is that no other Bond really works from an original script. Every single person who works on a Bond movie, be they sitting in a production office in London or in Los Angeles with hands on responsibility, has their version of what a Bond movie should be: either because they love it or because they think it will be commercial. So they're always applying a historical preconception onto something that you're doing now— me too. And that sort of hinders almost everybody in the process. For example, you know what a James Bond poster looks like, don't you? How many times has the poster changed? Why has it changed? Because ultimately there are a lot of commercial decisions made and there is a lot of molding.

And the other thing, of course, is that the character of Bond is somewhat taken for granted because of the historical background. He drives the story along, but you find that every other character in a James Bond movie is a new character. So they've often been written quite interestingly because they've often been written afresh. So he's less well written, and his purpose is to get us through the action sequences that together build the narrative of the story. And that's difficult. Pierce must feel that as well and I'm sure Roger did. You're there as the center of the story, but each script isn't developed to support that. The history supports that because we know he's James Bond. But in any other movie, you've got real scenes and real dramas going on, but not here. They're all different but the same. The other real question is: How important is it all? But I do not regret for a single second doing the Bond films. And there was the time that the boys in the coast guard took me for a ride in their helicopter and I literally hung down underneath it, much to the displeasure of the production. It was the most fantastic experience I've ever had. I do know that every single Bond movie beginning with Sean and ending with me, not one stunt was ever faked — it was done for real without any computer enhancement. Those people were real.

**What did it feel like to no longer be Bond?**

One day I was driving on Fairfax, and I saw the *GoldenEye* poster with Pierce pointing the gun… and I felt free at last.

# Pierce Brosnan

**What's Bond been like for you?**

When I did *GoldenEye*, it was a turning point for the franchise and the Broccoli family. Cubby was dying. Barbara and Michael were carrying on the torch. And for me, I was the new kid on the block. I had no say in it. I didn't even want to have a say. I didn't know what to say, even if I could say something. I just knew that it was an opportunity from an acting point of view. And it had been in my life before and had gone out of my life. I saw it as a glorious opportunity to go out there and do it. Because I was brought up on James Bond and wanted to be James Bond ever since I saw *Goldfinger* when I came from Ireland to London as a boy. So it came down to trying to make it real for myself, wanting to make it human but at the same time maintaining the fantasy and the mystique of the character. And there was a lot at stake for myself and for Martin Campbell. It was intense being up on the wire — do or die — and we did it and it worked. *GoldenEye* was a lovely success, and there was an audience out there, and a new generation that wanted to bring the romance back and the familiarity of something they had grown up on. And then, of course, the second time around they pulled out all the stops with wall-to-wall action.

**But with *The World Is Not Enough*, you've had an opportunity to go a little deeper with Bond.**

Yes, it moves like a bullet, and it's got content and style. And thanks to Mr. Apted, attention was paid to story and character, and it was a great time, actually. It was, for me, a walk in the park, really. It was not very stressful. All I had to do was show up. I saw an opportunity of articulating the human side and the mystique as well with Michael Apted, who's got a body of work that covers documentaries and character-driven dramas, and so much of his fingertips dealing with relationships.

**It's interesting how Bond functions as a catalyst for others to explore their demons.**

Bond remains a constant. He never changes. He's the one stabilizer within the whole genre. And he's the one who remains somewhat timeless, somewhat trapped within a period of time as well. My task was always trying to find my own reality within it: How do you make it human but still keep the fantasy and mystique of the character? What is his relationship with M? What is his relationship with the woman that he will encounter? And how far can you push those relationships in a Bond film to the point where he just closes the door and sits and reflects?"

**If it were up to you, what would you do with the character?**

If it was up to me, you would have scenes that have sex and violence. That's what this man is about. There would be lovemaking scenes that are palpable, like in *Thomas Crown Affair*, which were easy on the eye and exciting and erotic and tasteful. And I think you can work that into Bond as well.

**Kind of kinky?**

Definitely kinky. He was born from the pen of Fleming with a perverseness. There's always a shadow in those stories. And violence, too; this man has a license to kill. But how does he kill? And you [would] see that violence. We've reached a good part of it here in this film. But I would love to take the censorship off it without being gratuitous, without being distasteful. Just sort of, ha! So you could be more believable. So you could have both: the intensity of the killing, which is very clinical and matter of fact, and then you go into the humor. You go back to the flip side of things.

**Yet it seems you found a dark side emerging around the edges of this film.**

There's this ménage à trois that is rather perverse when you think about it. I mean, this secret agent who just goes through women, but for the first time he's kind of lent himself to this woman out of guilt. And not only that, she's a great seductress, too, and she knows it. And just when he's near the edge of the abyss, the worm turns.

**But it helps when you humanize the mission as you've done here.**

I think it starts with the mission. What is the mission? What is his relationship to his adversaries? And then back to the base. When Bond was introduced in 1962, the whole world was busting apart, sexually, and the exploration of drugs and music, and everything, so Bond fits snugly into that arena.

**It's getting more intense out there.**

I suppose. I mean, my first performance was terrifying. Martin Campbell said, "You've gotta be fucking great."

**What does that mean?**

Martin's a pretty intense guy and you're up on the wire. If you fell, there was no net.

**What was Roger Spottiswoode like?**

The script wasn't as well founded; it wasn't smooth in many ways. It was more difficult, and I think because *GoldenEye* popped out of the bag so well, there were second night nerves in the performance and it was very intense for Roger, too, because he was following in the steps of Martin. We got on well together, but I think his communications with Bond and the whole arena of dealing with so many units was probably difficult at times. Nevertheless, the film worked and what a ride. It was a success. And certainly Michael and I have known each other — not well — but we talk to each other and I've always enjoyed his company. So when we came to talk about Bond, it was terrifying. I had two under my belt. But this had a much cleaner line through it emotionally.

**I like how the title references *On Her Majesty's Secret Service*. Is it true you want to remake it?**

It would be good to have a crack at it, yes. I don't think they would. Maybe it's the best idea not. It's a great story and certainly one of the cornerstones of the character: it explains who the man is. It's an idea I had way back when.

**The great love story of Bond's life. And then Roger went lighter and Timothy brought it back down to earth.**

Timothy played it right down the fucking line there.

**The timing is so strange the way Bond has worked out for you.**

I wouldn't have been Bond if *Remington* hadn't happened, so everything has its purpose. I can go back to doing a Tennessee Williams play and Franco Zeffirelli coming to see me and offering me a play, which took me to the West End, which led to a progression.

**From destiny to dynasty.**

*Destiny to Dynasty*, starring… I think, at the end of the day, you're looking for things that stand the test of time. Nobody can take that away. That's what you're always chasing. But with *GoldenEye*, I was falling in love with my wife, being a family man, dealing with all the kids. I was very proud but anxious — anxious to do well. Huge place. I had nothing to lose and everything to gain, and knowing that if I pulled it off, it would change the course of my life. And it has changed my life. I can remember: I lost it on a Thursday evening. I remember it well: My wife was sitting on the deck and the phone rang. I was about the join her and sit and watch the sun set. I had six days to get out of this clause, and it was day six, 6:00, and we were having cocktails, and the phone rang and it was 6:30, my agent, Fred Specktor, said, "They want the option and Cubby said no. It's not going to work — it's over." The shock of it was unbelievable. I'd put my children into school back in England — it was a boarding school. We'd been five years in America and it was time to go back and become Europeans.

**With *Die Another Day*, you've been able to peel away the onion a little more.**

Yes, a little. That's the aspect that's the most

intriguing. Here's a man who has killed so many people, who lives with blood on his hands, sometimes messy killings. Dealing with death on a constant basis, [grappling] with the idea of his own death. And that's hard to do with something, which is geared now toward kids. [But here] you find the guy captured, you find the man on the run between friend and foe — a renegade — you find him outside the circle of his own people. The writing isn't as deep as you'd like, but there are beats that are a good throwback to the Cold War. Lee has brought a realism to it — a high volume of risk and danger and concern. The good thing about a Bond film is being on the curve or ahead of the curve of what is global amid all this fantasy. This film is a celebration of Bond at a time when we need to embrace heroes. To see Lee and Michael and Barbara pull Bond into the 21st century, to get them to use CGI, and get them to put Bond in tougher situations is so satisfying. And Halle — what a great player and what fun she is to play with. She has a maturity, sexuality, and sensuality that make men and women feel so at ease.

**But it must've been surreal after 9/11.**

We didn't adjust. The script came in at the end of summer; then 9/11 happened and it took me a while to come out of the paralysis of that and realize that, after a few days, we had a movie with Bond to make that deals with this planet, and blowing things up, and world domination.

**But it's always a struggle to do more, isn't it?**

There are some that don't want you to stretch that far. You're perceived in a certain way and it's typecasting that an actor deals with. I mean, it's a certain style in my acting, I suppose, that's manufactured but comes from the truth, hopefully. Bond has its restrictions; it has its own discipline and its own style, which has been built up over the years. And it has a rich tradition that you have to give up to and deliver. And it is a formula. So to go off and do *The Tailor of Panama* was highly enjoyable. It wasn't probably as much fun as Bond, but it was playing another aspect of the world of the spy game.

**You seem much more at ease with Bond now.**

There's a certain confidence that you gain after years of making Bond, a high degree of assuredness and relaxation that wasn't there in *GoldenEye*, which had its own fears and trepidations. Everybody has their own take on how to play Bond. For me, there's only one man who's played it and is Bond to this day— and that's Connery. He must've been blindsided by the whole thing. It's a big old train to step onto. It takes off really fast. You have to be prepared to go through many doors because you're not just as an actor. You become the front man for this franchise; you become an ambassador in different countries where you had no relationship before. You're certainly on the international map. For me, above all else, it's been about getting away with creating the role, having a love affair with the piece as a fan, and the pride in the work and being part of this legacy."

**Yet making it your own.**

I said it once and probably said it once too many times: there are situations where you can play with it so I can make it my own. How do I make it my own? Connery had such ownership over it. And there's only one. What Roger did was great and he did it well, but how do you do it so it's dangerous and sexy and free?

I just hope that it's truthful and believable, having the time of his life killing people, drinking martinis, and shagging his way through the high society of every country he goes to.

**There's talk of making *Casino Royale*. I'm sure the prospect of returning to Bond's roots must excite you.**

Yes, very much so. That's the template for Bond, the way Ian Fleming created him. Just the title on the marquee would say it all: *Casino Royale*.

# Daniel Craig

**Casino Royale is the Holy Grail for Bond. What does this mean for Bond and for you as a journey?**

There are a couple of simple equations that you can apply and that I have always applied to the work anyway. And that has to do with fallibility, which is much more dramatically interesting. People are saying that I'm showing his vulnerability, but I don't perceive it as vulnerability, because that would suggest to someone that there's a weakness. I don't think he's inherently a weak character, but his weakness lies in the fact that he's headstrong and he makes mistakes — and he makes mistakes that are severe. But his argument to M was, "You gave me the job — you gave me a Double-0." It's not that he's just been given a license to kill; he's been given a responsibility. He doesn't have to phone up before he kills somebody. If he's got the shot, and he feels it's the right thing to do, then he'll do it. I want an audience to question that and I want the audience to go, "Is that the right decision at this particular moment?" Because I want the audience to not only be on the edge of their seat with the excitement of the action, but also on the edge of their seat emotionally a bit and run ragged and go, "I don't know how I feel about this." Hopefully, at the end, we ultimately see that he was right: that there was a grander plan, there was something that he was thinking about. Then we're going to be covered. But during the movie it should go either way.

**He's learned something — he's attained some wisdom.**

But even then, with wisdom, we have to make the next situation even more extraordinary. And that's maybe why they went the way they did with a lot of the Bond movies. They had to get more extraordinary because when you have somebody who seems to know all of the answers, what do you do with him?

**Build a better mousetrap.**

Quite. But we've gotta find a way to make that work

each time as opposed to making it… I don't want to get lazy about this. I don't think of myself as a lazy actor. When I leave this one day, I want to leave something that's gonna last a bit because that's the way I look at the work I've done. That's all I can say at the moment. It's easy to say at the moment.

**Timing is everything with you getting to do Casino Royale.**

I know for Barbara it has been very important to finally get to do this.

**You have a wonderful opportunity here.**

For me, I couldn't have seen doing it any other way than with Casino Royale. If I would've just been stepping into somebody else's shoes and then handing it over to someone else at a later date — maybe that'll be the case in the long run — I couldn't have gone in feeling like that. I had to feel like we could begin again here, not in any broad way, but to try and find some of the subtlety of who this person is. And, therefore, hopefully, give us a springboard.

**Not even Connery had that opportunity.**

He defined it. It's that darkness that he brought into it. This is a complicated character — it's not two-dimensional. This guy has a past and there's a reason he's been made this way. That, for me, was one of the reasons I wanted to do this.

**The grittiness?**

Right. I think Bond had a lot of that in the beginning, then it sort of was lost, and then it came back again with Timothy Dalton.

**How do you define Bond today?**

As a hero figure, he's a guy that just knows what's what. And all of us struggle a little bit with that in life. But he walks into a room and sees a situation and says, "I'm gonna make this decision — and I'm gonna to make it now!" And that's kind of exciting. It gives him an unpredictability, and things are gonna be OK — he's gonna work it out. I try to point to this a little bit more so that maybe it isn't going to be OK because that's more dramatically interesting.

**But he's still larger than life.**

We're in a fantasy world here and that must remain constant because people come to see a Bond movie for that very reason. And that's why we owe it to make sure that the world we create is something out of the ordinary. And as long as you're on that level of fantasy, you can have as much reality as you want. We can hit you with the hardcore and we can hit you with the toughness.

**It's not *The Spy Who Came in from the Cold* or Harry Palmer or Jason Bourne.**

No, it's James Bond.

**But it's so surreal starting all over again but in the present.**

No, absolutely. But it's a testament to the writing that we've managed to get most of the Bondisms into the movie without belaboring the point about them and making them, hopefully, for a new audience to go, "OK, I've heard that that's the movie where it came from." But also for hardened Bond fans to say: "We accept it — we have to have them in there but take it this way." I don't see any reason why we don't get them into later movies. But we've set it up so that we don't have to hammer them home. The subtlety of always doing a gag comes out of the fact that there's been a very tense bit just previous to it. And that's what makes the gag work — that's what makes it funny, as opposed to it being a gag for gag's sake.

**So you prefer more of the droll, Connery-style humor.**

For me, it's funnier. I like black humor — always have. I know it's a British thing and a Scandinavian thing. I love the fact that it's under pressure making the joke — gallows humor — and that's really what

Bond was always to me. It's there even in this rather brutal torture scene. Bond may think he's going to die, but he doesn't want to lose. He likes making a joke when it's inappropriate and it gives him a kick, and, hopefully, that gives us a thrill. But you can't force gags like that. They're either right or they're not. But, again, we have to make absolutely sure that we get them spot on again.

**It's such a contrast to the brutal bathroom scene. I understand there was a lot more.**

Yeah, basically it's a choke hold that I put on him and I force him in and we shot a lot of that with me actually drowning him. It was very tough and I come through the door and throw him into the wall and kick him. I mean he just had to get him down.

**And it really bothers him, doesn't it?**

Yes, it's there — we did the shot where he has to take a breath. It's pretty nasty. We have to feel that it's his first one and he's been ordered to go out and do it.

**Is there a bit of a death wish for Bond?**

Yes, I think there's a slight undercurrent there.

**Did you have a lot of arguments with Martin Campbell about the character?**

We had our moments. But we had passionate talks. You always do that on films.

**What did you discuss?**

We discussed every scene. My criteria — and his — were: "Are we missing a trick here?" Things could get out of hand with a movie this size; the storyline gets out of whack. We had a great script and the one thing we had to stick to was that script and that piece of storytelling. The stunt scenes and the action sequences had to be part of the story: I didn't want to go and shoot two movies, where we're shooting the action one day and the storyline the following day. Each one had to fit into each other so we could get it as seamless as possible. I mean, we discussed things.

**What was the challenge of the poker scenes?**

With the poker stuff, it was trying not to confuse the audience. Of course, there'll be people in the audience that play poker and know what's going on, but we need to appeal to everybody. We need to have a sort of sparring and that was the key to making it work. There are lots of things going on with the hands, but, oddly, it's about, "I've got better cards than you." I know there was no money involved, but when you're playing for $25 million, it gives you a good feeling.

**Let's talk about the relationships. With Le Chiffre, it was all about the game and then the torture scene.**

It was like sparring; it was a fight. We never have a physical fight in the movie. That was our physical fight.

**It's interesting that you've got two central women in *Casino Royale* to help shape Bond: Vesper, who brings out a romantic side but then betrays him and hardens him further, and M, the mother figure.**

And I think that's crucial. We obviously didn't always have that: M was always a man. And some of those meetings are my favorite moments in the early Bond films in that office with that big padded door and coming in and throwing the hat and hooking it. And it was always a sort of dick-swinging exercise when he sat there and, "Hello, he's from the ministry," and all that bollocks going on. And I liked all that. But we have this opportunity — and I think Judi is an opportunist — with a relationship that is genuinely one almost of love, that where ever he is, in spite of everything, no matter how alone in the world he is, she's there for him. And that, in a way, gives him the strength but also allows him to be more chauvinistic than he normally is. Because, ultimately, we can go: "God, look at what a chauvinistic pig he is." But he

gets in her apartment, and even though he's, "Fuck you, mum," he respects her totally. And I like that feeling because that gives a balance to his other relationships in the movie. And I love that scene at the beginning in her apartment. He knows he's pissing her off and he likes that.

**And she's torn because of her complicity. She gave him the Double-0 and she's not sure he's going to work out.**

Completely. And we have her struggle a bit, which is very interesting.

**But it's all about Bond and Vesper being drawn to the mystery about each other. Talk about the shower scene.**

Well, the shower sequence is key: that vulnerability that she shows — she opens herself up and it's a shock to him. I don't think many people do that to him. And the fact that she says his soul can be saved: it's something she sees within herself. Her soul is unsavable, or so it would appear to be, and so is his. I love that. I haven't thought about it too much. But maybe she feels she can't save her own but she can save his.

**And we have to believe that she could fall in love with him.**

Absolutely, because she holds this secret, which, again, is part of Eva's skill as an actress because she has this sense of mystery about her and that's what he fell in love with. He was duped basically because there was something else going on. Bond has gained a sense of humanity and now it's been taken away.

I wouldn't have touched this movie if I didn't see an element of where we saw him change, where we saw him go through something — a revelation — and that revelation was Vesper. And he opened himself up. At the beginning of the movie, I don't think he cares if he lives or dies. It's his job, it's what he does, and this woman blows his mind — absolutely exposes him and breaks his heart. And it's that whole process and change that I thought was gonna make it an interesting movie, and also gives us a springboard. I never thought that far ahead, but when we get onto another movie, we have something to work with now.

**And it isn't until *On Her Majesty's Secret Service* that he gets a second chance at love. It'll be interesting to watch that movie again in light of *Casino Royale*.**

It's a good movie. Everybody sort of says, "Are you afraid of being a George Lazenby?" I love *On Her Majesty's Secret Service*. As I understood it, he chose to leave it.

**Yeah, he says he was advised that Bond wouldn't survive the sixties, so he didn't return.**

There you go. I mean, he does a great job. But what they do very cleverly is surround him with good people — Diana Rigg is fantastic and she gets him through it. I'm sure he would've gone on and learned how to act. I don't doubt it.

**Yes, but it's interesting to note the influence: Bond drawn to the suicidal Tracy after losing Vesper.**

And that's great that he gets drawn in again. It's exciting stuff, like you said.

**Has there been any serious discussion about redoing the books?**

Not to my knowledge. But it would bother me to try and repeat things. You'd like us to?

**I'm torn. I miss the character arc of the last three.**

Yeah.

**But *Live and Let Die* says it all as far as Bond's motto.**

Look, *Live and Let Die* was the first Bond movie I saw in the cinema and it holds a special place in my heart.

**So you probably don't want to touch that one.**

If there were a way to do that, I'd want to do it very differently. I think we have to rely on the fact that what we've created here we can get really good directors and writers involved. They can say, "I've really got something here." And we can move forward. You're the one bringing up the idea of repeating them. It's not something I want to do, but we have to get elements of the previous ones in there.

**Find analogous situations. In the meantime, you've introduced Felix Leiter and eventually Moneypenny and Q can get introduced.**

Again, we have to be very careful the way we do this. And I'm not scared of gadgets; we just have to get them in there in the right way. And with reason: not a gadget for gadget's sake. They shouldn't rule the movie. If they're not more than window dressing, then we're doing something wrong.

**Do you want to continue with this character arc?**

Yes, but I want to make sure that we continue questioning. And, of course, the story will take over, but, hopefully, that will become a different experience. I don't think he's formed at the end of this movie. I think he's just beginning to get his head around the fact of what he might have to achieve and what he might have to do. That doesn't bother me. I think everybody was saying he's now the person we know. He's not. He's somebody who's just been badly hurt and so his reactions after this are going to be extreme.

**He's going to want to be a killing machine.**

And we have to get that right as a consequence of what's occurred in this movie. The key now — and the relevance of it will take care of itself along with the action, which I will leave in the hands of other people — is it must be all tied together. Martin is very good at tying all these elements together and that's what we need in the next director.

*From Russia with Love.*

There you go. And the key was having in Robert Shaw somebody who could take him. And we've seen that already in that maze thing. So what you're basically saying is this man can kill James Bond. It's much more exciting.

**Or Oddjob, who pushes him around like a rag doll.**

It had to be convincing the way Oddjob picks him up and swings him around.

**It can't be all brawn. He's got to rely on his wits. It has to be a balance.**

There you go. A lot of it has to do with the physicality of it, which we started with this movie. What I'm interested in is a refining of the character. He can't go in guns blazing all the time, or whenever he'd like to. He's gonna have to start thinking. But still there's that possibility, when it comes down to it — and Sean was very good at it — he can pick up a table and smash it in somebody's face.

**Interesting how they toned down the cruelty after *Dr. No.***

Well, we had to tone it down with Sébastien Foucan in the [Madagascar sequence]. There should've been a head shot, but we couldn't for obvious reasons. There should've been two. But we weren't allowed that.

**How far along are you with the next one?**

We're definitely having conversations about it.

**Is there the possibility of doing this as a trilogy?**

That's not a bad idea. I haven't heard that one. It's kind of a nice thing to think about. I certainly want to carry on with what we've started. How we do that or what shape it takes on, I don't know. I think it would be interesting to take on the spirit of this one,

but things change. The world changes, and certainly the decisions to change can happen quite rapidly.

**But the way it's set up is topical and very SPECTRE-like: follow the money.**

Yes, that would be the key.

**Well, that's the stated goal at the end of the *Casino Royale* novel — go after the head and cut it off.**

I suppose, yes, you're right. I was looking at the movie again the other night. I had forgotten the character, who deals with the mundane stuff. He's got to go find the boss.

**A more realistic Blofeld?**

Well, maybe. I think if we set it up right. But the great thing about the Blofeld character is if he's done right, as in the early Bonds. It's not that he's mad for the sake of power; the madness is a psychosis for anybody who's got that much power — that craziness. If done properly, it could be fantastic. He's one of the great movie villains.

**It's too bad the Blofeld trilogy was messed up. You had a real psychological progression for Bond.**

There's definitely something to look at there. I would like to go back — I mean, I read them all years ago— my dad had them. When I picked up *Casino Royale* again, I was reminded what a lean and mean book it is. Funnily enough, I re-read it when I got the call [about becoming Bond]. It was on a Wednesday and I started it on Tuesday, and I only had two more chapters to go as I went to bed that night. The following morning I finished them in the cab on the way to my meeting. It's a really good read — it's a really good story. And I had forgotten how much it sets up and how complicated he makes Bond. That was one of the impetuses for me to actually think it was possible to do.

**What's it been like continuing the character arc in *Quantum*?**

We started off something with *Casino Royale*. We had a great storyline; we had a novel by Ian Fleming that was solid and had a really strong love story. And Eva Green played this great part, a wonderful performance. And when it came time to shooting this movie, it was like, we can't just push that aside, we have to develop that — we have to tie up the loose ends. And that's what *Quantum of Solace* is about — finding his quantum of solace. He's not on a vendetta, he's not after revenge. He's after finding his place.

**Talk about exploring his pain indirectly through the other characters.**

You've been talking to the director haven't you? His relationships with M and Felix and obviously with Mathis — and subsequently with Camille — are about solidifying his place in the world and who his allies are. And I think by the end of the movie we're sure and it's Bond and now we can do whatever we want.

**And his continuing relationship with M?**

It's a great thing to have. I think he can behave misogynistically, badly, he does the things that he shouldn't do — he's amoral or morally ambiguous. And M is the grounding. She drifts in and makes it makes sense.

**I looked at *Dr. No* again last night — it's just been released on Blu-ray — and it's interesting to compare you with early Connery and to see some striking similarities: The hard edge, the anger when he's fighting, the sadism, the ruthlessness. But then they immediately smoothed over the rough edges and started making it more effortless.**

That's what we're going to do… now we're going to get camp as hell.

**What was it like shooting the return of the classic gun barrel sequence?**

That was the scariest bit [laughing]. We did it twice. We did it once and it didn't work. And I thought it has to be right, it has to be aggressive, and it has to work.

**Where do you go from here, now that Bond has found his quantum of solace, has experienced this rite of passage, and is fully formed? Have you discussed a roadmap at all?**

No, no, no. We've got so much on our plate, anyway, trying to get one movie out. We have discussions, but there's never anything definite. [When writers come aboard], we want their creative input. And to suggest this is what we want puts up barriers, puts up walls. We want people with creativity and talent to come in and go, "I have a good idea."

**But you still have something to build on with the mission to discover the head of Quantum and destroy it.**

Yeah, we could do that. I definitely think there's some room for that and take it right up. We know it reaches into governments now. We can take it anywhere.

**Is the idea of Bond still making mistakes and not knowing all the answers still important to you?**

I think what we've got to keep doing is inventing new questions. There are characteristic guidelines that you have to adhere to because it's a Bond movie, and we try and do that, but within the parameters of that, you mess it up, and that's the challenge and exciting thing about doing this. It's a really good place to start: the books are good, Connery set the movies up and probably gave them what they needed to last a long time, and the Broccoli/ Saltzman partnership put the money on the screen. They put Bond on location, they made him stylish, and it's given it this impetus that's lasted this long. And Michael and Barbara love this franchise and protect it fiercely. And it's an unusual situation, but it's a very exciting situation as far as filmmaking is concerned.